PRAISE FOR 48 GATEWAYS TO THE ECSTATIC SELF

What if the answers you seek are already within you, waiting to be uncovered? In 48 Gateways to the Ecstatic Self, Kaelan Strouse offers a beautiful guide to reconnecting with the timeless wisdom of your soul. Through inspired practices and profound insights, this transformative book empowers you to heal, grow, and step boldly into your truest self. A must-read for anyone yearning to embrace their divine potential and live a life of purpose, joy, and wonder.

— DARREN MAIN, AUTHOR OF *YOGA AND THE PATH OF THE URBAN MYSTIC*

48 Gateways to the Ecstatic Self" reflects this deep journey and offers readers a thoughtful exploration of the inner landscape. With poetic language and contemplative wisdom, Strouse provides practical insights and guidance for those seeking deeper self-understanding, as he invites readers to explore the possibility of awakening to a more expansive nature.

— CHRISTIAN DE LA HUERTA, AUTHOR OF *CONSCIOUS LOVE, COMING OUT SPIRITUALLY,* AND *AWAKENING TO THE SOUL OF POWER*

All rights reserved. This book may not be copied, reproduced, or used in part or full without the express permission of the author! publisher—other than for "fair use" as brief quotations embedded in articles and reviews.

The author of this book does not dispense medical advice or prescribe the use of any technique as a form of treatment for physical, emotional, or medical problems without the advice of a physician, either directly or indirectly. The intent of the author is only to offer information of general nature to help you in your quest for emotion-al, physical, and spiritual well-being. In the event you use any of the information in this book for yourself, the author and the publisher assume no responsibility for your actions.

Copyright © 2025 by Ecstatic Self Press

ISBN Paperback: 978-1-7354689-7-6

ISBN eBook: 978-1-7354689-8-3

Printed in the United States of America.

First printing, 2020.

Published by Ecstatic Self Press, Washington, D.C., USA.

www.EcstaticSelf.com

48 Gateways to the Ecstatic Self

A Mystical Guidebook & Sacred Grimoire for Spiritual Awakening

Kaelan Strouse

48 GATEWAYS TO THE ECSTATIC SELF

A MYSTICAL GUIDEBOOK & SACRED GRIMOIRE FOR SPIRITUAL AWAKENING

KAELAN STROUSE

Illustrated by
ALFRED OBARE

CONTENTS

Introduction: The Deepening Sky	11
How to Use This Guidebook	15
An Optional Pause on the Side of the Path	18
I. Seek Peace	25
II. Let Go of "Supposed to Be"	31
III. Embrace Change	37
IV. Step Into the Unknown	43
V. Forgive Your Past Selves	49
VI. Embrace Your Desires	53
VII. Explore Your Shadows	59
VIII. Heal Your Wounds	65
IX. Purge Your Demons	71
X. Let Go of Control	77
XI. Wander Aimlessly	83
XII. Seek Wisdom	89
XIII. Invoke Protective Energies	95
XIV. Let Go of What's Not Meant for You	101
XV. Make Love	107
XVI. Root Into Your Body	113
XVII. Practice Being Present	119
XVIII. Turn Your Focus Within	125
XIX. Grieve What is Lost	131
XX. Uncage Your Anger	137
XXI. Set and Work Towards Goals	143
XXII. Forge Discipline	149
XXIII. Rest and Recover	155
XXIV. Pay Attention to Your Dreams	161
XXV. Trust Your Intuition	167
XXVI. Listen For Your Guides	173
XXVII. Practice Compassion For Self and Others	179
XXVIII. Embrace New Identities	187
XXIX. Let Parts of You Die	193
XXX. Get Comfortable With Chaos	199
XXXI. Enjoy Simplicity	205
XXXII. Develop Helpful Routines	211
XXXIII. See Yourself Through Another's Eyes	217
XXXIV. Find a Teacher in Everyone	225

XXXV. Let Your Body Move You	231
XXXVI. Reconnect With the Natural World	237
XXXVII. Find Moments of Retreat	245
XXXVIII. Seek Meaningful Community	251
XXXIX. Become Nothing	259
XL. Become One With Everything	267
XLI. Reconcile Your Masculine and Feminine	273
XLII. Embrace Joy as Life's Purpose	279
XLIII. See With Child Eyes	285
XLIV. Hold Paradoxical Truths	293
XLV. Be Grateful…For Everything	301
XLVI. Live With Integrity	309
XLVII. Reclaim Your Power	315
XLVIII. Just Be	323
The Brightening Sky	328
Also by Kaelan Strouse	331
Acknowledgments	333
Patron Saints of the Oracle	335
Thank you: Kickstarter Backers	337
About the Author	341

Dedicated to my beloved father, my first guide and protector.

It was an honor to read the first few pages of this book to you on the last day I saw you in this world. I will meet you on another road, in another time, someday soon. Until then, may this book serve as a remembrance of the paths you first encouraged me to explore.

INTRODUCTION: THE DEEPENING SKY

Greetings, intrepid traveler.

Thank you for joining me at this crossroads on this twilit eve. The road has been long and arduous to reach here, hasn't it? Filled with potholes, missteps, and unanticipated frustrations? This intersection only reveals itself to those who've reached a state of desperation, those for whom carrying on as they have has become untenable. This is an inflection point—a turning from what has been to what will be.

Onward, you've trudged, your footsteps haunted by false stories of your inadequacies, your path shadowed by errant beliefs in your smallness. You've come to think of yourself as mortal, flawed, and finite. The world has made you doubt yourself, burdened you with the notion that you are somehow less than whole.

But these are stories spun of cobwebs—ephemeral and lacking in substance. These are not your truths. Despite the thorns of doubt, you have dared to hope that you are something greater than the sum of your perceived failures. By choosing to challenge these lies about your worth, you have stumbled your way here. You've defied the modern world's escapist and self-medicating customs, refusing to simply avoid or dull your pain. Instead, you've sought a different path, dared to chart an unplottable course that you hope will lead toward liberation and wholeness.

Here, you can cease that search and set down your burdens. Here, you can surrender everything that does not serve your belief in your inherent magnificence. Stretch your spine; take a deep breath. This meeting was preordained; we were meant to collide here tonight, you and I—two bright stars intersecting in the fading light. I am here to remind you of something profound: you are so much more powerful than you can currently imagine. You, dear traveler, are something magical, vast, and brilliant.

And that's why you've come. You've dared to meet me at an abandoned crossroads, under a deepening sky, in a place where few venture because you've dearly hoped and dared to believe that you are more than your fractured parts. You are more than the mistakes and missteps that have clung to you like burrs. You've had the audacity to hope that you might, indeed, be something truly extraordinary. And I am here to whisper in your ear: *Yes*. You were right to believe in yourself. You are something truly special, indeed.

Crossroads are sacred; magic happens where paths intersect, where forgotten roads converge. *Shhh...* can you hear it? A wind is rising from the shadows beyond. A force is arriving, something deep and primordial emanating from the bowels of beginningless time like the sound of a titanic conch shell's moan. It's a force that has thrummed through existence since the stars first cooled and formed the lands beneath our feet. It is the call of divine remembrance, summoning you back to the wisdom of your ancestors, to the knowing of when your soul first spawned ages and lifetimes ago. It's a murmur in the dark, beckoning you to step off the familiar paths and into the wild, untamed lands of spirit.

Mere steps away, a shape grows in the suddenly-arriving fog. Tall branches strain upward and score the scarlet sky. A forest formed of soul-stuff manifests before us, and the mundane world dissolves.

We find ourselves standing on the precipice of a spectral woods—a place where who we truly are will be revealed. Furry and feathered creatures swoop and scurry in the periphery, ready to serve as our guides and companions on this adventure tonight. A soft, luminous glow sparkles within the depth of the woods, inviting us inward toward Forty-Eight Gateways. Each portal holds lessons we are meant to learn. This is a place where the impossible becomes possible. Are you ready to leave behind everything you know? Are you willing to wander away from what is comfortable and venture into a feral realm of transformation and growth?

Come, step with me now. The night is gathering fast, and this forest of soul won't linger long. We must make our way through these Forty-Eight Gateways tonight while the moon protects us and the stars stand sentinel on our behalf. Once nestled deep within these woods, time will slow, granting us the space we need to pass from portal to portal. But for now, we must hurry while the moss-lined path remains beneath our feet. Step over these fallen branches. Pull your cloak tight around your shoulders and steel your resolve. Smell the fresh, loamy air enticing us deeper, rich with the scent of peat and cedar wood. Listen for the cawing of the starlings and the rustling of the porcupines; they are here to encourage us on this journey we undertake tonight.

Carved into craggy crevasses, floating on lily-pad-covered ponds, or buried beneath gnarled hawthorn roots, the Forty-Eight Gateways lie glittering quietly. By passing through each, you will reclaim your divine heritage. You will reawaken to the knowledge of the eternal, blissful being that you truly are. You will uncover your celestial origin that has been veiled over by lifetimes of forgetting. You will reawaken to your Ecstatic Self.

For, you see, you are no mere human, trudging through life from one obligation to the next. No, you are a radiant shard of the Oversoul ensconced in the physical. You have forgotten your role as a divine creator of reality so that you could fully experience this human journey. But you have wandered far enough trapped in this self-imposed amnesia. Now is the time to remember your immense power and rediscover your vastness. For you are God incarnate—you always have been. This is what this forest is here to help you uncover.

Together, on this adventure tonight, we will drop our burdens and dance in firefly-lit meadows. We will wrangle with shadows and mourn our old selves in the quiet tidal pools of streams. We will climb mountains, embrace peace, and uncork long-buried emotions. We will laugh, cry, meditate, and make love in wildflower-filled glens. Embracing the natural world, we will find our place in it and its place within us.

Take my hand and step assuredly. This is a place few dare to enter, a place that demands courage, for it asks us to shed the self-limiting beliefs that have held us captive for so long. But you are ready—you will face your fears and set them free. You have courage enough to believe you are more miraculous than you even dared to hope. You are willing to accept your divine magnificence and reclaim your power as creator of the universe.

Let us step spritely; the first gateway calls. There, beside the tranquil pond, beneath the dancing branches of the willow, our portal awaits. Are you ready to enter and transform? Are you prepared to step through these gateways and emerge in the morning light, glistening and changed? Will you be like the dragonfly who goes through stage after stage of molting before it eventually climbs up onto a sturdy stalk of grass and sheds its larval skin, emerging glistening and new with the dawn? Will you be like the moth, clawing free of its cocoon to fly freely toward the sun?

The journey begins with a single whispered *"yes"*—a step forward into the heart of the unknown, into the depths of you.

Once you begin this journey, there is no returning to your former life. You will never shrink back into the confines you're about to expand beyond—there's no climbing back into the chrysalis. Once you know your immense power, the smallness of your reality will be torn asunder. Are you certain you're prepared to say goodbye to what you've known? Then be brave, dear traveler. Let us uncover what spirit has in store for you.

Once you step through, there is no turning back.

HOW TO USE THIS GUIDEBOOK

What you hold in your hands is a magical tome, both a guidebook for soulful reconnection and a mystical grimoire (magical text) for spiritual awakening. Together, we will explore the landscape of soul by venturing through forty-eight successive spiritual principals, or gateways. Each will challenge and encourage you to confront aspects of yourself that you have long ignored or kept hidden. They will entice you toward greater opening and softening. You will likely laugh, cry, and reflect on notions that have flitted around the periphery of your consciousness but perhaps never been considered directly.

In each chapter, you will find a deep dive into the lessons of each gateway. We will explore the terrain from various angles, using the creatures of the forest as examples of qualities we can manifest in our own lives and bearings. I encourage you to read slowly, to sip the words like hot broth on a chilly, rain-drizzled morning. We are not to rush through these concepts but to savor them. Perhaps read a paragraph or two, set the book aside, close your eyes, and breathe deeply. I would discourage sprinting from chapter to chapter, devouring the information like a ravenous raccoon who has discovered an unattended dinner table. Instead, slow down. Linger. Absorb the nuance inherent in each gateway. When you feel like the ideas have been digested, then move on. There is no haste, no rush.

Toward the end of each chapter, each portal, you will find:

RITUALS

These are practices to actively enact the principles of each gateway. They involve magical rituals, daily habits, and boundary-pushing challenges. These are sacred invitations for you to mingle spiritual ideas with your daily existence, drawing these lessons deeper in an actionable way.

JOURNAL PROMPTS

Writing gives our brains a different way to express themselves. Sometimes, we do not know what we are feeling until we grab a pen and set words to paper. I encourage you to find a gilded or leather-bound journal that feels beautiful and sacred to you in which to scribe your thoughts. Using our hands and a pen to write taps into different neural pathways than typing on a device. If you are feeling particularly romantic, perhaps seek out a quill and ink pot...something to get you into the spirit of this being a mystical adventure.

GUIDED MEDITATIONS

These are invitations to allow the messages to sink deeper, past the level of conscious thought. When our brain waves settle into slower patterns, different aspects of our minds are reached. I would suggest you read these sections softly aloud. Take a pause and a breath between each sentence. Then, when you reach the end, close your eyes and quietly let the words hum inside you. Do not strive to think or accomplish anything. Just simply allow yourself to be—experience whatever rises up within you.

MANTRAS

Mantras are repeated phrases or words that attune us to a specific vibration. While mantras in ancient languages are powerful and mystical, I decided to offer mantras in our spoken tongue for this journey. I encourage you to repeat these words as you go about your day. Envision them emanating from the center of your chest, flooding through your body, and making you hum with your intentions.

. . .

How to Use This Guidebook

There are many right ways to navigate this guidebook. You could progress from gateway to gateway in sequential order as they have been laid out for you. I have arranged the chapters in a progression that makes sense to me, as someone who has been exploring these wyrd ways for many lifetimes—but this is by no means the only route through the forest. You are your own best guide, and if your eyes light up when gazing upon one of the portals ahead, trust your intuition and follow. You may start on any chapter and skip to any other that calls to you. All options for exploring are available as you progress through the Forty-Eight Gateways.

Some of you may have also brought along the matching oracle card deck. Here, each piece of sacred artwork is emblazoned on its own card, allowing you to use your intuition or divine guidance to pull one for you. Cards are a powerful way to let spirit guide your choices and allow you to drink in the beauty of the artwork that harmonizes with the energy of each gateway. If you don't already have the deck, you can procure one at EcstaticSelf.com.

If you choose to use the card deck, you may decide to draw a single card to act as your guide for the day, the week, or even a whole moon cycle—allowing its energy and message to seep deeply into your awareness. You might seek the deck's wisdom in response to a specific question, allowing it to reflect your inner knowing back at you. Or, you might pull three cards: one to show where you've been, one to illuminate where you are now, and one to hint at where you're heading. You could even experiment with more intricate spreads, weaving narratives as you might with a traditional tarot deck. Every option is the right one.

You can achieve a similar effect without the cards by simply allowing the book to open to a random page, inviting providence to guide the choice of where to head next. You can flip from cover to cover, allowing your finger to land on a particularly meaningful passage your soul needs to explore. There are countless correct paths to progress through this forest of soul. However you decide to move forward, take your time. Pause. Listen. Linger with the gateways before you.

Trust that this journey is unfolding perfectly for your development and growth. Wander at your own pace. Some chapters may resonate deeply, like a temple gong shaking the walls of your heart, where you need to pause for a season before moving on. Others may feel familiar, encouraging you to progress swiftly, like a hummingbird's flight. Trust your inner guide, for it knows the way.

Now that we have these suggestions in mind, shall we continue on?

AN OPTIONAL PAUSE ON THE SIDE OF THE PATH

Before we delve deeper into these woods together, I wish to offer a glimpse into what lies ahead. If you prefer to jump straight into the gateways themselves, skip this and feel free to return whenever you'd like. But if you're curious about the roads that led me here, how I uncovered these forty-eight portals, then please, read on.

These gateways are more than principles and lessons; they are the accumulation of decades of study, travel, and soul searching. I first became interested in spirituality and soulful knowing as a child. I would find myself wandering out into the woods behind my parents' house, communing with the trees, meditating by the nearby lake, and relishing a sense of awe and majesty I felt for a force far larger than myself. I would peruse the library stacks, my fingers gliding along Dewey Decimal-ed spines, searching for arcane knowledge that would deepen my understanding of the divine. I would have out-of-body, almost orgasmic experiences by simply following the flow of my breath. When I entered university, I began taking courses in various spiritual traditions and visiting local religious sites in the hopes that they could teach me tools and practices to connect more directly with the cosmic Oversoul.

During this time, I uncovered a past-life connection with a spiritual community in the Indian yogic tradition. For seven years, I took residency in one of their ashrams (meditative centers), where I attended daily pre-dawn meditation classes, undertook hours of scrubbing floors and other forms of "selfless service," and strove to learn as much as I could from its teachers and its sacred texts. It was a profound time of personal growth and spiritual awakening, for which I am dearly grateful.

However, the time came when I outgrew the confines of this tradition. While there was much good there, the leadership proved too manipulative and controlling—and I knew I could never manifest my full potential as a spiritual seeker if I stayed within their grasp. With a heavy heart, I bid farewell to the structure and certainty it provided me and struck an uncharted path, following the compass of my longing to intimately know God. I decided to search as broadly as possible, to seek varied perspectives and practices for connecting with spirit. From plant medicine retreats in an Ecuadorian jungle, to healing ceremonies in the Vilcanota Peruvian mountain range, to ancient temples in India, I learned from various wise women, shamans, medicine men, sages, and spiritual leaders. By exploring this multitude of traditions and perspectives, I began to see a commonality flowing between them, threads that remained constant no matter the culture, language, or context. Through much contemplation and reweaving of these spiritual ideas, I eventually uncovered a path that felt expansive and universal.

It is these commonalities that grew into the landscape in which we find the Forty-Eight Gateways. You will find influences and allusions from numerous traditions but direct appropriation from none. The goal in offering these portals ahead is to provide ubiquitous truths removed from specific cultures or faiths—timeless principles stripped of dogma that can resonate with a variety of soul-seekers.

We will explore timeless notions such as forgiveness—both for ourselves and others. We will strive to bless those who have hurt us most. We will endeavor to realize that everything can be viewed from multiple angles, and there is seldom one "right" answer. We will come to regard our bodies as sacred places in which we will uncover a sense of home and belonging. We will dance, we will weep, we will mourn, we will celebrate.

The wisdom these portals bring us can apply to a soulful journeyer regardless of their background, faith, or level of spiritual progress. Many traditions state that timeless truths are floating in the ether, just beyond sight and out of earshot. They will reveal themselves to any of us if we just quiet our minds and become very still. These truths remain constant regardless of the viewer or listener, their spiritual heritage, the epoch or the part of the globe where they find themselves.

To be fully transparent and specific, the traditions that have inspired me the most are:

- Kashmir Shaivism: a non-dualist branch of Shiva-Shakti Tantra

- Vedanta: a tradition based on the "conclusion of the Vedas," the Upanishads
- Bön: an Indigenous Tibetan religion
- Vajrayāna: a Buddhist tradition of tantric
- Taoism: a diverse philosophical and religious tradition Indigenous to China
- Animism: a universal belief that objects, places, and creatures all possess a distinct spiritual essence
- Druidry: a tradition inspired by folk traditions of the Celts
- Mystical Christianity: an esoteric and non-dualist branch inspired by the Gnostic Gospels
- Various American Indigenous Traditions, specifically from certain Andean cultures of Ecuador and Peru

As someone born in the Midwest of the United States of America, I am cognizant that I have no faith tradition native to me. Christianity is the faith of my parents, but it is not indigenous to my homeland or the races of people from which I am descended. I have no living connections to the folk spiritual traditions my European ancestors would have practiced. And the land of my birth, the area of the Great Lakes, gives me no blood connection to the First Nations people whose lands are presently being occupied, such as the Council of the Three Fires. Therefore, I have had to set about cultivating a spiritual path that is native to me—respectful of all cultures that have lent me their wisdom but tied to none.

My hope is that this adventure will be particularly resonant for those who are similarly experiencing a sense of spiritual orphanhood, offering a way for those who likewise long to cultivate their own mystical spirituality without directly appropriating another's. I aspire to share a proto-spirituality that comes directly from observing nature, witnessing life's unfolding, and being present in the experience of sentient embodiment. It strives to be stripped of the historical events and cultural contexts that make something a religion. Instead, it offers a simple, human-centric approach to knowing spirit.

Each gateway provides a lesson that I have explored numerous times—and through this repeated wayfinding, I feel confident to guide you. I consider my role of guide to be akin to that of an usher or doorman: I am here to point out the portals, but it is up to you to step through and do the soulful work that awaits. This is your adventure; I am merely here to point out vantages worth examining. You are the true master here, and I am but the servant. It is always critical to remember that the greatest teacher and guide a person can find is the one that already dwells within the cockles of their heart.

I would be remiss not to include that another profound aspect influenced my understanding of spirituality, which comes from identifying as an outsider throughout my life. Being born queer, neurodivergent, and with a physical deformity that others would routinely mock, I quickly learned that I existed outside the bounds of normal society. I was forced to sit alone most lunchtimes, I was bullied and perpetually harassed, and I very rarely found belonging in any group or clique. Even before I fully understood how I was different, I recognized that I was separated from my peers and even my immediate family by these differences. This status as an outsider forced me to examine the world through a unique lens.

The spirit realm is often described as the "other world." When you are born into a marginalized community, you are forced to dwell on the fringes of the mainstream world. Because of this, we have one foot placed in the realm of communal experience and one foot in that "other world." I have come to believe that being queer, being differently abled, being an immigrant, being an outsider of any variety is an immensely sacred place to reside. In fact, numerous spiritual traditions across time and cultures have put those gifted with outsider perspectives as the central pillar of religious or spiritual life. I began to see these differences that I initially viewed as limitations or burdens to be tremendous blessings. This ability to shift my perspective from one reality to another has become a gateway to divine understanding.

I believe that divinity dwells in the margins, within the unexplored areas, on the untamed roads. When we open up to that which feels taboo, that separates us from the mainstream, we near the divine. It is in the stranger, the shadow, the lost, the ignored, the forgotten, and the abandoned that God dwells. Throughout our adventure together, I will encourage you to challenge norms, seek uncomfortable truths, and stake out uncommon positions from which to gaze. By facing that which feels unfamiliar, we begin to crack open the barriers that separate us from the spiritual realms. By dancing on the periphery between this world and the next, we find our places as children of both heaven and earth, spirit and flesh. We invite unseen forces to become our confidants, intangible beings to grant us wisdom. We will learn that our bodies are not the totality of us; we exist as part of something much larger than our limited selves.

As a young man wandering into nature, I would find myself sitting alone (I was often alone) and meditating. I had not yet been formally taught meditation, but I would cross my legs into a lotus posture while balancing on a fallen tree and attune my focus to my breath, to the present moment, to the energy around me. The forest became my first guide and friend; trees have been some of my most insightful teachers. My journey has been a life of seeking to understand the mystical web that interconnects all life, and this exploration through the Forty-

Eight Gateways to the Ecstatic Self is what I now share. It is a sincere honor and a privilege to walk you to them tonight.

I do not have the answers; all I have are questions. I am still continuing to seek, to strive, to know better. I am a fellow explorer who is also wandering these roadways. I strive to share the perspectives and tools that have served me well in my own spiritual foraging, seeking my own Ecstatic Self. Herein, you will find the ideas that have nourished me on this quest. This journey is about being curious, being open, and being willing to listen to the whispers dwelling in the shadows and on the periphery, lingering under moss-laden archways and within slivery, lily-covered ponds. This guidebook and grimoire is a tool to help you connect with the divine, not in some far-off heaven, but here, in the earth beneath your feet and in the sky above your head. It is in the water flowing in your veins, the fire burning in your belly, and in the sacred open space of your vibrant heart.

With this all in mind, let us begin. The star-spangled night is now truly upon us, and the first portal has called us with its glowing archway. It is time.

I. SEEK PEACE

The road has been wearying, hasn't it? The noise, the hustle, the constant grind to always do and achieve more—has it left you with a headache and a dull pain of dissatisfaction? No matter how much you accomplish, there's always more: more to attain, more to reach for, more to do. Don't you feel exhausted? Perhaps you feel it in your body, a lingering ache, or in your mind, restless with never-ending to-do lists. Don't you wish to escape the relentless pace of modern life?

Come, sit beside me, here, at this tranquil pond. Watch the moon shimmer in the ripples, reflecting off the softly undulating currents. Breathe deeply and draw in the stillness of the night. Observe the swan effortlessly gliding across the water's mirrored surface, radiating peace and tranquility. Everything here is serene. It almost feels like you could set down all your weariness and finally relax.

Take another deep breath in. Allow yourself to sigh out. How do you feel now? A bit lighter? A little more settled?

Few people actively search for peace in our modern world. They search for awards, acclaim, riches, and fame. But how many friends or acquaintances answer with "I just want a peaceful, contented life" when asked about their long-term goals? Advertisements and influencers compel us to seek excitement, distraction, and success—but seldom peace. Yet peace is one of the most beautiful and essential qualities we can cultivate. When you find it, you find home within yourself. There's little more you can desire, for you are contented. Peace is the soft surrender to what is, the letting go of all the burdens you don't need to carry. When peace flows through you like a gentle stream, what more could you want? You have everything.

It's essential to recognize how the modern world is not set up to facilitate this awareness. Capitalism and consumerism thrive by encouraging perpetual dissatisfaction. When you are separated from your peace, you buy clothes you don't need, consume snacks high in calories but empty in nourishment, and take vacations to escape the bustle, traffic, and ceaseless demands of modern life. The barrage of pings, dings, whooshes, and alerts from emails, messages, phone calls, and notifications creates a never-ending hum of anxiety, drawing us into a relentless cycle of wanting and chasing. Our world keeps us on a proverbial hamster wheel of striving, promising contentment if only we buy one more thing, reply to one more email, or take one more yoga class.

The irony is that most of us spend our lives following these distractions, hoping that one day, in the distant future, we'll relax and finally start living meaningfully. But why wait? Peace is available to you now. We know not what the future holds—far too many squirrel away their happiness in the hopes that one day they can finally enjoy it. But what if that day never comes? What if illness or injury claim you before you are ready to step into your retirement from the hustle, to reclaim your peace? Choose peace now.

For how long have you been seeking things that won't bring true contentment but only fuel the need to strive and produce more? How often have you neglected the path to peace, instead pursuing the flashing glamour of modern life, only to find those moments hollow and lacking in sustenance? There is nothing wrong with setting and pursuing goals, but it is foolhardy to believe that lasting happiness will be found in the transient nature of the material world. Everything comes and goes; fortunes accumulate and deplete, beauty fades, health waxes and wanes. But your sense of peace is eternal. How can you prioritize that over the fleeting satisfaction of momentary experiences?

Sit here with me a while longer. Taste the tang in the night air; smell the fertile earth, ripe with promise. Life is blooming here—do you taste it? Do you realize how much is happening in this present moment that we often miss because our gaze is fixed on some distant horizon? Can you slow down and see the satisfaction waiting for you, here and now?

Choosing peace is an active decision. It's stepping off the treadmill, taking a step back from the relentless pursuit of "more," and accepting the contentment already within your grasp. Stop for a moment and ask yourself: is this a decision you're ready to make?

Take another deep breath, watching your breath cloud the cool air with your

I. SEEK PEACE

exhale. The moon hangs bright and heavy, like a ripe peach on a fruit-laden branch. Notice the stars glimmering beyond the willow branches above us. Be here, now. Let go of your striving. Accept the peace that is already within you.

It has always been here. Now, you are remembering it. Make the choice to surrender to the peace available to you in this moment.

RITUAL:

Create a "peace corner" in your home or workspace. This is a dedicated, sacred spot to remind you to check in with your feelings of peace and contentment. It is a place you can retreat to whenever you are feeling stressed or overwhelmed. Decorate it with items that make you feel calm—plants, crystals, candles, incense, artwork of nature, or anything that feels peaceful and uplifting. Make a dedicated effort to visit it regularly—ideally spending ten minutes there a day or more.

JOURNAL PROMPTS:

- What does peace mean to me physically, emotionally, and spiritually? How does it show up in my life right now?
- When have I felt the most peaceful in the past? How can I bring more of that feeling into my daily routine?

GUIDED MEDITATION:

Take a deep breath and envision yourself sitting in the most tranquil abode possible. Perhaps you're surrounded by fog-laden mountains or beside a quiet burbling stream. Maybe you're on a sun-drenched, sandy beach or suffused in an ethereal light that shines from all directions, penetrating a gauze-like haze. Imagine that there are figures of golden light standing before you, at your ideas, and behind you, protecting your peace. They are guardians of your peace, standing stalwart, ensuring that nothing that disrupts your peaceful state of being can enter.

As you breathe, feel yourself inhaling peace and exhaling tension. Every breath in is an opportunity to infuse your body with the vibration of peace.

Allow it to settle over you like a comforting blanket on a chilly morning. Release any negative thoughts or feelings that are keeping you from that peaceful state of being. You are a creature of peace. Let it fill you and surround you. Stay in this space for as long as you are able.

MANTRA:

"Peace is within me; peace is around me."

II. LET GO OF "SUPPOSED TO BE"

Notice the glowing light ahead, nestled in the gnarled roots of an ancient oak. A rabbit's burrow shines with an inner luminescence. This should not be, and yet it is. A warren doesn't typically glow, yet somehow, this one does. The golden light beckons you inward, into a place of impossible things. Nearby, a fox watches with its eyes filled with curiosity. This is where the path leads into an unexpected place—a land where all expectations fall away.

For most of us, we feel burdened by all the things that "ought" to be. Since childhood, society has told us that life should follow a certain script. There are rules to concede to and expectations to meet. We have internalized destinies shaped by others—family, teachers, and neighbors—who have placed expectations upon us from as far back as we can recall. We have been told how to act, how to behave, what careers to pursue, whom to marry, how to dress, even how to wear our hair. We have been given standards to uphold and milestones to meet.

But none of this belongs to you. Whoever told you that you "had to be" anything in particular was mistaken; anyone who said that life "ought to be" a certain way was foolish. There is no one right road, one eventuality toward which we strive. In fact, most often, the things deemed impossible (like a glowing rabbit warren) are precisely the things that life lays before us on our path.

It's time to release all expectations. Now is when we set down the baggage of the "shoulds" and "oughts" and embrace whatever is. The totality of yourself, just as you are.

Step closer to the base of the tree. Feel the cool, packed earth beneath your feet, the dampness of the moss that cushions your steps. The doorway before you glows with the promise of something new—something implausible and yet real. To enter, you must set aside all perspectives on propriety, right or wrong, or even possible versus impossible. We must surrender the lives we thought we were "supposed" to live.

Certainty is a comforting companion. When we think we know where we are going and how we'll get there, there is a part inside ourselves that can relax. But the truth is that we have no certainty in the road ahead; twists, turns, and unexpected sights are guaranteed to await us. We convince ourselves that we comprehend the totality of what we are, where we are headed, and who we will become. But, like this centuries-old tree, our roots burrow deeper than our minds can trace. What you thought your life would be—who you believed yourself to be—was only a story. It was never the full truth.

It's time to let go of what no longer fits.

I speak from my own experience. Growing up, I clung to tightly held notions of the person I "needed" to become. The inside of my high school locker door was plastered with a timeline of all the roles and achievements I was supposed to check off. I had a well-constructed plan cobbled together via my own ambitions, advice from counselors, and hopes inherited from my parents. I was going to be a famous actor, a politician—I was "supposed to be" a great many things that were not in alignment with my truth. I was supposed to be heterosexual; I was supposed to marry and provide my parents with grandkids. I was supposed to take advantage of my expensive schooling in performance art and win awards for my roles on film sets and stages. I was supposed to be... the list was lengthy.

It took many years of soul-searching, self-inquiry, and brave experimentation to begin deconstructing the apparatus of my identity. I had to hone in on the things that felt genuinely aligned with me and separate them from the hopes and wishes placed on me by others. I had to dismantle internal paradigms as well as societal roles and expectations to uncover the person I truly was within. It wasn't easy—I had to challenge deep assumptions, confront rigidly held beliefs, and give a generous "screw you" to anyone who demanded I be someone I wasn't. Because, at the end of the day, the only person I could genuinely be was myself. Anyone else would have been a forgery.

Many of us go years or decades presenting a facade that is societally approvable but inauthentic. We get so comfortable roleplaying that we don't know where our truth ends and the lies begin; we have been performing as someone else for so long that the mask has begun to feel real. Living in this way, however,

II. LET GO OF "SUPPOSED TO BE" 33

has dire consequences for our health, vitality, and joy in life. Though we may not even admit it to ourselves, living according to other people's expectations rather than our own truth creates an inauthenticity in the world; people can feel our fakeness. Our health suffers because we are miserable, our relationships suffer because there is little genuine to latch onto, and our sense of fulfillment in life ends up severely stunted. In my experience, living as a fabricated version of yourself is one of the greatest curses a soul can endure.

So here we are tonight, instead, choosing an unexpected path. We are bravely stepping forward into our truth and surrendering whatever isn't ours. We are realigning our lives toward intrinsic fulfillment rather than outward approval.

The fox turns to you, urging you forward as if to say: *There is more than this story. There is more than what you were told.* Winking, it bounds into the rabbit hole and disappears in a cascade of sparkling light. That, too, should not be possible, yet somehow it is. Trepidatiously, you step forward to follow. You step into the light of possibility, into the unknown. You follow the unfolding path before you without needing to know where it leads. You trust, and you let go to wherever the next steps head.

When you let go of "supposed to be," you allow yourself to become who you truly are. The journey ahead is uncharted, yes, but that is where the magic lives—beyond the maps, beyond the scripts, beyond the old definitions of self. You simply need to trust that the path before you is the one you are meant to walk.

This is where you begin again. Let go, and step into your own becoming.

RITUAL:

On a piece of parchment, write down a list of things you believe you "should" be or do (e.g., "I should have a certain job," "I should be married by now"). Take this list to your sacred space, or sit before an element of nature like a lake, an ancient tree, or a mountain, and ask for its assistance in releasing these expectations. One by one, tear up each item on the list, envisioning divine energy guiding your hands. With each rip, feel the weight of those "shoulds" falling away, leaving you lighter and more free. When you are done, thank the universe for its support, and then go out and try something meaningful—something that feels aligned with the person you are becoming.

JOURNAL PROMPTS:

- What "supposed to be" expectations have I unconsciously carried throughout my life, and how have they impacted my decisions?
- How would my life be different if I completely let go of any expectations about what I "should" be doing or achieving?

GUIDED MEDITATION:

Close your eyes and imagine all of your responsibilities and expectations before you. Give them forms or bodies—maybe human, maybe just shapes and colors. After you feel this gathering of "shoulds" before you...invite in an energy of destruction. Maybe a wind comes and begins to blow them away. Maybe a storm gathers in the heavens and demolishes them with torrential rain and lightning flashes. Maybe the desert heat comes and bakes them, causing them to flake and crumble.

Allow this gallery of expectation to dissolve little by little, and as they depart, notice the empty space that remains. Notice how much more room there is for new things to take root, grow, and bloom. Notice how much more space there is for YOU. Let go of any and all expectations you may be feeling and open up to the vastness of your potential. You are so many more things than you can presently conceive. Remain in this vastness for as long as you are able.

MANTRA:

"I release what no longer serves."

III. EMBRACE CHANGE

The wind bites at the nape of your neck, heralding the arrival of change. Leaves patina with hues of crimson and gold as autumn sets in, transforming the lush greenery of late summer into the fiery shades of fall. It's as though a collective of painters dipped their brushes into ambers, cinnamons, and ochres, coating the seeable landscape in a blaze of color. The air whirls crisp and lighter, summoning images of cozy, fireside nights huddled under blankets.

This is the natural order—life transitions from one thing to the next. Seasons shift, tides ebb and flow, the moon cycles through its phases. Nothing remains constant for too long.

You stand in the middle of this transition, observing the world with curiosity. Perhaps you feel a pang for what has been lost. But as you gaze at the crimson boughs, you recognize the beauty in the change. What once existed was beautiful, yes, but so too is what is arriving. When we surrender what has been, we open ourselves to appreciate what is. Fighting to resist change is futile; flowing with it brings peace and a deeper sense of belonging.

Somewhere ahead of you, a massive bird erupts skyward, its tail crackling with fire. A phoenix, you realize—a symbol of transformation and growth. It streaks across the moon, its wings ablaze with golden light, smoldering in transformation. Once its fiery molting is complete, it will be reborn as something new and beautiful. It demonstrates our need to let go of what has passed and embrace the sanctity of what is coming.

We live in a time of great upheaval; the pace of change is accelerating at an exponential rate. For our great-great-grandparents, the entirety of human knowledge doubled approximately every hundred years. For our grandparents, it doubled every quarter-century. And for us, the scope of human understanding doubles nearly *every day*. We are forced to experience a rapidity of change at such a breakneck pace that it often feels entirely overwhelming.

In order to survive and, indeed, thrive in these times of great upheaval, learning adaptability is the key. We must surrender our need for control, for certainty, for knowing all the answers—we must accept that we will always know less than whatever is to come. We must reprogram ourselves not to see change as dangerous but as an opportunity. We must reframe it, moving away from viewing it as destructive and instead seeing it as beneficially transformative. In the wise words of Bob Bitchin, "The difference between an adventure and an ordeal is attitude."

Flowers don't cling to their petals once pollination has run its course; they let them wither and blow away. A snake does not hold onto its old skin once it's grown too tight and restrictive; it slithers out, shedding the past. We, too, are being called to release old patterns, beliefs, and identities to make space for what is arriving.

Just as rivers carve new channels over time, so too does life carve new paths for us. Resistance only causes a backup or stagnation. Change can definitely feel unsettling, so we must refocus on the opportunities for renewal and discovery that arrive with it. We must train ourselves to recognize that resisting change often causes suffering. The phoenix, blazing against the night sky, reminds us that transformation isn't only natural—it is entirely necessary. Life is change. From the ashes of what was, something new and vibrant eventually always arises.

Where are you holding onto outdated patterns and beliefs in your own life? Where are you refusing to accept that things are different than you anticipated? Perhaps you grew up with rigid ideas regarding the ways of the world or what you were entitled to because it was something your father or your grandmother were guaranteed. *It was always this way, so it must continue to be so going forward.* How can you let go of these outdated modalities that are no longer serving you but only causing further pain and frustration? How can you accept what is and let go of what was? How can you step into the new, the now, whatever is before you?

This gateway invites you to release all your long-held structures and rigid certainties. Embrace a more fluid, flowing, evolving mentality when it comes to life. Hold tight to your essence, to that which is eternal within you, but be willing to adapt. You cannot step into the same river twice; nothing is as it was. The only constant is the timelessness of your soul. You have existed since begin-

III. EMBRACE CHANGE

ningless time and will endure past the destruction of this known universe. You have survived great upheaval before, and you will again.

You are the divine made flesh—you created this reality. Therefore, you chose to incarnate in a world where change is prevalent. Let go of holding onto solidity and embrace the dance of life. Throw back your head and laugh at the uncertainty of it all. Shout "Yes" to the wild moon; embrace whatever comes. Know that, like a bird in a storm, you can rise or fall to counter whatever forces come your way. Trust that change is not the end—it is the beginning of something new and unexpected. It is the start of something wonderful.

May you find your peace while immersed in the flow of change.

RITUAL:

Go outside and collect fallen leaves (or use another natural element, depending on your location). Sit with them and study their forms, shapes, and colors. Notice how they used to be pigmented differently or had other shapes when they were younger. Reflect on how nature effortlessly transforms from one season to the next. Consider how you can embrace the current season of your life, letting go of what no longer serves you, just as the trees release their foliage.

JOURNAL PROMPTS:

- How have I responded to major changes in my life—both positive and negative? What have those experiences taught me about myself?
- What changes am I resisting right now, and why? How could I embrace them to open to new possibilities?

GUIDED MEDITATION:

Lay back and close your eyes. Envision yourself floating in the water...in the midst of a large, swiftly moving river. The current is strong, and the shore is far to either side. You could struggle and thrash and fight against the current, or you could simply give over and let it carry you. You take a deep breath, and as you exhale, you surrender any feeling of control that you have regarding your destiny. Give over to the river; trust it to guide you.

As you release your control, something amazing happens. You realize that you are being guided around any driftwood or debris. You realize that it requires no effort to stay afloat. This river is sentient; it is guiding you toward where you need to go. There is no strain involved; you are precisely where you need to be. You smile to yourself because you realize that all the energy you have historically spent fighting the flow was not needed. Had you just given over sooner, life would have gone so much better, and you would have been closer to your destination.

Continue to float, continue to let go of control, and just let yourself breathe. Stay here for as long as you need.

MANTRA:

"I flow with change. I am transforming."

IV. STEP INTO THE UNKNOWN

There is only fog before you. Any sights past a few paces are cloaked in mist; everything beyond is obscured. Sweat prickles on the back of your neck as uncertainty gnaws in your gut. What if you misstep? What if you fall into an unseen sinkhole? All you can discern is the next step—and yet you feel called forward, into the unknown, into the place where all plans fall away. You summon your courage, give over to the mystery, and step into the fog.

For so long, we have clung to what is familiar, known, and tried. But the pursuit of growth calls us to venture beyond well-worn paths; we must step into an undefined space of possibilities. We must brave uncertainty and accept the sparkling magic that lingers therein.

So, "screw your courage to the sticking place," march into the mist...and know that in the not-knowing, the true adventure begins.

I remember a camping trip from when I was around thirteen years old, a trip I will likely never forget. As dusk fell, a dense fog suddenly rose out of nowhere, shrouding everything in a thick, silvery blanket. In just a few steps, I was separated from the rest of my scout troop. I felt isolated in an unfamiliar, vast, and secret world.

My initial reaction was terror—a cold sweat erupted across my body, and I began to pant. Holding a hand out ahead of me, I could barely make out its contours, let alone anything a few feet beyond. I didn't know where the other boys were, where to go, or if it was even safe to keep walking. But then, as I asked my breath to slow, something shifted.

The world that, only seconds ago, had felt terrifying suddenly felt filled with wonder and possibilities. Anything could be out there in the mist: magic, mystery, untold adventures. What was a dread-inducing landscape transformed into a mystical realm of unimaginable possibilities. That fear turned into a thrill, into a sense of awe. The world became genuinely mystical—who knew what lay just beyond the next stride?

That wondrous moment has stayed with me ever since. It taught me that when we surrender to what is unknown, when we embrace uncertainty, we invite magic into our lives. We open to divine intercession, to the hands of fate intervening, and in doing so, we discover possibilities beyond what we could have ever conceived. We aren't stepping into danger; we are stepping into celestial serendipity and discovery.

Things align themselves so much better than we could have plotted or devised when we simply let go and trust the unknown. We begin to dance with forces beyond our imagining; we cavort with spirit as a co-creator in our lives. By surrendering what is defined and labeled, we invite the divine to present us with things more wild, unfettered, and incredible. We become open to miracles and divine arrangements.

There is little sadder in life than someone who faultily believes that they know everything, that they have complete mastery of their course. By claiming full expertise, we leave little room for growth, wonderment, and discovery. A truly wise person knows that there will always be an infinitely greater number of things that they will never know than things that they do. The person who thinks he knows all goes through life heavy and jaded, missing out on the endless discoveries that make life beautiful.

To step into the unknown is to willingly enter a state of un-knowing. It is to mindfully travel forward with child-like wonder, with a curiosity and willingness to be surprised. It is to marvel at the face in the craggy stone, the spirit in the twisting tree bark. It is to taste the dew droplets in the air and feel the soft grass between your toes. It is to ask bold questions, challenge our assumptions, and explore openly. It is to step beyond the boundaries of our "comfort zone" and into untamed lands that are yet undiscovered. For, in that unknown space, we evolve and grow.

It's tempting to stay where it's safe, to cling to what we know. But in doing so, we limit our potential. The most significant growth happens beyond the borders of our well-examined lives, in the realm of uncertainty. Here, where the mist hangs heavy, the air is laden with possibilities. All you have to do is take the next step…and then another after that. Though the path ahead is unclear, simply trust that you are precisely where you need to be. Each step reveals the next, and the unknown calls you to explore the mysteries it contains.

IV. STEP INTO THE UNKNOWN 45

Yes, you may feel fear. Yes, you may wish to retreat, but don't. Take a deep breath. Surrender your uncertainty and remain where you are—linger on the edge of what you cannot ascertain. Take just one more step. Find peace there, then take another. To embrace uncertainty is to give yourself over to the flow of life—to accept its wildness and its wonder.

You do not need to know; just trust the path and step. Walk into the mist boldly. Trust that it will reveal itself to you as you walk.

Magic lingers just out of sight, waiting to embrace you. When certainty turns to curiosity, wonder seeps in. Just keep stepping, and trust that the path will rise to meet your feet.

RITUAL:

Choose a night this week for a meditative walk in a place you've only ever visited in the daytime. Bring a flashlight, or simply allow the moon's light to guide you. As you step into the night, allow yourself to experience the thrill and tingles that come from reencountering a space that is suddenly transformed by the dark. That which was familiar is now foreign. Strive to remain calm and embrace a sense of wonderment. Notice how the ordinary now feels mysterious. Embrace the darkness and let it remind you that, even when the path isn't clear, you are safe, and all is well.

JOURNAL PROMPTS:

- What unknowns am I currently facing in my life? How do I feel about them, and what is my typical response to uncertainty?
- Reflect on a time when stepping into the unknown led to unexpected growth or joy. What did I learn from that experience?

GUIDED MEDITATION:

Take a deep breath, and as you close your eyes, allow yourself to settle into your body. Sense that you are surrounded by mist. Your feet are bare, and your toes dig into the dirt beneath them. You are standing on a moonlit path with a dense fog extending in all directions.

In your mind, you hold your hand before your eyes, and it's almost impossible to see through the dense vapor. A prickle of fear stirs in your belly; you cannot see the way to go. Take a breath, and as you exhale, let that fear go. As you breathe in, inhale trust. Exhale fear; inhale trust.

When you are ready, take one step forward in your mind. Then take another. Trust that the path will meet your feet; all you need to do is take the next step. When fear arises, let it release as you let go of your breath.

Trust that the universe is supporting you in your journey. You are precisely where you need to be. Everything is arranging itself to bring you toward your highest and best self. Just let go and trust. Step into the unknown and follow the next step that reveals itself before you.

MANTRA:

"I trust whatever comes. I embrace uncertainty."

V. FORGIVE YOUR PAST SELVES

You kneel on the lake's embankment, your fingers trembling, your breath coming in quick gasps. Inside of you, a torrent of feelings floods your body: regret, longing, frustration, and painful reminiscence chief among them. There are so many mistakes you've made, so many choices you wish you could make anew. But here you've come to the water's edge with your regrets written on sheets of linen paper, folded into boats, and you place them to the flow.

The water is still, save for the gentle ripples emanating out from the small ships. Within each, you place a lit candle and watch it flicker softly. One by one, they drift away, carrying the burdens of your regrets, past mistakes, and lost opportunities. You crouch low, your toes curling into the sodden riverbank, observing these little ships sail from view with the stories of who you once were.

Slowly, your breath quiets. Eventually, the emotions within you still. You did the best you could; had you been able to do better back then, you would have. You let the regrets be washed away by the water, burned away by the cleansing fire. It's time to let them go. You let them return to source as ash and pulp; they're yours no longer. They will eventually become soil that will nourish something new.

When examining our past mistakes, it is easy to see how we could have chosen differently. Hindsight is much simpler than foresight. It's simple to chide ourselves, to say we should have known better, done better. But, if we get painfully honest with ourselves, our younger versions of us were doing their best with the knowledge and resources they had available then. If they could have chosen better, they likely would have.

Regret is the past's way of hurting us in the present. But what is in the past has passed—it is no longer our present; it should no longer weigh down our hearts. Let the past be buried, keeping only the lessons that are left behind. We must strive to arrive at a place of gratitude—no matter how foolish or inept our past decisions were. We must strive to see that our past mistakes taught us valuable lessons; they helped us grow. We are who we are because of how our past choices shaped us.

Whatever you did or didn't do doesn't matter—what is important is how you relate to your actions now. Can you forgive your past selves? Can you bless the silly, sometimes stupid younger you? Can you see your mistakes and still thank yourself for trying? Can you welcome the lessons they gave you, even as you cringe in embarrassment or shame?

Yes, you were naïve. Yes, you were impulsive, arrogant, and probably selfish. But... isn't it marvelous that you can now see that? The very fact that you feel regret, that you feel shame, is a hallmark of your growth. It means you've learned, matured, and evolved to be able to hold this perspective. If you couldn't recognize your missteps, it would suggest that you hadn't learned or grown. It would mean that you were still in the same place of immaturity.

Forgive and release. Let the paper boats sail away from you and become something new.

Imagine the little ships drifting further, their flames flickering in the mist lifting off the water, and eventually fading into a dull glow in the distance. You have released the weight of your regrets. Your past has been set free—and a space is unfolding within you to support whatever you are growing into next. You are not who you were—you are who you are now, in this moment, as well as who you are becoming. You are greater for the trials and tribulations in your journey.

Forgive your past selves, bless them, and let them dissolve from memory. They were doing their best to help you achieve the life you thought you wanted. They were misguided, sure, but they meant well. Thank them for their lessons and then release.

With the weight of your past lifted, you are free to rise from the shore and march onward to whatever comes next. Your next iteration will be greater than any that came prior. Trust and believe in yourself.

V. FORGIVE YOUR PAST SELVES

RITUAL:

Find a body of water—a river, lake, or even your bathtub. On small pieces of paper, write down any past mistakes, regrets, or aspects of yourself you wish to forgive. One by one, release these papers into the water. As they drift away, visualize your past burdens being washed clean, carried off by the flow of life. With each release, feel a sense of lightness and self-compassion as you forgive and free your past selves. Finally, offer a silent blessing of gratitude to the water for its role in your healing.

JOURNAL PROMPTS:

- What version of my past self do I need to forgive most? What choices did that version of me make, and why was I so hard on them?
- How would it feel to forgive all parts of my past self completely, with no conditions or lingering guilt?

GUIDED MEDITATION:

Close your eyes, and in your mind, bring forth an image of a younger version of you. This version of you is one you might have a lot of judgment about. He or she comes from a time where you made a bunch of mistakes, where you failed to reach your goals. You failed to live up to your own standard. Notice how you feel about this time in your life, this iteration of you. Are you still disappointed? Are you regretful? Are you even ashamed of this previous self?

Take a breath, and as you exhale, imagine enveloping this person with the rose-colored energy of love. You can even imagine yourself wrapping your arms around your younger self and whispering, "It's okay. You did the best you could. I know you're disappointed, but I am still proud of you." When feelings of anxiousness, despair, or disappointment arise, allow them to be released along with your exhalation.

Keep surrounding your younger self in rose-colored light. Keep hugging yourself tightly. "It's okay... you did alright... we survived... we learned. That is enough." You are enough.

MANTRA:

"I forgive. I release. I grow."

VI. EMBRACE YOUR DESIRES

Glimmering, glistening seductively in the moonlight, a majestic peacock shows off its shimmering tail. Bold blues and emerald greens shine in iridescent, geometric patterns. You sit, crouched on a nearby rock, watching this enchanting display. The heavy bird waddles forward, its tail arrayed in a fan that captivates and entrances you. The peacock seems unafraid of displaying his splendor proudly, unashamed of his magnificence. The tail bobs and stirs up a breeze that wafts your hair and tingles your spine. You are pulled in and enthralled.

You pause and wonder: have you ever allowed yourself to be wholly unashamed about gazing at what transfixes you? Have you allowed yourself to fully feel your desires without guilt or fear? Have you let what grabs hold of you become a guidepost for what you wish to explore?

In many spiritual traditions, desire has been labeled as something dangerous that must be transcended. It is often cast as an obstacle to overcome in the pursuit of spiritual growth. For years, I subscribed to this notion. I believed that to pursue desire was to remain trapped in a never-ending cycle of craving and dissatisfaction. I was told that, once my mind got what it longed for, it would only create new longings to pursue. There's even a term called *hedonistic adaptation* that means, no matter how thrilling or exciting an attainment might be, we will always return to our baseline, eventually seeing it as ordinary.

Peace, we are told, is found only when we surrender desire fully. If we could just stop wanting, we would finally uncover contentment. Desire is the problem

—desire is a distraction from the spiritual path. Desire is what keeps us tethered to worldly suffering.

As time has gone on, I have developed a more nuanced understanding. I have begun to realize that, as spirits embodied in a human form, we have chosen to partake in this worldly life. We have chosen to incarnate in this physical realm to have experiences, learn certain lessons, and grow/evolve. Often, the things to which we feel pulled can be the lessons and the experiences we took physical incarnation to explore. If you are feeling magnetized toward something, it can sometimes indicate that there is wisdom to be gleaned from interacting with it. Desire can actually be a compass pointing the way toward our fulfillment. What if, instead of being an obstacle, desire could perhaps be a guide.

Yes, some individuals abandon spirituality altogether for the passing thrills of the mundane world. Yes, there is perhaps a danger of getting mired in issues that are too earthly. But, so too is there danger in becoming "holier than thou," in rejecting the gift of this physical reality in an attempt to transcend the body and identify only with spirit. I have seen many a spiritual practitioner who have rejected this earthly realm so thoroughly that they can no longer recognize it as a gift; they no longer see that they chose to incarnate here. They feel that this is a dangerous place to escape, not a place to dance, to celebrate being alive.

I believe this to be a huge mistake. These bodies are not meant to be transcended; they are meant to be adored. These human lives are blessings; it is a rare and precious gift to be here, in this form, at this time. Do not reject the gift of this mortal life. Instead, relish it, drink it in, and use up this body in pursuits that bring you joy and nourishment. A fabulous way to make the most of this human life is by pursuing the things that fascinate you. By mindfully engaging with what pulls on us, with that which we covet, we can find untold discoveries and lessons. Profound transformation and growth can occur by pursuing that art form, engaging with that person, and learning that hobby.

Ultimately, it is the decision to see this world as a blessing rather than a thing to transcend. Heaven could perhaps exist on a cloud somewhere, in some foreign realm, but it can undoubtedly exist here if we mindfully turn this world into a haven for what brings us joy. Heaven doesn't just exist on some astral plane or afterlife realm—it is here where we are. The goal is to realize the divinity here on Earth, not to escape from it. Desire can lead us to the very lessons our souls came here to learn. It is not something to suppress but something to study, explore, and follow.

Desire isn't inherently bad or dangerous—it is merely a tool for uncovering personal objectives and realizing growth. By listening to your desires, you may meet that person or go to that place that will change your life. Desire may leave

VI. EMBRACE YOUR DESIRES

you feeling inspired, fulfilled, and joyful. It can be a compass pointing us toward our soul's path.

Look at that peacock again. He doesn't question his beauty nor wonder if he's worthy of attention. He embraces it. What if you gave yourself the same permission to your desires—simply let them guide you forward rather than questioning their validity? What if you allow yourself to follow what pulls on your heart, to uncover pieces of your soul's purpose?

The things you long for may be calling you toward growth, toward meaningful encounters that will deepen and enrich your experience of living. Let desire teach you about who you are and what you need. It is a sacred force, part of the gift of living in a human body.

So, embrace what calls to you. Learn to see what pulls on your heart as a gateway rather than an obstacle.

RITUAL:

Take a moment to identify one thing you desire but have held yourself back from pursuing due to fear or shame. Create a small visual reminder (a drawing, a symbol, or a photo) that represents this desire and place it somewhere visible. Every day, spend a few moments acknowledging your desire without judgment or suppression.

JOURNAL PROMPTS:

- What desires have I been suppressing, and why? What fears or judgments are holding me back from fully embracing them?
- How would my life change if I allowed myself to pursue my deepest desires without fear of judgment or failure?

GUIDED MEDITATION:

Sit in a comfortable position, and in your mind's eye, imagine yourself in a cavern deep underground filled with treasure. Piles of gold, jewels, and precious antiques surround you. Take in the splendor. Notice all the choices you have before you. Today, you are allowed to go up to any one item, examine it, and take it with you. But only one. Tomorrow, you can come back and choose another.

We give value to things not only through their selection but by what we are willing to give up to get them. We only have so much time, so much energy—we have to be selective. What are the things in your life that feel worthwhile to pursue? Since you can only choose one thing right now, what are you willing to give up to have it? Go examine the item that has drawn your focus. Notice its shape and size. What is it made of? Notice that there is a price attached to it, something you have to pay that isn't necessarily money. Are you willing to pay it? Are you willing to surrender whatever is required to pursue this one course?

If you decide you don't like the price or would rather have something different, feel free to shift your focus. Take as much time as you need to decide on the one thing you will engage with today. What will you take home? What will you integrate into your life? Follow whatever seems to gleam and glisten most but also makes sense for you.

MANTRA:

"I honor my desires. I am worthy."

VII

EXPLORE YOUR SHADOW

VII. EXPLORE YOUR SHADOWS

The path ahead is a patchwork of shadows. Shades ranging from pale grays to inky blacks crisscross the dirt road. Unseen forces seem to tremble out of sight, eagerly waiting for you to arrive. Perhaps they are famished predators with their claws outstretched, their sinewy legs contracted. Maybe they are disembodied spirits, hungry ghosts, waiting to whisk you away to some underworld realm. Your mind flashes back to being a child, afraid to walk down the basement steps or to stare into the gap between your bed and the floor. You remember trembling, terror-struck, at what you could not see.

As an adult, your shadows have shifted and changed—no longer often lurking in dark rooms but in the attics and corners of our minds. They are the fantasies we have left unexplored, the fears we have never fully envisioned, the desires we have kept buried within mental concrete...forces that beckon with both dread and curiosity. They titillate and terrify us in alternating and equal measure.

But what if, instead of shrinking back, you choose to step into the darkness? What if you, like the proud wolf with her night vision, bravely made the shadowy world your domain? What if you permitted yourself to explore the unseen world within and venture into its murky depths?

What if you were unafraid of facing the totality of who you are?

Many of us choose to only present the aspects of our identity that are considered polite and socially appropriate. We share the "good" sides of ourselves that our colleagues, spouses, and parents will approve of—and sequester the other parts. We play a role that fits society's narrative of what makes us admirable and acceptable.

But that is not the totality of who we are. We also possess shameful bits, kinky parts. We have aspects of our identity that we consider inappropriate, wrong, or broken—and those we keep hidden from even our dearest loved ones who should know us best and accept us fully. And in so doing, we begin to wear a kind of mask. We don a papier-mâché facade that is only paper-thin and lacking the subtlety or depth of real flesh. We become fake persona devoid of the complexity and nuance that make up a human being.

We fragment ourselves into our "good" and "bad" parts and bifurcate our reality. And in so doing, we destroy any chance of having a wholly embodied existence. When we sever parts of ourselves, we can no longer be whole. We accept the fate of a half-life—being a wraith. Instead, we must make the radical choice to visit with our shadowy, naughty, entirely unacceptable aspects and choose which parts to boldly reintegrate into our larger sense of self. We must open the shutters to the attic, break through the concrete, and unchain the monsters hidden inside our mental basements. Some will fly away and some will take residence near our hearth and prove that they were never all that fearsome.

What would happen if you simply stopped hiding your shadowy parts? What if you brought them into the daylight and allowed other people to respond however they will? What if you explored and experimented and uncovered which parts were integral to you and which you could release? What might you discover?

Our shadow sides are not separate from us; they are us. The aspects of our identities that we have repressed can hold essential insights about who we truly are. Yes, we are the kind, polite, hard-working people who show up for business meetings and events with our families. And we are also the selfish, petulant, desirous people who we pretend not to be. How could you heal and evolve if you simply sat with all parts of your totality?

To become whole, you must welcome all of yourself. You must bear witness to the qualities about yourself that you have deemed as being wrong, harmful, or simply insufficient. We contain multitudes within. These hidden facets are not flaws to be hidden, but vital keys to unlock emotional and mental well-being.

How can you surrender the shame around the parts you have denied? How can you explore your shadowy desires, longings, and fears with kindness, gentleness, and reassurance—choosing which to keep and which to release? How can you allow yourself to go to that place, try that thing, or adopt that aspect of your persona that will bring you lasting joy and contentment? Even if it feels wrong. Even if it feels dirty. Even if it contradicts the narrative you've built up regarding who you are and who you are becoming.

VII. EXPLORE YOUR SHADOWS

The wolf is watching you, encouraging you on this journey. She wants you to step from the familiar, well-lit roads and explore the realms of shadow. Her eyes are alight with an inner knowing as she smells the footpath ahead; she is confident in the path you must take. She longs for you to confront the parts of yourself that you've long avoided. What if you simply allowed yourself to be your full self in your wonderful, contradictory complexity?

Throughout my teens and early twenties, I received feedback from people telling me I seemed inauthentic. They felt they couldn't trust me; they said to me that I didn't know who I was. I was routinely informed that it seemed like I was wearing a mask.

It didn't feel that way; I felt confident I was embracing my genuine self. But, lo and behold, I had yet to confront the fact that there were many aspects of my identity that I had banished beyond the scope of my awareness. I had unknowingly hidden critical elements of what made up my true self because I deemed them unacceptable. I hid my same-sex attraction even from my own mind. I hid emotions I felt were inappropriate—like anger—because they were in conflict with the man I wanted to be in the world. But, in so doing, I fashioned a half-life for myself. Until I became brave enough to ask difficult questions and tiptoe into my well-guarded and tightly-chained dungeons of soul, I failed to be a fully fleshed-out human being. And once I began to explore and integrate my shadow sides, the people around me began to behave differently.

Suddenly, I became the person who was praised for his authenticity. I became the person who was regarded as being well-adjusted and unashamed of his humanness. By embracing the parts of myself that I thought many would consider taboo, wrong, or sinful…I ended up becoming more light-filled. By embracing my shadow, a veil was removed from my inner luminance. By becoming whole, I became a beacon for others to accept their totality.

When you feel fear, disgust, or anger come up regarding other people…those feelings are often indicators of the direction you need to go to explore your shadow. Whatever piques your curiosity, titillates you with forbidden desire, or makes you uncomfortable…those are the things you ought to explore. These will lead you in the direction of your reintegration and wholeness. Whether or not you "like" these things is irrelevant. What matters is that they are somehow a part of you and must be allowed to return home. Only by reclaiming your shadow can you be fully integrated.

Do not fear the darkness. You will find wholeness by stepping into the abyss with the protective wolf at your side. In so doing, you will find an appreciation for the sacredness in all things. Release your terror—breathe deep and surrender. And, as you explore the shadows within, you may find that what you feared was never that ominous after all. It was just waiting to be seen.

RITUAL:

Plan a day where you engage in role reversal: adopt a trait or behavior you typically avoid but recognize in yourself and act it out in full. Pick a location, wardrobe, or group of people who would be supportive of this atypical expression of your identity. Note your feelings and reflections throughout the day.

JOURNAL PROMPTS:

- What aspects of myself have I been hiding from or avoiding? Why do these parts of me feel uncomfortable to confront?
- How can I begin to integrate these shadow aspects into my conscious self with compassion and understanding?

GUIDED MEDITATION:

Imagine yourself standing in front of a basement door. The door is padlocked and deadbolted. In your pocket, you find a key. Do you take it out? Take a deep breath and reach for it. When you are ready, slide it into the lock and turn. Unfasten the deadbolt. Open the door. Inside, the passageway down is covered in cobwebs; it's been a long while since you've treaded down here.

You brush them aside, turn on the light, and walk down the creaking steps one at a time. You feel your heart racing in your ribcage; you take a few deep breaths to slow it. As you reach the bottom of the stairs, you grab a nearby flashlight and shine a light into the abyss. Lining the walls of the subterranean vault are all the parts of yourself that you deemed unworthy, damnable, disgusting, inappropriate, or unlovable.

Step into the din and slowly explore the space. Shine the light on each hidden aspect of you, and send each part a feeling of love and compassion. These parts deemed reprehensible are also you. They are not bad, they are not wrong, they are not sinful, they are not dirty.

If you are ready, find one or two where you are ready to unshackle their chains and bring them back upstairs with you and into the light of day. Give these parts of yourself a room, a bed, and a hot meal upstairs.

VII. EXPLORE YOUR SHADOWS

Take as many trips as necessary down into the basement, emptying it out, until all your shadow sides have been released, integrated, or lovingly dissolved. Take as much time as you need.

MANTRA:

"I am whole. I embrace my shadows."

VIII. HEAL YOUR WOUNDS

We follow the noise of tinkling drops down a stepped path beneath gnarled roots of an ancient ash. Descending into the craggy bowels of the earth, we come upon a rivulet that grows into a stream and flows into a subterranean cave. Lit by a dim, ambient light that comes from some unseen source, you wade into the sparkling current that bubbles like champagne.

Come, sit with me in these salubrious, crystalline waters. Dwell here for a while in this place where healing begins. Notice how the current shimmers in opalescent lines, how it splashes like chimes over pebbles and boulders alike. Allow it to flow over you and wash away any bruised, burned, or broken parts.

In this space, wellness flourishes. Hope springs forth, joy bubbles anew, and scars fade. Allow yourself to lie naked in the healing pools, and let an effervescent glow spread through you. Gaze softly at the nearby mystical creature, a unicorn, lowering its pearly head to drink from the stream. Here, feats of wonder blossom like lotuses on the nearby lily pads. All types of renewal and healing are possible.

Bathing in these sacred ponds, a realization burbles into your awareness: healing is an active choice. To seek out the places, thoughts, and modalities that allow you to knit yourself back into wellness is a conscious decision. To cast away our limiting beliefs in our brokenness is an intentional action. You can opt to cling to your wounds as if they were prized possessions—or you could surrender them to the flow of life. You can decide to tightly grasp those old narratives of pain or, conversely, release into your wholeness.

Your physical form is ever-evolving. Some of your cellular tissues regenerate in days, some over years. But within a decade, mostly every part of your body is newly made. What happened decades prior no longer has a home in you. On a molecular scale, every atom in your body has been loaned to you from the oceans, from the mountains—they were originally forged in the bellies of stars. None of this is yours... not these stories of pain nor these tales of your brokenness. You are made of starlight.

You must choose to surrender the stories of your limitations and inadequacies. This is not to say that you don't have problems, that real traumas haven't happened to you. Some scars run very deep, indeed. But we learn from the parts of the story we focus on. And so, what stories are you telling yourself? Are you repeating tales of victimhood, of your brokenness? Or are you highlighting tales of your endurance and your ability to thrive? Outdated stories focusing on your limitations do far more harm than good.

The truth is that you are capable of having a tremendous life. You are entitled to feel vital, vigorous, and powerful. You can reclaim a space of wellness and empowerment. To do so, we must seek out those who can help us come back into alignment with those qualities.

Ask yourself: have you sought out the healers who you think can help you? Have you visited the shamans, the therapists, or the doctors who have expertise in your particular maladies? Have you explored the books, listened to the sages, or tried the modalities that may bring you back into congruency with your health? Even more importantly, have you consulted with your own body, asking it questions and listening to the stories it wishes to share with you?

A helpful practice I employ is asking the parts of myself that feel afflicted to speak to me. Whether it's a physical, emotional, or mental discomfort, I say, "What do you need me to hear? What are you trying to get me to learn?" I may ask these questions many times before I hear an answer.

We tend to think of the mind and body as separate things—and even more separate: our spirit. But, in actuality, the three are not only interlinked, they are extensions of each other. Where the mind goes, so too goes the body. Where your spirit flows, you will find your mind and body there too. Something that affects us on a mental or emotional level will affect our physical form, and vice versa. But by treating our bodies as being intelligent with wisdom to teach us, we can often begin to unravel the tensions that are keeping us in a state of unwellness. By seeking the aid of an experienced practitioner—whether they be an acupuncturist, a holistic medicine woman, an allopathic doctor, or a spiritual healer—they can often see or sense the stories that our bodies are striving to draw our attention to, hearing more deeply than our own ears sometimes can.

Healing is not a passive act; it is not just something that happens to you. To

VIII. HEAL YOUR WOUNDS

claim your place as a divine creator of this reality, you must also reclaim ownership in your ability to actively engage in healing. You can choose wellness, to a large degree. Our bodies are more resilient and regenerative than many people suppose.

There are interesting results in studies done on individuals with dissociative identity disorder (commonly known as multiple personalities). Different personalities housed within the same physical body can have different reactions to drugs—some even being allergic to ones the others are not. Studies have shown, through brain scans, that several personalities within one person can be legally blind (nothing lights up in the optically associated parts of the brain during an fMRI), while others can see. Studies have shown that moles can appear and disappear depending on which personality is expressed. In one studied instance, a person's irises actually changed colors based on which personality was dominant.[1]

This shows that our physical forms are not nearly as solid as we like to think. By engaging with yourself on a soulful level, miraculous changes can manifest. We must adopt a mindset of being well, actively asking for it, and then staying open to its arrival. It requires us to remember that we are shards of the Oversoul taking temporary residence in the physical, and our thoughts have the capability to create significant change in this material realm.

So, how can you better opt into a state of wellness? How can you claim ownership over your own healing? A simple way to begin is simply by expressing gratitude for whatever is happening to you. By saying "thank you" to our physical selves—including our injuries—we create a vibe shift. We begin to manifest a more beneficent resonance within ourselves—not one of suffering, but one of joy. The harmonious vibrations that emanate from a grateful state can work wonders. You must choose to let go of your stories of brokenness and instead embrace a narrative of thankful appreciation.

Next, cultivate a curiosity around healing and explore any/all avenues toward wholeness that call to you. Healing can occur in unexpected places, so stay open to a person, a book, a video, or a tradition that may provide you with essential information for your journey.

Healing is your birthright. Wholeness is your natural state. Open yourself up to your full potential—and allow the healing waters of life to flow through you. Bathe in their shimmering pools and allow yourself to emerge glistening, whole, and radiant.

You are, and always have been, whole. Or, as I often repeat to myself: All is well, all has been well, and all will be well. I *am* well.

---

1. Selbie, Joseph. *The Physics of God*. Red Wheel/Weiser, 18 Sept. 2017.

Healing isn't just a journey, it's a return. You are returning to your essential truth buried beneath the scars, pains, and limitations. You, at your essence, are whole, vibrant, powerful, and eternal. Embrace your wholeness and allow yourself to dwell in the healing that has been waiting for you all along.

RITUAL:

Identify a wound—whether emotional, mental, or physical—that still lingers. Prepare a healing bath with Epsom salts, essential oils (such as lavender or chamomile), and candles. While soaking in the water, visualize this wound healing, releasing any energy that holds you back. If you'd like to take this one step further, schedule a session with a therapist, acupuncturist, healer, or shaman who specializes in your specific area of desired healing.

JOURNAL PROMPTS:

- What emotional wounds do I carry that I haven't yet acknowledged? What is stopping me from fully confronting them?
- How can I begin the process of healing—whether through self-compassion, therapy, or seeking support from others?

GUIDED MEDITATION:

Envision yourself standing before a waterfall. The tinkling of water drops sounds like chimes; a healing mist rises off the water. Take a deep breath, and—in your mind's eye—dive in. Swim through these crystalline waters. Allow the shower to heal all wounds, hurts, and maladies.

Watch your psychic and physical bruises fade, and your cuts and lacerations disappear. In this sacred tidal pool, all that has been keeping you wounded dissolves. You are fresh and new. You feel purified, unburdened. Allow yourself to sit on a rock and feel the massaging downpour relax your shoulders. Let the salubrious waters clear your mind, heart, and spirit.

Stay here wading, swimming, and bathing for as long as you need.

VIII. HEAL YOUR WOUNDS

MANTRA:

"I am healing. I am whole."

IX. PURGE YOUR DEMONS

The climb has been arduous, each step heavier than the last. This journey toward the summit has been a test of both body and spirit. You're drenched with sweat from your exertions, aching through every limb, and nauseous from the strain. These physical discomforts, however, pale in comparison to the unrest in your soul. Within you, the traumas, regrets, and unresolved tensions from your past claw and gnaw fiercely. With the intensity of a festering wound, they twist and scream inside of you.

You stand at the precipice and survey the landscape below, struggling to still your ragged breath. You realize that this climb wasn't just physical. This trek was never about the rugged terrain beneath your feet—it was about the mountain within.

Each step has brought you nearer to the pinnacle of your pain. Each moment of exertion has brought closer the anger, the sadness, the bitter angst you've long kept hidden. But now, standing on this ledge, you feel it rising—that raw, jagged pain you've fought long to suppress.

It can no longer be contained.

You open your mouth, and from deep within, a scream erupts. It is primal, visceral, raw. You throw out your arms in a gesture of release, inviting the tensions within you to purge. And, to your great surprise, out of you erupts a mass of swirling darkness. An unfurling cloud pours from you, twisting and spinning into the sky. As the darkness rises, it transforms into an unkindness of ravens. A flock of black, shiny birds formed of vapors flap their wings and scatter toward the ominous clouds. You continue to scream, expelling more of the poison within you, releasing more of the pain.

On and on it goes until the final tendrils of darkness leave you. You feel emptied, hallowed/hollowed. The cloud of anguish and trauma dissipates, the birds disperse, and a shaft of moonlight shines down on you. Around you settles an eerie, unfamiliar quiet. There is no more clamor coming from within, no pulsing of despair. You fall to your knees, sobbing but lighter. You feel free of the internal demons that held you captive. In this stillness, flickers of peace begin to pulse. They feel fragile but real—something you haven't experienced in a very long time. You remember what it's like to live without being haunted.

In life, experiencing pain is unavoidable. Sometimes, the hurts are small and fleeting; other times, they are deep and existence-altering. The smaller pains resolve on their own after some time—those cutting remarks from a stranger will be forgotten, the selfishness of a friend will be glossed over, the rudeness of a coworker will be buried. But those deeper pains...the soul-etching traumas that follow us like determined ghosts...those we may need to actively deal with.

Sometimes, finding wholeness goes beyond mere healing. Sometimes, we must experience a type of exorcism of the traumas that have scorched themselves into our psyches. These deeper wounds need more than a balm or a salve—they require a purging. This is not simply about healing; this is about intense release.

These deeper wounds can warp our sense of self, distorting how we see ourselves and the world around us. These are the demons we carry—the unresolved tensions, the traumas we've never fully faced. They will not fade away on their own. They putrefy and grow tendrils of darkness into the landscape of our hearts. Purging them is an act of survival.

When I was growing up, I was bullied mercilessly—tortured, really—by my peers. From first through eighth grade, there was seldom a day where I wouldn't come to tears from the cruelty my schoolmates enacted. Middle school, in particular, was resoundingly terrible—not a passing period would go by without some hateful remarks being hurled at me multiple times, sometimes accompanied by physical objects.

In hindsight, I realize a big part of this was due to my neurodivergence—as someone whose brain operates differently, I was immediately flagged as "weird" and "strange." I became the class scapegoat, the person whom it was okay for everyone to make fun of. Being queer on top of that certainly didn't make things any easier.

Though I did the best I could to heal my wounds, an ever-present pit of darkness dwelled in my stomach well into my mid-thirties. No matter what I did, I

IX. PURGE YOUR DEMONS

could feel it there, pulsing. No matter how many affirmations, meditations, or medications I tried...nothing filled it, covered it, or made it fully dissipate.

A few months before my thirty-fifth birthday, I awoke one morning and heard a deep, rumbling voice calling me. I heard instructions to go to the mountains of the Vilcanota range in Peru. A friend of mine was hosting a retreat, bringing a group to work with the ingenious healers of that area. I went and quickly became sicker than I had ever been in my life. For six days and nights, I barely ate; I barely slept. In a tent nearly 20,000 feet above sea level, freezing from the glacial winds, the healers performed numerous ceremonies on me. In our conversations, they stated clearly that the sacred mountain we were visiting had called me to come. I had been summoned there to purge the trauma from my youth so it wouldn't consume me.

After several days of wondering if I would ever make it off the mountain top, I emerged a new person. Lighter, more healed than I ever remember being. The pit within me was gone—and years later, it still has not returned.

When the darkness inside has grown too great, when we have carried our pits of despair too far, we must do whatever is required to forcefully let them go. This is not time for a gentle healing; a violent reckoning is required. This requires raw intensity and willingness to face what has haunted us most viciously.

This is the time to seek out a healer with expertise in assisting with deep traumas. This may be a shaman, a wild woman, an exorcist, or a specialized therapist. This is the time to scream, shout, stomp, hurl things. Throw yourself off a cliff and into a salty body of water multiple times. Explore rituals, ceremonies, and cathartic movements to release. Strive to free yourself of the toxic energies within.

There is a significant cost that comes with ignoring our demons. They manifest in our bodies as illness, in our minds as mental disorders or depression, in our souls as disconnection. There are many who suffer from long-term conditions that can trace the onset to a traumatic event. The pain of keeping them within, however, is far greater than the momentary suffering that comes with finally lancing the proverbial cyst.

So yes, this is going to hurt. You will have to face things you've long sought to ignore, your deepest wounds. But the alternative is far bleaker. Once your inner demons have been freed, you will find your own liberation. You will find a quiet, a peace, a burgeoning of light in the space where the darkness once lingered.

It's encouraging to remember that our ability to experience true joy is predicated by the amount of sorrow we have faced. Philosophers have said this in ages past, and brain scientists are saying it now: your ability to enjoy life is directly predicated by the amount of suffering you've worked through. The fact that you have endured something terrible, that it has flown through you and out, means that you now have a vast space within to hold joy.

In the words of Khalil Gibran, "The deeper that sorrow carves into your being, the more joy you can contain. Is not the cup that holds your wine the very cup that was burned in the potter's oven? And is not the lute that soothes your spirit, the very wood that was hollowed with knives? When you are joyous, look deep into your heart and you shall find it is only that which has given you sorrow that is giving you joy."

Trust me, dear one. You are not broken. You are not beyond repair. You are a being of light, capable of transformation and tremendous growth. The time has come to finally confront the shadows veiling your inner light and strip them away. Cast them off and reveal your inner luminosity. Yes, it will be harrowing. Yes, you will scream, cry, and rage—but that's perfect. Do what you must to purge your shadows and set yourself free. A marvelous sense of openness and bliss is waiting for you. The light will shine through the clouds and make you dazzle.

RITUAL:

Grab a pen and paper, and write down anything that feels like a personal "demon." This could be an addiction, an un-ignorable pain, a bad habit, or a negative belief system. Once written, perform a small burning ritual in your sacred space: safely burn the paper in a fireproof dish, symbolizing the release and transformation of these demons. Take the ashes outside and scatter them to the winds, thanking them for the lessons they brought. Offer a blessing for their release and thank the universe for assisting you in letting go.

JOURNAL PROMPTS:

- What are some of the past traumas that still haunt me to this day? What sensations arise when I focus on them?
- How do these "demons" manifest in my daily behavior, and what triggers them? How would I feel free without them?

IX. PURGE YOUR DEMONS

GUIDED MEDITATION:

Envision yourself in a room with a long table. On this table are empty glass bottles of varying sizes with sturdy corks sealing them up. One at a time, grab ahold of one of the bottles, and holding it tightly between your hands, envision your inner demons flowing out of you and into the glass bottle. Once the demon is fully trapped inside, replace the cork and grab a new bottle.

Repeat this process as many times as you need; there is an infinite supply of bottles for you to use. Once you feel like you've caged as many of these inner beasts as you can, carry them outside. Nearby is a blazing fire, hot enough to melt glass and incinerate any living creature. Standing safely back, toss the bottles into the blaze and watch as they melt and destroy the demons within.

Once your arms are empty, offer some gratitude for the lessons these burdens have taught you. Give thanks for the freedom you're feeling.

MANTRA:

"I surrender and release all tensions within me."

X. LET GO OF CONTROL

Give yourself over; feel the caressing currents undulate along your body, tingling you from your toes to the many little hair follicles on your head. Allow yourself to float, glide along, swirl with the movements of the river. The current strokes every part of you, lulling you into a blissful state of surrender. There is nothing to do and nowhere to be...all you need do is simply release and give over to the hypnotic caress of the river. There's no effort here, no resistance...you can simply be.

Notice how tightly you've been holding on. Observe the tension in your shoulders and across your back. You sigh and release the white-knuckle grip you've maintained, striving valiantly to steer the helm that directs your life. Why have you perpetually tried so hard, you wonder? What would have it been like to have just given over and let the currents of fate guide you? What if you trusted everything was arranging itself to bring you the needed lessons and experiences to help you thrive and grow? You wonder how much energy you've wasted striving to fight against the current, to wade upstream, when everything you've needed has always been awaiting you if you simply flowed along.

Why the forcing things into place? Why the relentless need for control?

Control is a fickle friend. It often feels so comforting in the moment; it reassures us that we are doing the right thing. If we just try harder or strive more, we can surely cultivate the perfect existence. If only we could get everyone and everything to perform precisely as they should, then life would be easy. Oh, how encouraging control feels, whispering in our ear that we just need to push a bit harder.

Yes, it makes us feel briefly powerful. It permits us to feel like masters of our destinies—but, over time, we realize how exhausting it truly is. Striving for continuous control leads to burnout, chronic fatigue, relentless anxiety, and a host of other maladies. It doesn't matter how willful or strong you are; you will never have the capacity to mold everything to obey your will...and so exhaustion eventually comes.

The metaphor I return to again and again is that of the hammer. Imagine I give you a hammer and ask you to hold it at shoulder height. Perhaps you're very athletic; perhaps you can keep the hammer extended for a minute...two minutes...five minutes...or even more. No matter how muscular your deltoids are, eventually, they will fatigue. Eventually, that hammer, which initially felt so light, will come to be unbearably heavy. Then, your shoulder will seize up, your arm will sag, and you will have to let the hammer drop.

Control feels like an easy fix in the beginning. It feels like a comforting friend, egging us on to just do a little more, try a little harder. But even the strongest and most adept of us will flag and fail. There's an old adage that control is merely an illusion—which I repeatedly remind myself of and strive to take to heart. I may be an immensely capable person in the world—I may do a fabulous job in manifesting the life I desire—but I also recognize that my powers are limited...while the powers of the universe are unlimited.

Instead of drawing on my personal agency, what if I ask the universe for divine support and guidance? Instead of forcing the water to flow in a specific direction, what if I request the universe arrange the riverbed so that it naturally flows in the direction of my highest good? What if...and this is the heart of the issue: what if I realized that everything was already flowing in the direction of my highest good, greatest joy, and deepest enlightenment? I didn't need to do *anything* to make it so; it was already arranged perfectly.

It's easier to give up exerting control when you've observed practical examples of how life is working for you, not against you. When you realize that the universe is orchestrating situations and timing events in a way that feels serendipitous, and when you recognize that miracles are happening all around you (if you have cultivated the awareness to recognize them), it becomes easier to let go and trust.

Float and observe the koi fish circling around you, their graceful bodies gliding effortlessly. They aren't fighting the current, they are swimming with it. Their fins glint and shine, reflecting the sunlight above like golden silk in the water. Watch them and feel your soul relax. Allow their grace and ease to stir something deep within you. Trust that, if you give over, you will be precisely where you need to be. The divine hand of destiny (or karma) has arranged everything for you. Give yourself permission to surrender.

X. LET GO OF CONTROL

Yes, we are responsible for our actions in the world. We choose our reactions and next steps—but we cannot choose the events themselves. Do your work, but then let go—let the results be whatever they are to be. Strive to accept whatever comes, gratefully...knowing that in it are lessons and opportunities for growth, happenings that our soul called out to experience.

Yes, you will know troubles. Yes, you will know hardship. But releasing and flowing with life makes managing those situations easier, not harder. Let go and trust that everything will work out, eventually. Most of the things that worry us, that make us gnash our teeth and pull our hair, anxiously striving to fix them... will be forgotten entirely in a few years. Was it really worth all that stress and strain? We cannot decide what will or won't happen—life will toss blessings and storms your way, no matter your plans. It will send waves that we could never have anticipated. In the words of journalist Mary Schmich, "The real troubles in your life are apt to be things that never crossed your worried mind, the kind that blindside you at 4 p.m. on some idle Tuesday."

So, will you let go? Can you recognize that the tighter we strive to exert control, the more likely we will suffer? Like trying to dam a river with the force of your body—you're only creating more resistance, more pain. What if, instead of a dam, you strive to build a raft, a sturdy vessel that could rise or fall with the changing tides? What if we simply respond to the unfolding of events with grace and trust, flowing with the current?

Life is bringing you whatever it is that you need. Even storms can be blessings in disguise, clearing away what no longer serves you. Surrender your need to control each outcome. Let go of the fear that things won't turn out as they should, if you simply trust. The river knows the way—trust its flow.

I invite you to be like the koi, be like the water. Flow in the direction of least resistance. Trust that life will carry you precisely where you need to be. Let go.

RITUAL:

Practice a "trust walk" exercise with a trusted friend or partner. Let them guide you, blindfolded, on a short walk through your neighborhood or a park. As you walk, notice your body's tension and let yourself surrender control, trusting your partner to lead you safely.

JOURNAL PROMPTS:

- What am I currently trying to control in my life that may be causing stress or resistance? What would it feel like to surrender control in that area?
- Reflect on a time when letting go of control led to an unexpected but positive outcome. What did I learn from that experience?

GUIDED MEDITATION:

Lie down for this meditation. As you breathe, feel yourself getting lighter and lighter. Ever so gently, you become no weight at all, and a soft breeze lifts you up into the air as if you were a feather. Notice how you are carried out of your room and into a beautiful meadow. Floating and gliding over the wildflowers, notice how free you feel.

You need absolutely no control here; the wind is guiding you toward your perfect destination. You are completely at ease and trusting. Notice how you fly effortlessly over trees and bushes, avoiding any potential obstacles in your way. Eventually, the wind sets you down on a gently flowing river. As you effortlessly float, notice how the water guides you around any rocks or debris. You are effortlessly steered toward your perfect destination. Feel the sunlight against your eyelids. Feel yourself surrendering to the current.

Eventually, you end up on a sandy beach. This is precisely where you wished to be. Look how you were guided here in the most perfect way possible. Letting go brought you to where you belong. This is where you are at your best. Enjoy laying here and feeling the freedom that comes from simply letting go.

MANTRA:

"I surrender. I am stepping into the flow."

XI. WANDER AIMLESSLY

You've folded your map and tucked it away into your pocket. You've slid the compass in beside it. Onward, you walk with no direction in mind, no specific goal to achieve. There is only the path you are creating—one step making footfall, then another. With no destination at which to arrive, the journey itself becomes the focus; each moment is a new discovery. You know not where the path ahead leads, but somehow that feels right. Each pace forward is a delving into the unknown, an exploration of life without plan or pressure.

As you progress, the twilight hums with an enchantment you've never noticed before. The leaves on the vines and the petals on the flowers seem to glow, sending sparks of luminescence into the dusky air. The surrounding bushes and brambles shimmer as if alive, rustling with an age-old sentience. You feel their presence greet your heart and wrap it in a warm embrace. You are moving through a world of living beings rather than things. The magic of the forest is seeping into your skin, sinking into your bones.

A soft breeze whispers in your ears, sharing secrets you can almost discern. You feel it guiding you forward with gentle, knowing nudges. A hare scampers beside you, curious about your journey. He seems a fellow explorer, equally curious about what you'll uncover and where you'll end up. With a chuckle, you realize there is no rush to find out where that endpoint will be.

You wander aimlessly and, in so doing, uncover a vital truth: the journey has never been about the destination. Our paths in life have never been about achieving some gold ring, some final accolade…no. It has been about the discovery, the learning, the presence of mind that occurs on the route toward wherever we are headed. The winding roads you didn't expect, the deer path that veered off from the course you were supposed to take—they were the purpose all along. Each surprise, each discovery found tucked away between trees and under boulders was the meaty sustenance of life...not the end results.

When I was a young lad, I had a detailed timeline hung up inside my school locker. I carefully plotted out what achievements I wanted to hit by which year of my life. Many of the goals were audacious, like garnering famous awards and titles...things my young mind thought would bring me lasting self-worth and happiness. But now, a few decades later, I can confidently say that none of those epic plans have come to pass. My life has veered in directions I couldn't have conceived of—and though my younger self might be a little disappointed in that, I cannot imagine a more fulfilling and meaningful life. In order for me to have arrived at this place of true contentment, where I have a deep sense of belonging within myself and my wider community...I had to dare the unexpected roads. I had to allow myself to wander and explore things not scribed in the guidebook or marked on the map. I had to become aimless and tune into the wisdom present in the world around me. And, more importantly, become aware of the quiet murmurings within my own heart.

The world is vast, complex, and meandering. There is seldom a straight line from our initial inspiration to the fulfillment of our goal. Instead, life spirals, dances, and cavorts, diverting us into places we didn't know we needed to see. But wherever our feet take us, there will undoubtedly be worthwhile sights to explore that just might provide the information, the clues, or the answers to questions we didn't know we needed fulfilling.

There is an immense freedom that comes with letting go of plans, goals, and expectations. There is profound joyfulness in simply accepting where we are, not needing to figure out where we're headed. When we allow ourselves to explore the landscape around us, we open ourselves to so many more possibilities. We uncover beautiful lessons and fortuitous happenings that we would have missed on a linear, rigid path.

Nonetheless, so many of us crave certainty—we diligently set and follow carefully laid plans. We long for a map and a timeline to follow. But, as the Yiddish proverb goes: "You plan, God laughs." Life just doesn't follow a systematic unfolding. No, it vines, it creeps, it reaches like a tendril of new growth spurting from the soil. There are no detailed guidebooks laying out the precise course. We may catch a glimmer of insight providing a direction...but the truth unfolds moment by moment.

It's time to surrender our culture's obsessive fixation on productivity and maximizing gains. Instead of fetishizing your ROI (Return On Investment), synergizing your abilities, or hacking your potential...what if you just paused,

XI. WANDER AIMLESSLY

felt your bare feet in the dirt, and took a few steps in any direction you desired? What if you let go of your addiction to the hustle and grind culture, of charting your progress with an app or a planner, and you just let yourself wander?

When was the last time you let yourself meander with no goal, no agenda, no multitasking with a podcast in your ears or an update on your phone? When did you give yourself idle time to simply explore with no bigger goal to accomplish? When was the last time you gave yourself permission to simply play? Play is defined as being self-directed, containing adventure, having no larger purpose, maintaining worth in and of itself, bringing a state of joy, being pleasurable, active, and process-oriented. When was the last time you permitted yourself to enter a state that could be described with those characteristics? What if you let curiosity and joy lead your decision making rather than objectives, milestones, or deadlines?

When was the last time you set out on a path simply to see where it would take you rather than to reach a landmark? Life isn't a race to a finish line. It is meant for more than just checking off boxes and meeting your goals. Life is most fulfilling when we smell the wildflowers, explore the detours, and linger with the unexpected sights along the way. When we pause to have those unplanned conversations and meet those surprising individuals…that's when life gets juicy. Magic happens in the in-between moments, in the places we didn't anticipate, in the roads we never planned to walk.

So, let your heart and your bare feet lead you. Step from the path and allow whimsy to lead the way. The lessons, the discoveries, and the magic of life await you just beyond the hedge rows that keep you on the linear path. Step into the wild undergrowth, feel the pulsing of the mycelial matrix under your soles, and breathe deep the fecund air. The life you wanted was never ahead of you—it was always around you, right here, right now. Life isn't about arriving…it's about discovering the transcendent beauty already here.

RITUAL:

Take an aimless walk for at least 30 minutes. Let go of any destination or purpose and simply follow your curiosity—turning left, right, or pausing wherever something catches your eye. As you walk, observe what happens when you release control and allow yourself to be led by instinct and impulse.

JOURNAL PROMPTS:

- What does aimlessness mean to me, and how can I incorporate more aimless exploration into my life without guilt or pressure to be productive?
- When was the last time I allowed myself to wander freely, mentally or physically? What did I discover?

GUIDED MEDITATION:

Close your eyes and take a deep breath. Imagine yourself wandering down a winding forest path with no destination in mind. You are simply walking for the joy of it, letting your feet guide you wherever they wish to go. As you move, notice the sounds of the forest—the birds singing, the leaves rustling in the wind. With every step, you release the need to know where you're headed, trusting that wherever you end up is exactly where you're meant to be.

Breathe in the freedom of aimlessness and let yourself enjoy this unhurried journey. Notice the sights before you. Pay attention to the smells. Let yourself accept whatever comes, realizing that you've been hurrying through life too fixated on a destination. There is nothing to achieve, nothing to attain. There is simply enjoying this moment. Being in this moment. Being here. Trusting that life is leading you to wherever it is you need to be; you don't need to plan so much.

This is an adventure, and aren't the best adventures full of surprises and unexpected pathways? Let the landscape reveal itself to you, and discover how much there is here to learn, feel, and experience. This life is meant to be savored. No more rushing. Stay here for as long as you'd like.

MANTRA:

"I release the need for direction. I trust the journey."

XII. SEEK WISDOM

The night is thick with potential, and you approach an ancient oak tree before you quietly, with reverence. She is one of the "mother trees," one of the ancient ones who has predated nearly all the other trees of the forest. Through a mycorrhizal network within the soil, she connects with her offspring and shares nutrients as well as information. For many centuries, she has lovingly stood rooted here, the hub from which all the forest thrives, towering over all.

Ages have come and passed, and she has stood stalwart and observed. She has seen so much and learned far beyond what our mortal minds could comprehend. Tonight, she has generously offered to share some of that wisdom.

Come, sit amongst her roots which fan out like veins through the loamy earth. Feel the pulsing of her life-force in the bark as it cradles your back. Sense how her branches reach up, gathering starlight like a net. Her roots speak to the ancient treasures beneath us, absorbing stories from many millennia ago, long before our ancestors walked this forest.

An owl who calls this tree home sits perched on a branch nearby, gazing intently at you. It flutters its feathers and nibbles at its wings. There's something about its demeanor that makes you smile. As you continue to take in your surroundings, you discover stacks of old tomes you hadn't previously noticed. Hidden under and in the elbows of raised roots are leather-bound books that smell of forgotten dreams, papyrus scrolls that crinkle like cellophane, and loosely-tied sheaths of parchment with faded ink set down by long-dead scribes.

This is a place of profound wisdom. The owl's eyes glow with a light of knowing, watching you take in the pages before you.

You have been called to accept the wisdom of the ancients. It's an invitation to listen, to learn, to open yourself to truths that lie beyond the boundary of your current understanding. The owl blinks, and you hear a quiet, steady voice in your mind: *Be still. The answers you seek are already here, waiting to be uncovered.*

You open one of the weighty tomes and realize that these aren't new truths; this is wisdom we are simply remembering. Much of the wisdom we seek comes from within ourselves. Sometimes, that knowledge stored in our soul arises effortlessly. Other times, we must turn to external sources to help us recover it. Truths are eternal, and it only requires the right ear or the correctly tuned frequency to allow us to grasp them anew.

You realize that seeking wisdom isn't about gathering more information. It's about deepening your understanding of self and the world around you. It's about seeing the connections between all things, all people, and the sameness that resides within each of us—the same soul, the same divine sparks.

The leaves in the branches rustle, and again you hear a soft, verdant voice: *True wisdom cannot be forced—it must be accepted. Learning is a surrender, not a conquest.*

How often in the past have you forced yourself to learn something? Modern education systems are not set up for joyful, gentle unfolding of wisdom. They are frequently a harried, force-fed experience of absorbing and regurgitating information as expeditiously as possible. For many, the school system has doused the spark for life-long learning. But that is not here—that is not now. Learning is your birthright; you came to this planet to learn and evolve. It is one of the reasons you chose to take physical form and incarnate.

Wisdom isn't found in the accumulation of facts but in the practice of discernment, observation, and quiet knowing. It comes from recognizing the lessons that surround us every day and in every instance. The universe constantly provides us with teachers, guides, and wisdom holders from which to learn.

The trouble is that many people only see learning as being facilitated by a structured course or a credentialed teacher. In fact, some of the most profound teachers have been those who aren't even able to speak. Sitting with a gnarled, generations-old tree can teach me more in an afternoon than sometimes the most well-degreed pundit can. The animals I care for, the two dogs and the cat we keep in our home, teach me a great deal about kindness, humility, and listening each and every day. Sitting beside the ocean or another large body of water can reveal cosmic truths if you can attune your listening to the vibration of the waves, currents, and streams. There is sentience in each rock, each cliffside, each fern. We must expand our notion of what we consider being "alive"

XII. SEEK WISDOM

and grow our understanding of what it means to "communicate" beyond just the human and the lingual.

It's time to seek out greater wisdom. This may take the form of a contemplative practice and self-study. It may mean taking long walks in nature and learning from the spirits of the land, sky, fire, or water. It may mean hiring a guide or a teacher who can instruct you. Perhaps it means checking out resources like online videos or purchasing a book to read.

The point is to expand what our idea of attaining wisdom means—extend it beyond the typical notions of universities, courses, and degrees—and identify ourselves as ever-evolving learners. It is to embrace the perspective that living well means we are continually growing. Yes, there will be moments of clarity and moments of confusion. Yes, there will be times when you wonder if you have studied the right perspectives or absorbed the appropriate philosophies... but the point is to just go out there and learn from whomever and whatever entices you. Achieve mastery in the studies of the soul and the connection between life forms. Become ever-curious about the nature of reality, why we are here, and our purpose.

The owl in the oak tree whispers to you again: *The wisest amongst us are not those who claim to know everything. The wisest are those who know they are forever students, ever eager to learn.*

You feel the weight of this revelation settle into your heart. Attaining wisdom isn't about arriving at answers—it's about asking progressively nuanced questions. It's about the willingness to sit with uncertainty, to see many different angles on the same topic, and to hold conflicting notions with compassion. It's about knowing that you are never done growing, never done learning. The universe is vast, and it is an infinite classroom. Your teachers exist in every form—from the smallest ants to the mightiest sequoias.

The deepest truths live within you—use the insight of other wisdom holders to lift them to the surface of your awareness. Gaze at the stars and let them reveal their mysteries in hushed tones. Swing on the vines hanging from trees, and let them whisk you into a more profound understanding of self. Take a deep breath and feel the flow of life-force, of sentience within you. See this body as a fantastic, ever-changing vessel—that your life is enmeshed in the pursuit of growth and expanding self-knowing.

So, seek wisdom. Seek it in books, in nature, in dreams, in the words of others, in quiet moments of reflection. Seek the wisdom of your own heart and in the experiences of those who cross your path. And, most importantly, seek it with an open mind and a humble spirit, knowing that the journey toward true wisdom is the journey of a lifetime.

RITUAL:

Choose a topic that has always sparked your curiosity. Download or purchase a well-reviewed book that delves into this area of knowledge. For one week, dedicate time each day to immerse yourself in its teachings. Create a cozy, sacred reading space that fosters a deeper state of absorption. Light candles or incense, boil some tea, and lay out a cashmere blanket or wooly pillow. Choose a space that feels inviting, perhaps by a window or near a fireplace—somewhere that draws you into stillness. If you feel so called, take this one step further by reaching out to someone you consider wise. Ask them to share a personal story or a lesson that has shaped their journey. Listen with gratitude and an open heart, honoring the wisdom they pass on to you.

JOURNAL PROMPTS:

- Who are the key sources of wisdom in my life, and what have they taught me? How can I open myself up to receiving wisdom from unexpected places?
- Write about the top ten books, films, or podcast episodes that have taught you something meaningful. What are their commonalities?

GUIDED MEDITATION:

Close your eyes and envision yourself standing at the foot of a winding path up a mountain. Near the crest, you can see a small hut with lights glowing inside and smoke emanating from a stone chimney. Inside is the wisdom holder you've been seeking.

Taking one step at a time, begin the serpentine path upward. Notice the herbs that grow along the path, the medicinal plants that want to reveal their wisdom. Listen to the birds in the trees chirping secrets that they encourage you to learn. Watch the wise raccoons studying you from the shadows; they, too, have knowledge that they wish to impart.

As you climb higher, you notice giant stones with writings carved into their surface. Pause and try to discern the lettering. Do they teach you anything? As you climb higher, notice the dried plants hanging from the rafters of the hut.

XII. SEEK WISDOM

Notice the books piled up under the eaves. This is precisely where you need to be. Trust it. Let go and accept the knowledge that is waiting for you.

When you reach the flat land where the home is built, take a moment to pause and appreciate the gift of this moment. With a full heart, step inside and see what wisdom is waiting for you. Go within and uncover what you're meant to learn.

MANTRA:

"I am accepting truth and wisdom."

XIII. INVOKE PROTECTIVE ENERGIES

You have gathered your supplies: flowers for offering to the protective spirits, sticks for burning to ward off malignant entities, dried petals for consecrating the ground beneath your feet. Sitting on the crinkling, dried grasses, you bow to the four compass points; you sketch a circle with a hawthorn rod on the ground, and you invoke your ancestors to surround you and provide you protection. In the dry-baked soil, you trace a sigil with your fingertip—a symbol for warding, for strength, for prosperity. Candlelight flickers from the limbs of nearby trees where you have hung lamps; the air hums with anticipation.

The weeks leading up to here were filled with trials and tribulations; you felt as if you had experienced an undue amount of misfortune and suffering. It felt like the time had come to clear your energy field and ask for divine intervention, to ask for protection from whatever unfriendly vibes have been dogging your steps. You speak from your heart and ask for guardianship; you plead for a force to come and protect you from whatever negative energy has been lingering.

Out of the evening's fog steps a figure—tall in stature with horns on their head, lips pressed to the tip of a flute. Ancient and wise, he blows a soft melody into the night air. His song emanates a vibration of enchantment, creating a boundary between you and anything that would wish you ill. He is your guardian of the threshold; he will only allow forces that aid your wellbeing to pass by. You relax and settle into your meditation, communing with the forces around you and changing the flow of energy for the better.

Far too often, we encounter forces that do not serve us well. Perhaps these forces are quite literal: the intoxicating glow of our cellphones, the mind-bending allure of advertisements, the confounding delusion that spins out from the web of internet algorithms. Sometimes, the negativity stems from others who are jealous or vengeful, sending us negative vibes to feed their anger or dissatisfaction. Sometimes, the energies are more ethereal: spirits of the land who have been angered by our actions, rocks taken without permission, or energetic beings who did not want to trespass. In Tibet, there are lists of thousands of types of non-corporeal entities that affect humans negatively and must be placated, banished, or dominated in different ways.

Part of accepting that the world is animate and alive is acknowledging that there are forces beyond our perception that affect us daily. Some of those forces are helpful, some are neutral, and some can be destructive. While working to cultivate an open heart and mind is beneficial, we must also be conscious of whom and what we open to. Not every person or being should be invited into our sacred abode, our heart of hearts—there should be a level of discernment regarding who and what we let in. This is the process of recognizing and affirming our boundaries—standing up to protect our sanctity and wellbeing.

Some of these forces exist in our own head. How many of us have had self-destructive thoughts? How many of us have felt our brains run amuck and realized that we needed to do something to save ourselves from ourselves? While many spiritual traditions expound upon the benefit of non-doership and simply observing the mind experiencing itself...those are usually advanced practices that occur after the mind has been structured and placated through mantras, visualizations, and offerings. This book has been a conscious endeavor to break away from dogma and religiosity—and, at the same time, it is essential to acknowledge that nearly every spiritual tradition has always included practices for sanctifying and protecting ourselves, our homes, and our sacred spaces. Any ritual usually begins with some form of consecration and banishing of inimical forces. We ask for our guides, our ancestors, our spiritual relations to come and give us sanctuary, to protect us from the wild and whirling forces of the world that could damage our body, mind, or heart.

Spirit is in everything; everything is spirit. That tree you swung on as a child was a being with which you were (and perhaps still are) in relationship. That rosebush whose flowers you picked to present to a beloved on your first date was a sentient being with whom you were in relationship. The stones on which you step as you leave your home each day, they are also in relationship with you. Are you cognizant of the nature of these relationships? Are they symbiotic, predatory, or neutral? What is the nature, color, and texture of the energies you share? Are they helping you or hindering you?

My husband and I once bought a house in the country and learned a

XIII. INVOKE PROTECTIVE ENERGIES

profound yet uncomfortable lesson. We purchased the house because it logically made sense; it checked all of our boxes. But, energetically, it did not...it didn't feel welcoming. The land did not like having that house there. The previous owners' relationship ended in a messy divorce. The house cried and leaked water from many surfaces despite having the roof and walls repaired numerous times. It was a house where the energies of the land were not placated, happy, and welcoming. And we suffered; it was the most difficult years of our relationship when we lived there. In Japan, there is a concept called jiko bukken, where properties with a history of misfortunes like deaths and divorces make the property practically unsellable. Whether it was the sadness left over by the previous owners or the disgruntlement of the land itself, that home was never happy...no matter how many prayers I offered, sage I burned, or Feng Shui principles I employed. Never again will we purchase a property where we don't consider the energetic vibe and the feeling of being welcomed by the energy there.

The modern world needs to be warded against. Every notification, every shocking headline, every social media diatribe is fodder for our distracted, fractured minds. Our electronic devices are purposefully engineered to hijack our attention, keep us doom scrolling, and make us feel helpless amidst a flood of distressing information. Left unchecked, these energies can lead to addiction, mental health issues (which are at an all-time high worldwide), exhaustion, and burnout. We end up in ever-looping cycles of seeking distractions, self-soothing techniques, or numbing agents. We need protection from these nefarious forces foisted upon us by the tech bro billionaires and Madison Avenue advertising executives.

A rosebush has thorns, and so do kapok trees. Those that are the most beautiful and most succulent often also have forms of protection. So, too, is it with ourselves. This notion of always-open spirituality arose in the 1960s and 70s as Eastern spiritual masters arrived in America and was a response to the repressive and overly-rigid culture of the 1950s. It is understandable why it took root and flourished here—but it is only part of the story. There is a time for opening and a time for closing. There is a time for breaking down walls and a time for building them. There is a time to invite guests into your house, and there are times when it's necessary to shut and bolt the door. You are not required to be at the mercy of every passing influence; you are not only allowed but encouraged to practice discernment regarding what you let in and what you keep out.

This is the time to invoke protective energies to keep you safe and grounded so you can do the open-hearted, expansive work. It's time for you to shut the castle gates and retreat to your fortress, unperturbed by disorienting or unsettling influences. For in that stillness and peace of a protected space, we can better open to our higher and purer selves. If we are being maligned by negative entities pulling at our hair and scratching our skin, how will we ever find peace?

So, call on your ancestors. Ask the earth for support and protection. Clear away any forces that do not wish to aid you in your journey, and call close any who will assist. Learn to discern the uplifting from the destructive—whether in people you encounter, websites you visit, or unseen forces lurking in the corner of rooms and in forgotten caves. Claim responsibility for your well-being and seek the help of those who specialize in ritualistic purification of space and guardianship to aid you in creating a protected, vibrant, and healthy life.

You bow with respect to the horned entity standing sentinel on your behalf. You offer them smoke from your burning camphor and Palo Santo. You thank them in your heart. And you thank yourself, too—thank you for doing the work to keep yourself safe. Thank yourself for learning to discern helpful from harmful, supportive from destructive. This body and life are gifts, and we should do what we can to ensure they remain safe and well.

RITUAL:

Find your sacred space and acknowledge the four directions. Turn to each, saying:

"May I be protected from the East, the South, the West, the North, above, and below. May I be protected on all sides and from within."

Visualize a glowing orb of light surrounding you, a shield that allows only kindness and clarity to pass through. At each compass point, envision a being of golden light standing sentinel—whether warrior, ancestor, animal guide, or something formless yet strong. They are here to hold the space, to ensure that only love reaches you.

Light incense or a burnable offering. Use the smoke to cleanse yourself and your surroundings, watching as any lingering negativity dissipates into the air. Offer the remaining incense in gratitude, acknowledging the protective forces that surround you. Envision a radiant presence above, pouring down blessings and guidance. Breathe deeply. You are safe.

JOURNAL PROMPTS:

- When have you felt truly safe? Who or what made you feel this way?

XIII. INVOKE PROTECTIVE ENERGIES

- Where in your life do you need stronger boundaries? What steps can you take to create them?

GUIDED MEDITATION:

Close your eyes and breathe. Envision an army of protectors gathering around you—whether animal, human, celestial, or something you cannot name. See them clad in glistening battle armor, carrying weapons forged from moonlight. Watch as they take their places at the borders of your home, your mind, your body.

Feel them fortify the spaces in your life where you need strength. See them standing watch at every threshold, every doorway, every vulnerable point. Imagine a rose-hued energy blooming in your chest, flowing outward to empower them.

This is a symbiotic relationship—you offer love, and they offer protection. You are safe. You are shielded. Sit in this presence for several breaths, knowing you are held.

MANTRA:

"I am protected on all sides, above and below."

XIV. LET GO OF WHAT'S NOT MEANT FOR YOU

The wild wind whips the hem of your cloak, twining it around your shins. Sand blows into your eyes, into your mouth—but you squint and carry on climbing up the powdery dune. You grasp the strips of paper you've brought, holding them to your heart, as you struggle to find footing in the undulating sand. Inscribed on each piece are the failed dreams, unobtainable desires, and forgotten ambitions that you've carried for far too long. Listed are the people you coveted but could not have and the achievements you aspired to but could not reach. All the things you hoped were for you—but were not.

Slipping and stumbling more times than you'd care to admit, you arrive at the crest of the tallest dune. Lowering your cowl, you shut your eyes against the bright, setting sun and breathe. Bringing both hands toward your heart, you whisper a prayer of release. You ask that the universe cut the strings tying you to these unreachable attainments—you ask to be freed from the burden of wanting things you cannot have. You whisper to the wind, "I wish to surrender everything that was not meant for me." As the words fly from your lips, you release the papers into the wind. They flutter on the strong currents, lifting higher, shimmering and flapping like small, winged creatures.

You stare in awe as you realize something magical is happening. These long-held longings have transformed...they have become fluttering butterflies. Bright, iridescent wings form from what were once simple parchment strips. What were once burdens are now colorful and jubilant beings that fly into the twilight.

You marvel as these pieces of your past, once laden with longing and heavy with expectation, dance freely. You yourself feel lighter, you notice—less burdened. All the things you thought you needed, the dreams you believed were yours to claim, have been surrendered. Flying to wherever they need to go, you admit they were never meant for you. They were not your gifts or blessings to receive; you have wasted too much energy focusing on your lack rather than the abundance already in your life.

You watch until these surrendered ambitions fade from sight, aware of the miracle that has transpired. The winds have fallen with the sun, and as you climb back down the dune in the dusk, you smile at the sense of internal buoyancy. By releasing that which was never yours, you are making space for what is. Arriving back into the still of the forest, you wriggle your toes and scrunch your nose. Blossoming within you is a gratitude for the life you have been gifted, for the tremendous joy you've always carried but could rarely see. You were blinded by your coveting, missing the miracles that were already yours—and now you can see them more clearly.

We are too often grasping for things we believe should be ours: accomplishments, accolades, relationships, etc. But what if they were never meant for us? What if karma/fate/our spirit guides were directing us another way? Why do we always assume that we know what is best for us?

Focusing on what we do not have and being envious of other people's gifts and hard work only proves burdensome. Jealousy is like a red-hot coal that burns in the pit of our stomach. It glows so brightly that it blinds us to the awareness that we have qualities that untold others would be thrilled to attain. We are all so blessed—but we often ignore our abundance by focusing on what we lack. We become fixated on goals that may or may not be obtainable and outcomes that may or may not be aligned with our highest good.

I remember these feelings well. Until my mid-twenties, I was intensely driven to become a successful actor. I studied theatre at the prestigious Northwestern University; I spent a year training and performing at the comedy giant The Second City. I spent countless hours in private coaching sessions with some of Chicago's most eminent directors and acting teachers. But no matter how hard I worked, how fiercely I strove, it felt like I was meeting with far more obstacles than successes. The harder I pushed, the more resistance I encountered.

I watched others receive the roles and opportunities that I coveted. "But I work harder than them," I would moan. "I deserved this more than they did." Instead of accepting that the universe was nudging me in a different direction, I ignored the hints and strove harder. The results were maddening; all I felt was growing resentment. I have come to believe that if our actions align with our mission, purpose, and talents...things will flow smoothly. In this instance,

XIV. LET GO OF WHAT'S NOT MEANT FOR YOU

however, the universe kept telling me "no." Despite my dedication to self-improvement and honing my craft, my career never clicked into gear.

After years of striving, the opportunity presented itself to move to Hollywood. I quickly got picked up by an agent and manager in Los Angeles; I booked a bunch of projects—but I began to question...*is this pursuit of a career in acting actually aligned with my spirit?* I had woken up enough to pause, take an objective look around, and see that things had been so hard because I didn't truly want this life. I realized that the things that really mattered to me (connected community, meaningful and honest relationships, making the world a better place) were antithetical to the culture and ethos of the industry I was striving to work in. If I aligned my actions with my values, I would need a different path to walk down than that of the entertainment industry.

Just when I decided to leave acting and move back to Chicago, big acting opportunities began to come through. I booked a few high-profile projects—I even had to leave my car at the Denver airport halfway through my road trip home to fly back to LA to shoot a well-paid commercial. It was as if the universe was saying: *Now that you don't want this, we are showing you that it wasn't that you weren't talented or deserving...it's just that this career would have diverted you from your life's work.* I see that now. Had I gotten the things I thought I wanted (which, in hindsight, were due to early-life traumas leading me to seek validation in unhelpful ways), I would never have evolved into the soul guide that I am today. The universe wouldn't give me those things because they would have derailed my reason for taking physical incarnation and disrupted my purposes here on Earth.

It was a sincere blessing in disguise that things I coveted did not manifest. I am deeply thankful that my guides and spiritual protectors didn't let me head down a path that, while alluring, would have been to my detriment. By aligning myself with a life that the universe provided for me, I am far happier, more contented, and deeply nourished than I would have ever been in an industry that felt diametrically opposed to my more authentic values.

Learning to let go of what is not meant for us is not a "giving up"—it's a "giving over" to divine guidance. It's about trusting that gifts that are truly ours will never miss us; they will always arrive in the perfect time. If it's meant for us, it will show up. We don't need to push and pull at the fabric of reality, trying to mold it into a particular shape. We can just trust that everything is working out in the best possible way for our thriving.

Let me repeat: this is not giving up—it's about realigning ourselves with our path. It's about recognizing that getting things that aren't in your best interest would only be (at best) burdens and (at worst) catastrophes. Remember that saying: "Be careful what you wish for, you might just get it?" It's best to just wish for whatever is in the highest good for ourselves and others around us. Let go of specific outcomes and just request that the best possible path manifests, wherever it leads, whatever direction it takes. When we release what is not ours, we open ourselves to the vast abundance of the universe.

Take a deep breath and surrender your attachment to those longings that are frustrated, to those desires that are not coming to fruition. Are they taking a long time because it just takes a while—or because it does not align with your highest good? Ask yourself: "Is this something I need to release?" If so, let it go with blessings and grace. And in so doing, open to newfound freedom and space.

Letting go is an act of trust. It's telling the universe that you are willing to dance with it, to co-create with the wisdom of your guides and your deeper self. It's trusting that what is meant for you will arrive in the perfect fashion—and what is not will make way for something even more incredible.

In so doing, you open to far more potential than you could have ever conceived. Trust that what is coming is far better than what you've left behind. Be free—free to receive, free to expand, free to become. Open to the many blessings that are indeed meant for you.

RITUAL:

Find a quiet space in nature and bring a small collection of objects that symbolize the things you've struggled to release: dreams, relationships, or desires that no longer serve you. Dig a shallow hole in the ground before you. One by one, hold each object in your hands, close your eyes, and ask the universe to help you let go. When you're ready, take a deep breath, whisper a blessing of gratitude for what these longings have taught you, and gently place them into the hole. Finish by covering them with soil, saying, "I trust that what is meant for me will never pass me by." Pause to feel the blessings that are now making their way to you.

JOURNAL PROMPTS:

- What are some things, relationships, or goals that no longer serve my highest good? Why am I holding onto them?
- What would my life feel like if I released them, creating space for new possibilities?

XIV. LET GO OF WHAT'S NOT MEANT FOR YOU

GUIDED MEDITATION:

Visualize yourself standing in a meadow, sunlight filtering through the trees. In your hands is a small cage filled with butterflies. Each butterfly represents something in your life that was not meant for you. Maybe one butterfly represents the career your teenage self wished to achieve. Another might be that person you so desperately wanted to date in college. Perhaps another is an award you worked so hard to achieve but never procured. Feel with your heart the longings present in this cage, things that have gone unsatisfied, and give yourself permission to let them be present again.

We often try to deny these feelings of regret, to bury them. Let them be here as these magnificent, multicolored winged creatures.

When you are ready, open the door of the cage. One by one, the butterflies fly out. Slow down your awareness so you can acknowledge each as they depart. Say goodbye to these parts of your story that never came to pass. They were never meant for you. Were they meant for you, they would have manifested. Now is the time to wish them goodbye. May they have safe travels wherever they need to fly to.

With each exhale, feel yourself release—let go—even more. Watch as the butterflies flutter away, their delicate wings catching the light. See them rise higher and higher, carried by the breeze, until they disappear into the vast sky. Feel the weight lift from your heart, leaving you lighter and freer. Stay here for a moment, breathing in the fresh air, basking in the freedom of letting go.

MANTRA:

"I release what isn't mine. I accept my blessings."

XV. MAKE LOVE

Feel the breath catch in your chest as the pleasure flows through you. We are built for connection—with ourselves and with each other. We are meant to accept and share feelings of tenderness, elation, and love. You gaze into the eyes of your beloved and see a universe of stars swirling within their depths. This galaxy in which we reside was formed through the force of love—a vast cosmic web connecting every one of us.

Smell the orchids and array of flowers around you. Gaze at the tender buds, feeling your love for them racing across the space between you. Feel the outpouring of love that exists in all beings, all times, and all spaces. It is the reason we are here; it is the essence of all that is.

Making love transcends the physical (though, yes, it includes that too). It is to dwell in a state of ecstasy, a state of wild appreciation for the life around us. It is to cultivate an orgasmic state of being that wells up unprovoked. It is to feel a sweeping connection with another lifeform as being both an extension of you and also your divine mate. It's time you reclaim your power as a loving being—and share that love with the broader world.

We exist in a time where more people are disconnected than ever. People live lives of isolation and desperation, afraid of their neighbors, terrified of being vulnerable or seen in their entirety. They hide behind usernames and keyboards, unable to expose the fullness of their hearts. People behave in ways that can be so unkind, so cutting, so unconcerned with the well-being of the beings we encounter, the people we meet. We often go through our days feeling separate from everyone around us, a lone voyager adrift in a frigid sea—a polar bear stranded on an island of ice.

People long for love but know neither how to give it or receive it freely. Many are disconnected from their own bodies, unable to speak words of loving kindness with themselves or engage in nourishing self-touch. Much of the world is experiencing an epidemic of loneliness and unkindness. To remedy this, we must begin by speaking loving words, performing loving actions, and opting into meaningful connections.

To make love is to step into this current of connectivity—to become part of the larger ecosystem. Beneath the ground of the forest is a matrix of mycelium (fungal strands) that unite all living creatures rooted in the earth. No plant in the forest lives in isolation—they all communicate and share resources with one another. We must realize that we exist in a similar web. We ought to strive to be fully open with one another, the world, and the divine. Loving connection is one of the greatest purposes in being, and we enact it through the ways we touch, support, and cherish one another.

How would the world be different if we held this desire for loving connection at the forefront of our actions? What if we treated each being we encounter as a manifestation of divine consciousness? What if we freely engaged in affirmation, tenderness, and appreciation? One of the greatest gifts a person can receive is to truly be seen by another. When was the last time you allowed yourself to be fully taken in by someone else—or offered it in return? When was the last time you freely and unapologetically provided caring, tender touch with another human—or even your own body? When was the last time you used your sexual vitality as a means to connect in deep and loving ways—again, with yourself or with another?

How are you making love to the world? How can you come to see love as a potent healing force? For it is through love that we fulfill our purpose. We are here to help one another grow, evolve, and enliven. Through sharing love, tenderness, kindness, and pleasure, we transform not only our lives but the lives of those around us. It is the reason we are here, the reason for our existence.

Imagine yourself being a lover pressed against your mate, entwined in an embrace. Yes, there is a physical act of loving, but there is also an unspoken language of connection. That sizzle of affirmation that sees the being before us, not as only flesh and blood but an incarnation of the divine. When we make love, we acknowledge that divine light within another. That connection, soul to soul, is the essence of love, the essence of creation itself.

In the modern world, physical lovemaking is often deemed as something sinful and dirty. Many spiritual traditions ask us to transcend our bodily urges for pleasure and connection—seeing them as distractions or even damnable.

XV. MAKE LOVE

How wrong they are! Our desire for sexual connection (with ourselves or another) isn't base or banal—it is a profoundly sacred part of ourselves! The universe was formed from the divine lovemaking of God with itself—the cosmic foam was churned through the orgasmic undulating of the divine.

When we connect with our ability to make physical love, we are connecting viscerally to our abilities as divine creators of this reality. It is a connection with our life-force, our ability to create new life, and it is deeply spiritual. Making love is ultimately the most sacred act we can undertake—for it is an act of reconnection, of coming home to our larger self.

It's time to step boldly into the realms of embodiment, lovemaking, and tenderness. It's time to make love to the world, starting with yourself. This is an encouragement to explore love through touch (massage, masturbation, sex), through affirmation (words of kindness, encouragement, tender messages), and through intention (letting your heart shine, thinking of others as loved ones rather than strangers). It's an invitation to become a being of love, dwelling in ecstasy, and reclaiming your power as a divine creator of this universe who expresses themselves through their loving energy. You are a creature of love; it is both your purpose and your existence.

So, make love with your words. Make love with your touch. Make love with your actions, thoughts, your presence. Let love be the guiding force in everything you do, and watch as the world around you transforms. For love, above all else, is why we are here.

Make love.

RITUAL:

Dedicate one entire evening to an activity that allows you to express love creatively. This could be writing a love letter, creating a piece of art for someone you care about, or preparing a meal with love for friends or family. This could also be creating a deep connection with a partner or yourself. Dim the lights, play music that soothes your soul, and spend the evening being fully present with your body and emotions. Allow this to be an act of love—whether physical, emotional, or spiritual.

JOURNAL PROMPTS:

- What does making love—both physically and metaphorically—mean to me? How do I invite love into my life in ways that nourish my heart and soul?
- How can I bring more love, compassion, and intimacy into my daily interactions with others and with myself?

GUIDED MEDITATION:

Find a comfortable position and rest your hands on the center of your chest, palms facing in toward you. Feel this space—breathe into it. Learn the contours of your heart-center; feel its shape, color, and vibe. And as you breathe into the space underneath your hands, feel it begin to glow with love and gratitude. Envision this inner light becoming stronger and stronger, sending out waves of loving energy like ripples from a stone dropped into a pond. Let this love-light shine out of you, bathing everyone and everything in near proximity with love.

Also, let it nourish and spread through your own body, sending love to all the parts of you, including the parts that you view as shameful or unlovable. Accept your divine right as a creature of love. It is your purpose, your duty, and your right to give and receive love freely. You are a creature of love.

When you've expanded this love as much as you're able, let go of sending out love and, instead, simply observe. Whenever a gift is offered, a reciprocal gift is received. Notice the feeling of love flowing back at you from your friends and dear ones, from your ancestors, from the sentience of the land and entities around you. Notice how you exist in a web of love. There is always so much love flowing in one direction or another. You are a being enmeshed in love. Own it. Celebrate it. Drink in the love that is offered to you; you deserve it. Stay here, soaking in love, for as long as you'd like.

MANTRA:

"I give and receive love freely."

XVI. ROOT INTO YOUR BODY

Wade into the crystalline waters with me. The lake is so clear, and the surface is so still that we cannot tell where the sky ends and water begins. Clouds ringed in fire shine both above and below us, only disturbed by the small ripples our progress makes. Feel the slippery mud under your soles, the kelp brushing your calves. Stand here, feel yourself rooting down, descending into the sludgy depths. Breathe...

A small, shining turtle swims up lazily, curious about us. Its eyes are studying, assessing what we are doing. His fins send shimmering waves of gold across the opalescent blue. His presence extends toward you a feeling of place—a belonging. You feel yourself sinking deeper within, into yourself, into the water, into the mud beneath us. You are fully within your body, but also extended into the surrounding environment as well.

You feel something tickling your ankles—an eel, maybe? You do not stir from your place. The sensation winds its way up your legs, then your waist. From the depths of the lakebed, long tendrils break the water's placid surface and wind their way up your torso like searching tentacles. You are not afraid. The tendrils are not binding you or holding you captive; they are supporting you. They are gently connecting you more firmly to this place, to the natural world. With their presence, your sense of self extends well past your physical frame and into the vast ecosystem of the lake. You are not separate from the world—you are part of it. The earth is rising up to meet you, claiming you as part of itself.

The turtle glides in closer, circling. It seems to almost smile, suggesting that this is precisely as it ought to be. You are grounded and being held by forces as old as time itself. You are coming home to your body, home to the earth. The earth is not merely something on which you walk; it is a part of you. You remember hearing stories about great sages and meditative masters who would cry out when people would step on nearby grass—they were so attuned to the surrounding lifeforms that they became extensions of themselves. You understand that viscerally now. You are in yourself but also part of something so much vaster. The water of the lake flows through your veins; the pulsing of the undertow is the beat of your heart. You are home.

For many of us, our bodies have become foreign spaces. In his book *Dubliners*, James Joyce said, "Mr. Duffy lived a short distance from his body." Many feel as if their sentience exists only in their head—or, worse, entirely separate from their physical form. I have heard people claim that their bodies are merely ambulatory machines to sustain their brains and move their heads around. They have become so disconnected from their physical forms that they do not even identify them as parts of themselves.

The ancient Greeks, in contrast, believed that fitness of the body was a reflection of, and deeply tied to, mental fitness. Where one went, so did the other. In fact, modern science is showing that there isn't so much a mind-to-body connection as it is a mind-body continuation. These bodies are extensions of our mind-structures. Studies have now found that we have neural cells in our hearts and in our guts. Have you ever felt the pangs of loss or elation in your heart? Have you experienced flashes of intuition in your belly? That is because we process information with our physical form, not just our heads. Our bodies are wisdom holders, and we do them tremendous disservices by not treating them as such.

Ancient Egyptians liquified and discarded the brains when they were embalming the other organs during the mummification process—they held the gray matter in our skulls in such little regard. When asked where their "self" exists, Tibetans point to the center of their chests. Other cultures show that they identify less with their heads and more with the rest of their physical beings.

Much of this bodily disconnection in the modern era comes from becoming so externalized in our experience. We read, scroll, and watch with our eyes for much of our days—our work takes place on screens, in devices, and in technological spaces. Very seldom does modern life ask us to return to our breath, to the sensations in our physical form, to pay attention to the happenings in the analog world around us. The more technology gallops forward, the more forcibly we must choose to slow down and observe where we are.

Additionally, many of us grew up in cultures and faith traditions that demonized our physical forms. We were told our bodies were base, sinful, and dirty. We were told that we must transcend our humanness to attain something heavenly. We are told the divine exists outside of ourselves, and we will never be able to understand (let alone attain) that state of being. We are told we are separate, insignificant, and disconnected in our relationship to God. Spirituality becomes a mere mental exercise when it comes to prayers and scriptures—they tell us understanding divinity does not come through our body, through the present moment, or through the earth.

These perspectives have done us a tremendous disservice. We have learned to treat our bodies like tools, things that must be trained and honed but seldom listened to or understood. Even our exercise regimens, which should draw us back into connection with our physical forms, serve almost as a form of corporal punishment—forcing the body to exceed its healthy limits, pushing it to its very edges. We train for ultramarathons, for Olympic-level feats, and to "survive the zombie apocalypse" (said one gym poster I saw)—seldom for wellness.

Too many spiritual circles view heaven as something outside of themselves rather than something that can be cultivated here and now. "We are spirits having a human experience," is a maxim repeated oft by those wielding incense and candles...but they often overlook the second part of that statement. We aren't just spirits longing to return to some astral realm—we chose this human incarnation for the enjoyment of it. We were blessed with these physical bodies—they are not things to be escaped or devalued. Every part of it is sacred—from your nose to your toes to your sexual organs. No part of it is sinful—each aspect is a divine gift. Every single part.

It's time to reclaim the divinity inherent in your legs, arms, torso, and everything in between. Give yourself a massage, make love to yourself, dance, and roll around in the grass. Pull yourself back into your physical form and shout "Thank you!" to the heavens for this remarkable gift! Run your fingers over the little hairs on your forearms, marveling at the patterns they make. Hold your palms to your ribcage and count out your heartbeats, giving soft thanks to each one. Provide stimulation to your sexual organs and feel the waves of ecstasy flow through you, pleasure that is your birthright.

When I was younger, I experienced immense shame regarding my physical form. I couldn't even take my shirt off in front of others without shaking. My disconnection was so thorough that if a massage therapist tried to touch anywhere south of my diaphragm, I almost couldn't feel their touch. It was as if my body had gone numb from the waist down. I had learned that my body was an unsafe thing that could betray me, that it was worthy of derision. This comes from the tension of being bullied as a child for being scrawny and having a convex-shaped ribcage—things I could not control yet were perpetually mocked.

It took many years of touch-related therapy, exploring public nudity, and reclaiming my divine right as an embodied individual before I could call my body my "home." Accepting my own touch as well as from another person has been a significant component in my bodily reconnection. Learning to lovingly caress, embrace, and nourish myself has been critical. We are not just minds floating through space. You are a vast and integrated being whose sentience extends into each part of you and even the space around you.

So, root into yourself. Run with bare feet through the grass. Tickle your skin. Breathe fully and deeply. Shake rhythmically in time with music. Sweat. Have an orgasm. Have three.

Come to understand that you truly are a spirit having a delightfully human experience. See this human vessel as the most excellent gift you will receive in this lifetime. Feel yourself connecting with the larger world around you—the trees, animals, and people nearby. Allow yourself to become part of everything—and everything becomes part of you. You are not separate, and you never were.

Come home to yourself. You belong here.

RITUAL:

Set up a time for a self-massage. Light some candles, turn on some soothing music, and sit on a towel, clad only in your skin. Choose your favorite lotion or oil and tenderly, lovingly massage it into each section of your body. As you proceed, strive to stay present and express gratitude for whatever part of you is under your hands at that moment. If so desired, allow this practice to evolve from merely sensual into erotic touch. Finish by giving yourself a hug and saying, "Thank you for this care."

JOURNAL PROMPTS:

- In what ways do I disconnect from my body during times of stress or uncertainty? How can I begin to honor my body as a vessel of wisdom and experience?
- Reflect on a time when I felt fully embodied—grounded and in tune with my physical presence. How did that connection impact my emotional and mental state?

XVI. ROOT INTO YOUR BODY

GUIDED MEDITATION:

Sit comfortably with an erect spine. As you close your eyes and breathe, envision your mind's eyes sinking down within you. Let your attention drop from the space in your forehead down into your throat and then into your chest. Let your seat of awareness, this space from which you look out to observe the world, go even further down. Sink into your belly. Sink into your hips. Come all the way down to the spot where your pelvic basin makes contact with the surface beneath you. Take a few deep breaths, breathing all the way down here, envisioning your breath traveling all the way down into your perineum.

Once you feel settled here, let your mind's eye go down even further. Envision roots growing down from your pelvic basin and into the earth beneath you. Even if you're sitting on a chair or a bed, envision the earth directly below you. Go down further, feeling that the earth is part of your body. As you go deeper and deeper down, realize that you have a much bigger body than you supposed...you are the whole world. You are part of this planet, and this Earth is part of you. Feel yourself reconnecting with the totality of what you are. Feel yourself spreading out sideways, taking up more and more space, becoming more and more girthy. Become as big as you can be, appreciating the totality that is you.

After you've extended as far as you can, become aware of your physical body. Notice how much more "in it" you are. Notice how full you are. Notice what a magnificent vessel this physical form is for getting to experience the world within. Appreciate your physical body for a few moments, filling it all the way through every finger, toe, and hair follicle. Then, when you're ready, open your eyes.

MANTRA:

"I am in my body. I am within myself."

XVII. PRACTICE BEING PRESENT

Your fingers tingle with electricity; you're alive with a quiet pulsing that flows through your body. Each heartbeat, each breath feels exquisite. The wind caresses the nape of your neck like a lover's whisper, and you feel glisteningly, radiantly alive.

Beneath the soles of your feet, you sense that the soil churns with intelligence. Overhead, the crackling of tree branches and cackling of crows forge an entrancing melody. An emerald dragonfly hovers close, and without needing to follow its flight with your gaze, you trace its path in your mind's eye. You are so deeply attuned to the world around you that everything hums with connection.

Every falling leaf, every gust of wind, every exhale feels poignantly present for you. You have entered a state of flow—you have moved beyond the typical cascade of seconds and minutes to enter a place of "deep time" where each moment expands toward infinity. You are here, now.

You watch the comings and goings of your thoughts with relaxed curiosity. There's no need to latch onto any of them. You are simply in this glorious moment. You are present. You smile as the thrill of being fully alive roars through you.

Mindfulness has become such a buzzword in recent decades that it almost feels cliché—and it has likely lost much of its impact. We see it in so many places (particularly in advertising slogans, which, ironically, are designed to entice us into dissatisfaction so we consume more) that we may have become numb to its true meaning. At its core, mindfulness is about bringing your awareness fully to the present moment. It suggests abandoning our desire to reflect on the past or anticipate the future—to remove ourselves from the actions of worrying or regretting. It is about simple, nonjudgmental observation. We breathe, we watch, and we listen. We surrender the need to label or dissect. We let go of categorizing or planning. We simply witness whatever is occurring.

"Isn't that interesting?" you might silently say to yourself. It's both simple and challenging to enter this state of being a watcher. The benefits of being able to objectively take in the passing moments are both obvious and profound. It takes time—and yet no time at all—to experience this state.

Staying mindful should be light and easy. We shouldn't endeavor too mightily or employ force to make it happen. I lived in an ashram (a meditation community) for nearly seven years—and during that time, I routinely witnessed people who became zombie-like from overly striving to always stay present. They tried to turn themselves into mindfulness machines. They lost their character, sense of humor, and joy. They became tedious to be around, always focusing on just the precise moment at hand to the exclusion of everything else.

Being present shouldn't disconnect us from life—it should tether us more deeply to it. Mindfulness shouldn't diminish our joy, it should expand it. We must let go of the effort involved in trying to be present and just allow ourselves to be.

The ability to dance lightly with the present moment makes us easier to be around, more playful, and more resilient to stress. As a bonus, it increases our productivity, efficiency, and sense of awe. Practices like seated meditation, mindful walking, tai chi, Zen calligraphy, or ecstatic dance can help you train your mind to rest peacefully in the here and now. I regularly employ several of these techniques to draw me into a more harmonious experience of life.

Each morning begins with silent meditation and out-loud chanting. Afterward, I grab my two pups, leash them up, and head out for our morning walk. I strive to observe the colors of the leaves, the shapes of the clouds, and the sensations in my feet as I step. At the gym, I choose to keep my phone in my locker so I can be present to the sensations within my body as I exercise. When meeting with clients, I continually remind both of us to come back to the present. When I make love with my husband, I focus on the bodily sensations and energetic flow passing between us rather than getting caught up in fantasizing or imagining. Sitting down to play my gongs, I strive to feel the sensations and reverberations ricocheting through my skeleton. Doing these things helps me maintain a more balanced and meaning-filled life. It allows my mind to quiet so I can tap into a transpersonal joy that is often covered over by the clattering of distracting thoughts.

Becoming present is an essential skill for anyone on a spiritual journey—a

XVII. PRACTICE BEING PRESENT

disquieted mind makes for a poor traveling companion on the path. Learning to settle into the moment allows us to see beyond life's surface and gaze into a deeper reality. When we get past all the commercials, social commentary, and parental prescriptions for how things "ought to be"—and simply observe the world as it is—we realize that everything is much less concrete. The rules of how the universe functions and how reality operates are not as solid as they want us to believe. By watching the world with no agenda, we can gain the ability to stretch and bend the rules of it a bit. We realize that our thoughts are sculptors of this reality. Where our mind goes, so goes everything around us.

By being present, we reclaim our awareness of being divine creators of the universe—we regain the ability to mold it. This cosmos sprung from thought and is maintained through mental energy. Many spiritual traditions agree: in the beginning, there was a thought, and that thought created the universe. From the Christian Bible (which uses the term *logos*, which can translate to "mind, thought, or breath") to the Indian *Rig Veda*, this idea of reality arising from the thoughts of the Oversoul reoccurs across cultures.

When we quiet and still the mind, we rediscover the power our thoughts have to change reality. In fact, we are always manipulating the world around us...but because our minds are often so chaotic, we aren't typically able to witness the direct effect we have on the world. In a very straightforward way, we can see this expressed in the words of Lao Tzu, the founder of Taoism: "Watch your thoughts, they become your words; watch your words, they become your actions; watch your actions, they become your [...] destiny."

When we quiet our minds, we see layers of life that were hidden become visible. When we settle into the now, a new world reveals itself—one brimming with magic, depth, and untold beauty. We begin to see the connections between things—between people, actions, cause and effect, past and present. It's as if an invisible web glimmers into view, and we see how everything, absolutely everything, is interconnected. The boundaries between ourselves and the wider world melt, and for a moment, we slip into the transpersonal flow of existence. A mystical experience of life isn't hidden away in some crumbling scroll or far-off monastery—it's right here, right now.

The trees speak in languages older than words. The wind carries messages from distant ages. The stars above whisper of mysteries beyond our current reckoning. When we are present, the universe opens its heart to us, and we glimpse an infinite intelligence that has always been here, waiting for us to notice. Every moment is a portal. Each breath is a gateway to another layer of life, shimmering just beyond the surface.

So, watch the dragonfly as it dances through the air. Feel the pulsing of the lifeforms all around you. Breathe—and simply be. In that stillness, a more beautiful world will open before you.

RITUAL:

Choose one simple activity—such as eating a meal, taking a shower, or brushing your teeth—and approach it as a sacred ritual of presence. Before you begin, take a deep breath and set the intention to be fully immersed in the experience. Pay attention to every detail: the sensations, the smells, the sounds, the textures. Feel the water on your skin, the taste of your food, or the bristles of the toothbrush against your teeth.

Whenever your mind begins to wander, gently bring it back to the task at hand. Imagine the act itself as a form of meditation, with each moment being an offering to the present. As you finish, offer gratitude for the ability to be fully here, alive, and engaged with the world around you.

JOURNAL PROMPTS:

- How do distractions and multitasking affect my ability to stay present? What can I change in my daily routine to foster more moments of mindfulness?
- When was the last time I was fully immersed in the present moment? How did that experience feel, and what can I learn from it about my capacity for presence?

GUIDED MEDITATION:

For this meditation, get up and be ready to walk—if possible, do this outside. Before beginning, take a moment to scan your body from the inside. Notice: how are you feeling? How are your joints, your belly, your heart? What's going on inside of you today? Once you have a good sense of your starting point, allow your gaze to transition to half-open, enough to see where you are stepping but so that you can still keep your focus within.

As you take your first step, silently or quietly say: I am stepping into the present. Let your foot touch the ground and transfer your weight. When you're ready to take your next step, again say: I am stepping into the present. And then repeat. With each breath, let go of thoughts about the past or future, anchoring yourself in the now. If your mind starts to wander, gently bring it back. Keep stepping, simply being fully immersed in the experience of now. I am stepping into the present. Over and over.

Walk for as far or as long as you'd like.

MANTRA:

"I am here now. I am rooted into this moment."

XVIII

TURN YOUR FOCUS WITHIN

XVIII. TURN YOUR FOCUS WITHIN

The evening crackles with the calls of cicadas. You sit comfortably surrounded by piles of books, cradled in an ancient forest library that smells of incense and waxed leather. Firelight flickers from nearby braziers, and a tiny kitten lies curled on a nearby window ledge, purring quietly. The room's coziness invites you into a deep state of reflection and self-awareness. The world beyond the panes of glass stretches into the distance—but in here, your attention is attuned to what is within.

Dipping your feathered quill into an ink pot, you jot down in your journal some remembrances about your day. You reflect on what transpired, how the events made you feel, and how those unfolding relate to deeper, more meaningful introspections. As you weave a larger story about how you've come to be where you are in life, memories rise and fall, coming into and receding from your awareness. Each thought is a thread tying you to your past and weaving you toward your future. You realize that none of what has transpired in your life is random; each event has been like a stitch in an enormous tapestry. Each twist of fate, each knot in the plan has created a larger embroidery that you can only discern once you step away and gaze from a distance. Your journey has been divinely arranged, each part becoming a bright stitch in the pattern.

You pause, close your eyes, and sink your awareness deeply within. You breathe and feel the pulsation of your life-force. Focusing in your heart, your awareness drifts into a state of profound presence. Everything you have been, everything you are, all that you will be begins to merge as time dilates. There is no past or future here—only now. You witness yourself spreading before you in a magnificent, glittering expanse. All the pieces connect—each moment leading to the next. Everything is woven together with divine precision.

Within yourself, a vastness unfolds. This is not merely a mental exercise; you are experiencing something profound, something beyond the mind. You have dipped into a well of soul that dwells outside of thought and beyond the scope of time. You have become the watcher—the divine observer of your existence. You have become consciousness itself. You are all things.

The outside world provides endless entertainment. Between our cellphones, computer screens, artificially intelligent robots, flashing billboards, 24-hour news cycles, and unending social media feeds...there is a dazzling array of distractions. Our attention is pulled in countless directions over the course of a day. While some of these external engagements are meaningful—forest paths, sandy beaches, and heartfelt conversations amongst them—many are pure noise. They don't feed or nourish us; they merely trigger a dopamine or cortisol burst, which does little to make us more well or lastingly satisfied.

If our focus is always directed outward, it becomes difficult (if not impossible) to truly know ourselves. The constant buzz of notifications and endless refreshing of updates keeps us looking outside of ourselves. We search for validation, approval, and meaning—we seek out stimulation to distract us from our internal disquiet. But home will never be found lastingly outside ourselves—true belonging occurs within. We exist *in here*, not *out there*. Real meaning, real knowing comes from inside.

Far too many people are afraid to gaze inward. There was a study done where men were given the choice to sit alone with their thoughts for under fifteen minutes or endure an electric shock just to end the experiment sooner.[1] 67% chose the shock. Individuals are deeply uncomfortable facing the dissatisfaction, the memories, the swirling emotions that arise when they focus inward. They can feel overwhelmed by the unresolved tensions, the disquiet from knowing they are not aligned with their values, principles, or purposes. What does it say about our culture that we'd rather experience physical pain than be left alone with ourselves for even a brief expanse of time?

The path to lasting peace and contentment lies in doing the very thing that we often avoid—turning inward. Try this with me: close your eyes and take a deep breath. Notice how it feels. Notice the quality and length of the inhale, the feeling and duration of the exhale. Observe where you experience breathing within your body—is it localized to your lungs, or do you experience this else-

---

1. Wilson, Timothy D., et al. "Just Think: The Challenges of the Disengaged Mind." *Science*, vol. 345, no. 6192, 3 July 2014, pp. 75–77, science.sciencemag.org/content/345/6192/75, https://doi.org/10.1126/science.1250830.

XVIII. TURN YOUR FOCUS WITHIN

where? How does this make you feel? Does attuning yourself to your breath make you feel more relaxed—or does it spike your anxiety? Does turning within make you feel more or less comfortable?

I first became aware of the tremendous power of turning my focus within when I was around eight years old. I vividly remember sitting at my desk in Mrs. Ferris' second-grade classroom, staring at a poster hung above a chalkboard, and becoming enthralled by my breathing. The sensations heightened to such a degree that an orgasmic-like ripple ran through my body, and the world began to spin. I distinctly felt myself leaving my body and entering some sort of other plane. Though no one had taught me meditation, I had stumbled into an ancient esoteric practice for transforming consciousness through breath awareness.

I half-jokingly say that my greatest ambition in life is to get to a point where my husband and I can sit on our back deck with our dogs and watch the sunset progress each evening—holding one another's hands and observing the joy that wells up inside us. There is no greater comfort than exists in our own heart when our soul is at peace and we are fully accepting of ourselves. To achieve this state, we must do the inner work. Practices like meditation, journaling, spoken word therapy, automatic writing, and breath practices can help us delve our inner world.

When we turn our focus within and slow our rate of respiration, the vagus nerve gets stimulated. The longest nerve in the body, it is responsible for engaging the parasympathetic nervous system—which is basically like a brake pedal for our stress response. We heal and soothe ourselves when we slow down and focus on our breath. Becoming aware of this internal state opens a gateway for divine knowing. The more we practice inner focus, the more we begin to understand the deeper levels of ourselves. Reality itself begins to take on new dimensions—we begin to see the connections between thoughts, memories, emotions, and the future that is manifesting. We begin to parse together the meaning behind the events in our lives.

If we go even deeper, the boundaries between us and the wider world dissolve. We experience something called mystical or transpersonal consciousness—we become part of a sentience much larger than ourselves. We realize that the inner and outer worlds are not separate at all: they are reflections of each other, woven together.

This is why nearly all esoteric and mystical spiritual tradition has initiates practice some form of meditation and go on retreat. When we focus within, when we quiet the mind and open our hearts, we see through the veil of illusion. We see past our limited perspectives on space and time and come to know cosmic truths that are enteral and everlasting—truths that cut across culture, religion, and time itself. We connect with the divine Oversoul from which we sprung, which is in every sentient lifeform. We become one with all.

It is interesting that by going within, we connect with a force far more expansive than ourselves. But so it is. What is within is without—the inner and outer worlds are mirrors of one another. By sinking deeper internally, we expand vastly. And in so doing, the mundane becomes sacred, the ordinary extraordinary. Time and space dissolve, and we reclaim our heritage as eternal, cosmic beings.

So, take time daily to turn away from the noise and redirect your focus within. Our inner world is filled with profound wisdom, waiting for us if we will pay attention. It is here that you will find the deepest insights, the clearest guidance, and the purest sense of who and what you are.

RITUAL:

For one week, as soon as you wake up, devote five minutes to an inward reflection ritual where you do nothing but simply observe the state of your body. Notice your breath, notice any physical sensation. Then, turn your focus to the emotional sensations you experience within: are you feeling joy, pain, fear, anticipation? Then, turn your focus to the state of your mind: are you agitated, serene, focused, or fuzzy? Take full stock of your state of being and then get up and start your day.

JOURNAL PROMPTS:

- What external influences have been pulling my attention away from my inner world lately? How can I create more space for self-reflection and introspection?
- Reflect on a time when turning inward brought me greater clarity or peace. How can I cultivate a deeper relationship with my inner self?

GUIDED MEDITATION:

Sit comfortably and turn your focus within. Begin by simply noticing how your body feels. Start from your head and work your way down. How is your jaw, your neck, your shoulders? How does your back or your belly feel? Your hips?

XVIII. TURN YOUR FOCUS WITHIN

Turning from the physical, begin to observe your breathing. Does it feel rapid or slow? Is there more emphasis on inhaling or exhaling? Does the breath feel easy or restricted?

From here, move to the state of your mind: does it feel relaxed, tense, calm, or agitated? Are your thoughts bouncing about, or are they more tranquil? What is the quality of your thinking at this moment?

After a few moments of examination, turn your focus to your emotions. What are you feeling? What are the colors of the emotions, and do they have a physical residence in your body? Are you feeling joy in your heart, grief in your gut, celebration in your shoulders? Realize that, with all of these things, there are layers. You may experience a quality on one level, but the longer you sit with it, the more layers unveil themselves to you.

After some time, home in on the area at the center of your chest. This is the seat of consciousness, the seat of your soul, some might even argue. Invite your awareness to settle here. Sink as deep as you can into the middle of your chest. And in this rooted place, envision a pinprick of light shining there. Allow it to be brilliant and glittering. Maybe it grows with each inhale. Invite all of yourself to settle into this space of calm and quiet, knowing that this is a safe haven for you. Here, you can rest. Here, you can find peace. Stay here for as long as you wish.

MANTRA:

"I find home within."

XIX. GRIEVE WHAT IS LOST

The surrounding woods pass by in a blur as you stagger toward the water. Collapsing onto the ground, digging your fingers into the mud, dry heaves overtake your body as your tears mingle with the stream. A heaviness pulses in your chest, and a nauseous ache gnaws in your belly. You feel it beneath your skin, behind your eyes, in the hollow of your throat. Grief. It's woven through your being, tangled up in everything you lost. You feel the pain of what should have been but isn't—what you counted on but has vanished.

You curl into a hunched crouch, the wind wrapping itself around you. You stare into the water, watching the ripples catch the fading light. Not too far ahead, you hear a rustle in the bushes across the river. A forlorn-looking bear placidly emerges onto the bank opposite you. The two of you meet eyes—hers are dark and shining. You feel no danger here, only comfort. Her eyes shine as if saying, *I've lost something I loved, too. Let us mourn here together.* You sit in silence, watching the fallen leaves float downriver until they disappear from sight. Someday, you hope, this grief will flow away and leave you, too.

Grief isn't something we choose. It arrives uninvited, a force that pulls us under before we even recognize what is happening. It can feel like drowning, like you're trapped beneath the surface and unable to catch your breath. Or, it can feel like a numbness, like the world has gone silent and the colors have faded to ashy grays. Or perhaps it is deep and hidden, churning far below, affecting you in unknown and mysterious ways.

However it manifests, grief is a natural part of life. It is as inevitable as the turning of the seasons or the riptides hidden beneath the waves. Just as the trees must let go of their leaves, just as the river must surrender its glacial melt waters to the sea, so too must we let go of the things that have been lost to us. We mourn for people, for places, for dreams, and for the versions of ourselves that no longer exist.

We cry for the people who promised to journey beside us the whole way but departed abruptly, whether by choice or fate. We weep for the homes to which we had to say goodbye, the sacred abodes that provided us solace but were swept away by the floods. We grieve the plans we laid, the goals we set, the dreams we harbored. We mourn the innocence we lost, the parts of ourselves we had to jettison to survive. To continue along the pathway of life means to surrender so many parts of ourselves—to give over so many things that once brought us joy.

Even though we all experience loss, many of us resist the act of grieving. We push it down; we endeavor to outrun it; we numb ourselves to its presence. Our loved ones tell us to keep moving forward, keep our heads up, and "be strong." Many of us have heard that crying is a sign of "weakness"—that we should get past our losses with alacrity, that we shouldn't burden other people with our grief.

But these are all falsehoods. Grief cannot be rushed or ignored. It cannot be neatly boxed into private areas of our lives, away from other people. It is a process that must be allowed to unfold in its own way and time. By grieving, we honor that which has been lost; we give it space in which to be remembered and celebrated. It provides us room to focus on the love that was shared, a feeling that we ought to drink into our marrow. Grief allows us to move forward with the loss, honoring and contextualizing it so it integrates into our larger life narrative.

As you sit by the water, allow the waves of grief to wash over you. Surrender the internal dams you've built to keep the feelings at bay. Allow the memories to flow in like the tide, one arriving after another. Feel anew the love you shared with the people who left, the opportunities that slipped through your fingers, the dreams that never came to fruition. Allow the feelings to come—resist the urge to push them away. This grief is yours. It is part of your story and deserves to be felt.

So let the tears fall without chastisement or shame. Mourn what could have been. Grieve for the things that will never return, for the parts of your life you once thought you couldn't live without. Allow the grief to flow through you… allow it to be like a river: cleansing, purging, softening the sharp edges of your

XIX. GRIEVE WHAT IS LOST

pain. And when the tears finally subside (do not rush them), notice the emptiness that remains. It's not a hollowness but an openness. A space for spirit to occupy.

Because that is what grief does—it creates space. It makes room for something new, something vibrant and real. Something that may be even greater than what you lost. In the words of spiritual author Richard Bach, "The space for what you want is already filled with what you settled for instead." Perhaps this purge has created the room necessary to have a life beyond your wildest imaginings. Perhaps it is creating the space for more joy, love, and bliss than you could have ever anticipated.

We must let go of what is no longer serving us—and, in so doing, open to the potential for greater.

Feel the tears drying on your cheeks; lick the salt from your lips. The bear is still here, her presence a grounding force—she is bearing witness to your sorrow. Her eyes are filled with compassion—for love knows no boundary between species, ages, or times. She understands that loss is a part of life, just as love is. And in that understanding, there is peace.

Grieving does not make you weak—it makes you fully human. It connects you to the cycles of the earth, to life itself. You become one with the hermit crab who abandons his shell home when it's been outgrown; you join in with the aspen trees shedding their shining, yellow leaves when it's time for winter snows. Grief reminds you that you are part of something larger than yourself. And, in time, the heaviness will lift—the pain will become softer, more manageable. You will find that with the rivers of loss that flow inside there are similar streams of hope and possibility. You will eventually feel greater joy, for the sorrow has carved more deeply into you, allowing you more space to hold light.

Grieve what is lost—and in so doing, create the space for what comes next. Open to what life is teaching you—and embrace this moment with a full heart.

RITUAL:

Once you've identified what it is you need to grieve, create a personalized ritual to honor and release it. This might mean visiting a place tied to this aspect of your life. As you step anew into these familiar haunts, visualize yourself blessing and severing the energetic ties that connect you to this place, allowing it to become part of your past. Perhaps your ritual will involve writing a letter to the person or situation you are grieving and reading it aloud under the full moon. Maybe it means gifting an object that once held significance but now feels like a remnant from a former life, symbolizing your release. Allow yourself to sit with the grief, honoring what has passed. Surrender in whatever way feels right for you—whether through tears, silence, or words.

JOURNAL PROMPTS:

- What loss have I been avoiding grieving, whether it's a relationship, a phase of life, or a part of my identity? How can I give myself permission to fully feel and process that grief?
- How has unprocessed grief impacted my life? What would it look like to create a safe space for that grief to exist and heal?

GUIDED MEDITATION:

I invite you to bring to mind three things you have lost along your journey. Maybe they are physical objects: treasured possessions, trophies won, sentimental mementos. Maybe they are people: loved ones who departed too soon, family members from whom you had to cut ties, friends who fell out of favor. Perhaps they are long-held hopes or ambitions: that dream job you never attained, that body you coveted but never achieved, that life goal that always remained out of reach.

As you uncover those three things that you are mourning, give them a physical representation. Allow their essence to be represented by a physical object that you can hold in your hand. Maybe that person that you miss is represented by an egg-sized jade figurine carved into the shape of a rabbit. Maybe that award you strove for is represented by a golden teacup. Perhaps that cherished lost object is now represented by a piece of fruit.

Gather up these three items and carry them, in your mind, to the edge of a cliff. One by one, set them free by envisioning winged baskets waiting to receive your burdens and carry them away. Tenderly, lovingly, set your items of grief into three separate baskets. Bless them. Thank them for what they've taught you. Envision them surrounded by love. Then, when you're ready, allow the baskets to fly over the edge of the cliff and off to wherever they need to go. They are being tenderly brought to wherever these energies can gently resolve.

These burdens are no longer yours to carry. Sit on the cliff's edge and watch them fade into the distance. Breathe deep and congratulate yourself on letting go of something that you no longer need to carry.

XIX. GRIEVE WHAT IS LOST

MANTRA:

"I honor what was. I allow it to flow through me."

XX. UNCAGE YOUR ANGER

The storm gathers dark and thick, pulsing with raw energy. You feel the electric tingle in your bones; the building pressure will be contained only a short while longer. Your chest tightens, your breaths come rapid and shallow, and your skin prickles with the intensity of it all. This tempest reflects the fury you've kept bottled inside for too long. You've pressed down your anger beneath layers of "goodness." You've striven to remain in control, stay calm, and be composed no matter what. But no longer.

Anger isn't something that can be contained indefinitely. It's a natural force, like a storm, that builds silently. It strengthens with every slight, each betrayal, every injustice that goes unaddressed. It is wild and untamable—even the strongest resolve cannot hold it back forever.

Inside of you, it feels like a convocation of frenzied eagles is clawing and cawing, desirous to escape. They rage, screech, and beat their wings against the cage that is your ribs. You've kept them prisoner for too long, and now they rebel. Their cries say they will be constrained no longer.

Tonight, the imprisonment ends. Tonight, you will release your anger.

You stagger to the edge of the cliff and unlatch the cage. The birds—your anger—explode into the night sky. Their wings beat fiercely as lightning crackles; the sky itself seems to rage. As they fly out and away, they are no longer your burdens to carry. They scream and twirl, rushing into the storm—leaving you trembling in the wake of their release. The winds howl, the rainclouds burst in a downpour, and everything turns chaotic. Everything now feels so much worse than had you kept everything caged tightly.

But, eventually, the sheets of rain stop falling. The eagles have taken roost somewhere distant. The storm clouds dissolve. And what is left is silence—a stillness, deep and profound. It's as if the mountain has sighed in relief.

You stand taller and lighter, your back no longer aching from the emotions you've held for too long. Your mind is no longer clouded by words you couldn't say or feelings you couldn't acknowledge. Now, the air feels fresh—the skies are clearing. And for the first time in a long time, you can breathe deeply.

Anger is not the enemy we've been taught to fear. It's a necessary part of the human experience. It's like a forest fire—scorching and burning—but once it dies down, it will have cleared space for new growth. We are told to suppress our anger, to keep it hidden. We are encouraged to be calm, nonreactive, and intentional when displaying our emotions. But, like an electrical charge building in a storm cloud, it needs release. Anger requires a space to break—and then to dissipate.

The problem is not the anger itself—it's how we express it. Do we offer it up in moments or in ways that are unhelpful, merely destructive? Do we vent our anger to people who are undeserving of our fury? Are we scorching innocent bystanders? When the heat of our rage is delivered to those who deserve the blast—is it meted out in a way that can be constructive, or does it merely sear? Can we process and refine our anger so that we can deliver our frustrations in a more compassionate and useful way?

The worst option is to keep the anger bottled in, pretending as if everything were alright. Do we deny our disquiet; do we pretend we aren't experiencing rage? When we trap our fury within, it festers. It sours into resentment, bitterness, and even hatred. It singes the soul, turning us into someone who is no longer just angry—we are despising and blinded by loathing. We become prisoners to the anger, unable to soothe or abate it. We become entrapped by the very thing we are striving to ignore.

If we are able to release it—if we give our anger permission to exist—we can set ourselves free. Just like a storm, anger can be cleansing. It cleans the air, washes away the build-up of tension, and can allow us to start anew. To permit ourselves to feel our anger is not to lose control but to reclaim it. It's to recognize that this emotion is like any other and is an inexorable part of you. It is a necessary part of you.

I spent much of my life disconnected from my own anger. As a young person, I was viscously tortured by my peers for being neurodivergent, queer, clumsy, gangly, and socially awkward. I learned quickly that, were I to express my anger or rage at my tormentors, their cutting remarks would only become more brutal. So, instead, I learned to turn it inward and bury it. I became a "good" boy who never got angry—I "rose above the torments."

XX. UNCAGE YOUR ANGER

My ability to dissociate from my anger became so adept that by the time I entered my later teenage years, I completely lost the ability to become angry. Something terrible would happen, and I would feel no response. I was just numb. Certain people applauded me for my composure—but I had the wherewithal to realize that something was very wrong. There are moments where fury is an appropriate response—and for me to feel nothing was a huge red flag.

I didn't disconnect from my anger—instead, I had turned it against myself. I had learned to hate myself for everything my peers had mocked me for. I, on a subconscious level, attacked myself for being too feminine, weak, not rugged enough, and not suave enough. I adopted manufactured personas to become the kind of person I thought others would approve of; I donned social masks.

In my early twenties, I embarked on an adventure to reclaim my anger. I began exploring ways to allow myself to feel it again and express it healthfully. I meditated, and I raged at the people who hurt me. I stomped my feet, cried, and howled with fury. Sometimes, I took to expressing my grievances directly to those who had injured me. I also learned the art of forgiveness.

As part of this process, I also worked to reclaim the parts of myself that I was told were shameful. I accepted my same-sex attraction; I began exploring social nudity as a way to reclaim my body as something beautiful and sacred—not something to be mocked or jeered. Over time, I became someone who developed a healthy relationship with my anger—though, at times, it is still difficult for me to express my disappointment and fury for fear of hurting others. It is a journey I am still undergoing and coming to terms with.

Anger, like all emotions, must be honored. And when we honor it and let it flow, we allow the rest of our emotions to flow freely, too. There is little peace to be found until we have allowed anger to take residence inside of us. There is no calm without first opening to the storm.

Release your shame around feeling anger. Let go of your guilt around allowing your anger to rise, crest, and release. What matters is how we uncork it, how we let it out. Do we let it simmer until it boils over and scorches everything in the vicinity? Or do we open the valve gently and carefully, allowing it to expel without consuming us all?

This is a gentle invitation to let it out. Uncage it. Stand on the cliff's edge and release the eagles of your fury. Let the storm rage and then pass. In the quiet that follows, feel the lightness that remains. Feel the freedom. Know that you are whole, even with your anger, especially with your anger.

Remember the words of the Buddha: "Holding on to anger is like grasping a hot coal with the intent of throwing it at someone else; you are the one who gets burned." Allow the coal to drop. Let your rage release.

RITUAL:

Find a private space, indoors or outdoors, where you feel safe to release any pent-up anger. Set a timer for 10 minutes, dedicating this time as sacred space to allow the energy of your anger to fully flow through you. Express yourself freely —yell into a pillow, punch the air, throw rocks into a river, shout to the heavens, beat on a drum, or stomp your feet against the ground.

As you engage, let go of any judgment, trusting that this energy is natural and deserves release. Allow your anger to move through and out of your body, feeling it dissipate like mist with each movement and sound. When the timer ends, take a deep breath and feel the space you've created within, honoring the strength it took to let go.

JOURNAL PROMPTS:

- What situations or relationships trigger anger in me? How can I acknowledge and express my anger in a healthy and transformative way?
- Reflect on a time when I allowed myself to fully feel and express anger. How did that experience impact my sense of power and agency?

GUIDED MEDITATION:

Close your eyes and envision yourself standing in a potion master or apothecary's shop. Lining the shelves and tables are hundreds upon hundreds of bottles. They are of different sizes, shapes, and opacity. Some are green and slender, others are dark and opaque. Some have long stems; some are short and squatty. You notice there is a label on each bottle.

Moving closer to the ones nearest you, you realize that in spidery handwriting on the bottle is a note detailing its contents, and each represents a bit of resentment, anger, or betrayal that you bottled up. These bitter potions have been sealed for too long and have been collected here.

Nearby, there is a blazing fire in the hearth. You have permission to gather up however many of the bottles that you would like and toss them into the sparkling flames, where they will shatter, and the trappings within will dissolve.

XX. UNCAGE YOUR ANGER

Let your eyes fall upon a bottle representing some particularly pernicious anger that you've kept sealed, and grab ahold of it.

Carrying it to the flames, toss it in. Hear the satisfying shatter of the glass fracturing from the impact. Hear the hiss of steam as the contents within evaporate. Good. Now, take another bottle and repeat. And then another. And then another.

Stay here in this shop, breaking as many bottles as you wish, creating empty space for new potions to be brewed, this time ones that bring healing and happiness rather than bitterness and resentment. Then, the space you clean out today will be filled later with feelings of love and belonging. But you must first empty out the rage that you have been storing within.

MANTRA:

"I feel and then effortlessly release my anger."

XXI. SET AND WORK TOWARDS GOALS

The road has been a long and arduous trek, but you are resilient. You had set a course, marked your maps, and set out with a determined spirit. Passing one goalpost after another, your milestones mounted as you climbed higher and higher. Sooner than you anticipated, you find yourself taking in views from dizzying heights that take your breath away. You're nearing the summit and venturing into landscapes that few before have ever trod. Though you cannot yet see it, you can sense the pinnacle approaching.

When you pause and look behind you, you see something remarkable: each step you've taken has left behind an illuminated path. The road you walked is sparkling with a golden aura, as if you had literally been blazing a trail. You set a goal, worked hard, and your determination has left a ribbon of light at which others can gaze in wonderment.

There are times when we let our hearts guide us, and we wander aimlessly. There are moments where we simply let go and trust in the divine guidance. Then, there are times like this where you choose a specific route and determinedly work toward following it to its conclusion. Through dedicated effort and methodical progress, you've achieved something profound. And although the journey is not yet complete, you can savor the satisfaction of a job well done. Few would have had the tenacity or grit—you must feel so proud.

Setting a goal and accomplishing it feels good, doesn't it? It makes us feel vital and powerful—as though we are fulfilling our life's purpose, using our life-force well. Your achievements spin out behind you like a golden thread of light. You've traveled so far, and a deep sense of pride sets your heart aflutter. Through briar patches, over fallen logs, wading through swamps—you've endured. And now, you approach the mountain top, breathing in the rarified air. Ah, how good it feels!

Drink it in and savor the view. Draw the feeling of a "job well done" into your bone marrow. These are the moments that make life sparkle.

What are the things you dream of—what is the type of life you wish to cultivate for yourself? Then, what are you willing to do to achieve it? What do you discern as being meaningful exchange for your life-force; what do you think of as being deserving of investing your time, tears, and "sweat equity?"

It is said that we live in a mental universe—that creation itself was formed from an initial thought. As shards of the divine Oversoul, we have the ability to manifest and change reality with the power of our minds. Each of us creates our world anew each day—and as we change our thoughts, our reality shifts. So, what sort of world do you wish to live in? Each thought you entertain, each intention you set, eventually becomes the reality you experience.

When you envision, daydream, or vision board, you are attuning yourself to a specific frequency and inviting that vibration to manifest in your life. There is no one objective reality—each of us experiences our own flavor of it that may or may not overlap with another person's. So, if you dwell in vibrations of camaraderie, joy, wellness, and abundance, those qualities will begin to unfold around you. If you focus on them, they will slowly and subtly be summoned into being.

But are you doing this consciously? What are the goals and outcomes you wish to see more of in your world? What are the experiences you are holding yourself back from because you believe they are unattainable or you are undeserving?

For a long time, I had a deep desire to develop my musculature in a way that I could be proud of. For years, I followed training manuals and diet plans, to little avail. Little did I know that I was holding myself back because I was deeply tied to the narratives others had foisted upon me as a younger person. I believed I was unworthy of having my goal fulfilled; parts of me even thought I was selfish for wanting something so banal. *You should be focusing on higher things, like enlightenment,* I would chide myself inside my head.

Eventually, I began to work through my self-limiting beliefs and, indeed, discover that I was worthy of having a physical body that I found beautiful. Though it took many years, it eventually did come to pass. Our intentions are invocations that never go unanswered. If we ask for something and diligently work toward achieving it, it will come. It may not arrive in the time frame you desire—or in the way you anticipated—but it will come (so long as it's not in conflict with your life's mission or highest good). Though it took well over a

XXI. SET AND WORK TOWARDS GOALS

decade longer than I would have chosen, by putting in daily effort, I was eventually able to manifest my goals in this area.

Now, this is one simple example. Time and again in my life, I have identified objectives and developed plans to achieve them. My husband says it's one of my superpowers: breaking down a project into smaller, manageable tasks and methodically proceeding through them. But this skill is not unique or rare—any one of us can do it. It begins with identifying what it is we really want, making sure that all parts of ourselves are in alignment in working to achieve it, and then taking one step at a time in the direction of our dreams. Ensuring that all aspects of your conscious and subconscious mind are onboard is often the most challenging part—that, in itself, can take years, sometimes.

I often describe it as having an internal committee sitting around a round table. Though sixty percent of the committee may be onboard, until I convince the rest of the members to find consensus and get behind this objective, little progress will be seen. These members will be actively resisting. It's like playing tug-of-war with yourself; certain parts want to go one direction while other parts are opposing that progress.

This process of naming and striving to achieve goals is a sacred endeavor. It is part of our divine right as humans on this planet, as embodiments of the creator to manifest the lives we want. It is a ritual of becoming, of transforming thought into reality. You don't need to have every step ahead of you figured out before you begin the journey—you just require courage and faith in your determination and resilience. Yes, there will be detours, unexpected roadblocks, unforeseen twists in the road, and moments of doubt—but that is part of the fun of the adventure. Each step brings you into alignment with the life you long for, and you are more capable than you might believe.

Too often, we settle for the current state of things because we believe it's all we deserve—or it's all we are capable of. But this is not so! You are entitled to a fabulous life filled with wonder and joy. You are worthy of having an existence where you wake up each morning, smiling and marveling, "How blessed am I?!"

This is the power of setting goals—it really isn't about the achievements themselves so much as the transformation the pursuit of them provides. In setting out and working toward what you desire, you will learn about your strength, tenacity, and worth as a human being.

The path forward is illuminated by your intention; the path you've already traveled is glowing from your results. Trust in your vision—trust in your steps. Know that with each breath, you are creating a golden thread that leads you ever closer to your highest potential. In the words of the mystic Henry David Thoreau, "Go confidently in the direction of your dreams! Live the life you've imagined."

RITUAL:

Choose a goal—small or large—that you've been putting off. Break it down into three actionable steps. Start with the first step today, treating it as a sacred act—whether it's sending an email, making a phone call, or drafting a plan. Set intentional deadlines for the next two steps, marking them in your calendar or planner as a commitment to your future self. Each time you revisit these steps, return to the original intention you set, honoring the journey you're creating.

JOURNAL PROMPTS:

- What are my most meaningful goals right now? How do they align with my values and desires for the future?
- Reflect on a past goal that I achieved. What was the journey like, and how did working toward it shape my personal growth?

GUIDED MEDITATION:

Close your eyes and envision yourself standing at the base of a winding path. It is serpentine and heads steadily upward. Your eyes trace its course as it switchbacks up the steep hill before you. Notice how there are certain milestones along the way, demarcated points that indicate a definite stage of progress. Perhaps they are lanterns glowing brightly or large stone monoliths. Maybe they are signposts declaring the achievement of having reached so far along the road.

Once you have a clear vantage of some of the landmarks that you are going to hit on your journey toward the crest, begin your ascent. See yourself consciously and slowly marching up the path toward the first landmark. See yourself nearing that lantern, that sign, that monolith.

Feel how good it is to be reaching the first stage in the pursuit of your larger goal. You aren't trying to tackle climbing the whole mountain in one go; you are taking it stage by stage. Maybe you'll get to the first milestone and rest for a day or longer. Perhaps you'll continue walking. It doesn't matter how long the ascent takes. Just keep walking.

Reach the first landing and feel the light of achievement erupt in the middle of your chest. How does it feel to have made it this far? Do you want to pause

XXI. SET AND WORK TOWARDS GOALS

here or keep going? Allow yourself to envision taking this journey up the hill at your own pace, taking as many pauses as you need until—someday—you eventually arrive at the summit. There is no rush to get there. Just keep taking the next step before you.

MANTRA:

"I move effortlessly toward my dreams."

XXII. FORGE DISCIPLINE

Everything quiets as your focus hones to a single point. You pull the arrow back, feeling the feathers nearly graze your cheek as a familiar tension builds in the bow. Your arm holds steady against the resistance, as it was trained to do. With a total cessation of breathing, you release—and the arrow flies true, cutting the air to strike the target with a satisfying thud. You smile with pride, and not just from the shot's accuracy. You feel a deeper sense of accomplishment well up within you over showing up time after time to hone your craft and develop your acumen.

There are days when showing up and cultivating your talents feels effortless. Days when drawing the bow and letting the arrow fly feel like an innate skill with which you were born. Then, there are those days when it feels tedious and burdensome. Getting up, heading out, picking up your bow or paint brush or laying down your yoga mat seems about as enjoyable as walking naked through an ice storm. Days when your mind and body resists, where discipline feels onerous.

It's important to acknowledge that both ease and effort are experiences on the road toward skill acquisition. You understand the road toward self-mastery is long…but you are committed. You have learned to find joy in the small wins and in reflecting on how far you've come. The road you have set out is long, more akin to an ultramarathon than a fifty-meter sprint.

You observe a hawk gliding through the air above, scanning the ground for its prey. The hawk didn't become a skilled hunter immediately—it took countless attempts and months of practice to become the deadly marksman he is today. But even he isn't perfect—he, too, has plenty of misses and failed attempts. Your journey is very similar. You are not expected to be perfect every day, nor are you meant to relentlessly push well past your limits. You are meant to improve, little by little, day by day. Perfection is not the end goal—we are not striving to become machines. Instead, we embrace the pursuit of excellence: not to be *the* best, but to be *our* best. We strive to develop our potential as well as we can, irrespective of how it compares to others.

True discipline is about finding balance—between effort and ease, striving and resting, ambition and contentment. Discipline is not about pushing through at all costs, regardless of who you hurt or how you injure yourself. It's about regularly showing up with intention, attention, consistency, and a light heart. Some days, the work will feel dance-like: joyful and floating. On other days, it will feel like lugging an iron ball. Either way is alright—both are part of the process of development. What matters is that you stay true to your long-term commitment to your chosen path.

Now is the time to check that you are still committed to your goals, that you are showing up and putting in the effort. It is time to hold yourself accountable that your actions are in alignment with your intentions and desires. Are you trying hard enough? Are you striving too hard? Do you need to invest more time? Do you need to back away and cultivate an unrelated hobby? What we ought to aim for is balance and consistency, showing up regularly over time.

I remember a story of an aspirant asking a spiritual guru about how long enlightenment would take. "What if I meditate for 2 hours a day?"

The guru replied, "You will reach your liberation in 25 years."

"And if I meditate 5 hours a day?"

The guru thought for a moment and then said, "50 years."

To attain anything of value requires a balance of patience and stamina. Being able to work for hours on end and exceed your limits is all well and good—but is it sustainable? Will you still be invested in pursuing that same goal months, years, or decades from now? It is better to invest a manageable daily effort to achieve what you seek. Effort over time equals growth. Honor the ebb and flow of your energy. There will be days when you need rest—and you should take them. That is not failing at discipline; that is just part of the practice. We must honor the wisdom of our spirit and body for when it's time to push and when backing away is called for.

If you are truly aligned with your purpose, if you are pursuing something that adds to the quality of your life, bringing you greater joy and vitality, then showing up daily shouldn't be a chore. It should feel like a blessing to have the opportunity. *I get to sit in meditation every day. I am lucky to practice my quilting each*

XXII. FORGE DISCIPLINE 151

evening. How blessed am I to have the time, health, and resources to meaningfully work to cultivate the skills that matter to me?

Regular, disciplined practice should eventually evolve into something called the flow state. In the words of author Mihaly Csikszentmihályi, "Flow is a state in which people are so involved in an activity that nothing else seems to matter; the experience is so enjoyable that people will continue to do it even at great cost, for the sheer sake of doing it." You enter a space where time dilates, thinking abates, and everything not a part of your pursuit fades away. In this space, we become pure conscious energy—we tap into our innate state as creators. It becomes a magical state of possibility.

As you practice, you should strive to tap deeper into that state of flow, where the world blurs and everything proceeds with an effortless grace. Instinct takes over; all actions feel primal, almost second nature. You look forward to getting to practice again because you get connected to something greater than yourself, something timeless.

Too many people have the misconception that discipline must be hard—that it must be forced and demands willpower. And, of course, there are times when we need to light a fire in our bellies to get motivated. When showing up at the cushion, to the canvas, or picking up the bowstring takes some self-motivation. But, overall, it should be enjoyable. Zen master Paul Reps once said, "Until it's fun, better left undone." If pursuing your goals always feels like a slog, like you are constantly running into walls...maybe it's time to reevaluate? Maybe this desired accomplishment is not in alignment with your talents or higher interests? Perhaps this is not something that all parts of your subconscious want to come to fruition.

When fully aligned with purpose, our work should become a form of play. You find yourself drawn to it, eager to engage because it feels so good. Do not force yourself into unnatural, rigid routines because some master somewhere said you must. Instead, find your own way—find how you thrive. Choose practices and modalities that light you up inside, that make you feel inspired and connected. Rather than imagining yourself pushing through, feel yourself being pulled toward your goals. Then, the work becomes a part of you, a natural extension of who you are. What if every step forward felt like an adventure in and of itself?

The key to unlocking discipline is knowing it's okay to be human. Enjoy your messy complexities—forgive yourself for your shortcomings while you simultaneously hold yourself accountable. Realize that everything is always perfectly imperfect—let go of the relentless pursuit of being faultless. The goal is merely growth, a growth that never reaches a conclusion point. That way there will always be something to hone, improve, or develop. And that is precisely how it should be.

So, what goals do you have? What dreams light you up and draw you into a state of flow? What desires are worth the effort of showing up daily with energy and enthusiasm? Keep them at the forefront of your heart. Be disciplined but also gentle with yourself. Trust that every small effort you make is building toward something greater. Discipline isn't about hardness or sacrifice. It's about creating the space for something beautiful to unfold—a life that feels blissful, a path that feels right. Work diligently and lightly in the pursuit of your ambitions.

RITUAL:

Pick one small habit that you've wanted to develop, such as drinking more water, waking up earlier, or meditating daily. Light a candle or hold a grounding object and set an intention that this practice will help you cultivate the life you desire. Commit to practicing this habit for 40 days without skipping a day. Use a habit tracker, journal, or small stone to mark each day completed. Reflect on how discipline feels as you build momentum, and allow this practice to be a steady anchor, reminding you that discipline is a pathway to personal mastery. At the end of the 40 days, hold a small celebration, offering gratitude for the progress you've made and the commitment you've honored.

JOURNAL PROMPTS:

- In which areas of my life do I struggle with maintaining discipline? How does this lack of structure affect my overall well-being and sense of accomplishment?
- Reflect on a time when discipline brought me closer to achieving something important. How can I rekindle that sense of purpose in areas where I'm currently feeling unfocused?

GUIDED MEDITATION:

Close your eyes and envision yourself standing before a pile of massive granite stones. Some are cut into oblong rectangular shapes. Some are more freeform,

XXII. FORGE DISCIPLINE

more rough-hewn. These are the materials for the tower you are building. Before you are a stack of stones; one day, they will become a magnificent structure. But it is going to take patience and discipline to arrange them as such. Fortunately, you are strong, wise, and capable of great feats of strength.

Approach the stack and pick out your cornerstone block—the first piece that you will lay. With some effort, pick it up and carry it to the level ground nearby, carefully setting it down to become the first piece of your foundation. Return to the pile and choose another, carrying it over to set it beside the first.

One by one, begin arranging this assortment of stones into place. Creating a tower one stone at a time is no easy or quick act. It takes determination, patience, and a willingness to sit with monotony. For many trips back and forth, you will be doing more or less the same thing: carrying and arranging stones. But to you, you find joy in this. For in building this tower, you are learning valuable skills. You are achieving something that few would have the tenacity to cultivate. You are honing your abilities and building your strength.

Notice how, with each return trip, things become a little easier; you become more adept at choosing and arranging the materials. Stay with this image of building your tower for as long as you can or until your structure is completed.

MANTRA:

"I am committed to my personal growth."

XXIII. REST AND RECOVER

Ahh, a mossy crux of where two branches meet forms a perfect bed to cradle your body. It's time to lie down, set aside your worries and hopes, and simply rest. Allow yourself to sigh as you settle into your place of renewal. Hear how the forest hums with the symphony of crickets chirping, cicadas clicking, and bullfrogs bellowing? Notice the lullaby of the owls, the ravens, and the starlings.

Above and around you, luminescent mushrooms softly glow, creating a dreamlike haze—you feel suspended in a twilight. You rub your shoulders against the moss-covered bark, worn smooth from sheltering countless centuries of travelers like yourself. The air smells damp of earth and distant rain.

At this moment, there is nothing to do, nothing to achieve. You have nowhere to go—no destinations, no arrival times, no deadlines. You've surrendered all your ambitions and have entirely given over to rest. All that is being asked of you now is to simply be—to stop doing and just be. Set down your plans, abandon your ambitions, and allow yourself to recover.

You've journeyed far—you've climbed mountains, waded through rivers, navigated through dense forest undergrowth. Your body feels exhausted from everything you have asked of it. Allow those knots to untangle, those aches to dissolve, and your spirit to return to a place of tranquility. Feel cozy as you curl in on yourself, exhale fully, and drift into that beautifully nourishing place between wakefulness and dreaming. Let everything become soft, hazy, and beautiful. Allow the hum of the forest to be your serenade. Your eyelids grow heavy, and you let yourself drift, knowing that what you need most is a true, restorative rest.

Our world never ceases its turning. In a society that prioritizes achievement, busyness, and "the hustle," rest has become a radical act of self-care. We are constantly being prodded to be more—more productive, more successful, more highly achieving. The pressure to engage with "grind culture" is relentless. We have become hardwired to our devices, unable to detach from the endless barrage of notifications, updates, emails, and messages. We are encouraged to fill every waking hour with something "useful" or "important." It's as if our value has become tied solely to our output—meanwhile, our nervous systems are being fried from constant overstimulation.

We have been taught to believe that rest is indulgent or wasteful, something we are only entitled to do after we've exhausted ourselves in a lifetime of constant action. But this couldn't be further from the truth; rest is our birthright. Look at any other living creature on this planet; be it plant or animal, there is a time for growth and a time for rest. The jaguar hunts intently for a period of time and then returns to her lair to recover. The sacred hazel tree grows rapidly in the spring and into the summer months, and by autumn, rest has taken over. There are seasons for action and creation; there are times for new growth and pushing outward. But equally important are the times for dormancy, stillness, and renewal. And by dwelling in a modern culture that has become antithetical to rest, we must actively reclaim it.

To understand why rest feels like such a radical idea, we must look at the history of how we came to be here. Going back to the era of pre-industrialization, most people worked for themselves as farmers and sharecroppers. While the myth is that they worked harder and longer hours than we do in the modern era, this is far from the truth. Not only were they limited to solar-lit hours that varied by latitude (since there was no artificial illumination), they also had more "festival days" (holidays with no labor) than working days.

When industrialization came around, however, the notion that a person's time was owed to an overseer became preeminent. A boss owned a laborer's hours for a set percentage of the day, and there was a relentless push to eke out more productivity, more hours of focused efforts, and as little downtime as possible. We began to be viewed like the machines that had been introduced to society—and time suddenly became something we never had enough of.

With industrialization and capitalism also came the notion of scarcity. We were taught to consume, to purchase, to covet things we never saw need of before—and it brought us into a debt cycle. We never had enough money to buy all that we desired—so the remedy was to work more and grease the wheels of industry. Our society forced this upon us as a way to grow capitalism, to get us to spend our earned money so more goods could be produced to meet demand.

Flash forward a few centuries later, and many alive today work two or three jobs. I personally know many advanced degreed professionals who have multiple side gigs because their primary profession cannot support their livelihood. Thousands of podcasts, books, YouTube channels, and motivational speakers are dedicated to the topics of efficiency, productivity, growing your brand, achieving more, and making more money. Seldom does anyone stop and ask, "Why?" Why do we need more? Why do we need to be so productive? Why is our society built this way?

There was a time in the early- to mid-twentieth century when economists analyzed the speed of automation that was occurring and concluded that, within a few decades, most humans would only need to work for a small portion of the week. This did not come to pass because industry took the profits of automation and, instead of paying them back to their workers, sought more growth—new products, grander innovations, more models to consume. That time that should have been ours for rest, idleness, and enjoyment got devoured by profit margins and hungry investors.

So, we must be the revolutionaries and claw back our time for rest. We must find ways to say "no" to grind culture and prioritize naps, daydreaming, sitting idyl, exploring hobbies without wanting to turn them into side hustles, and simply being. Getting eight hours of sleep each night shouldn't be aspirational but a given. Having time to walk barefoot in the grass, play with your dog, and make love to your partner...those moments are your birthright. You are deserving to have them.

You are no machine; you are not here to function endlessly without pause. You are here to live, to experience, to feel. Rest is where our body, mind, and soul flourish. It's where discovery and joy blossom. When was the last time you felt true wonderment at life's majesty? Genuine awe and appreciation for the gift of living? If you are overworked, overtired, and overstimulated, experiencing those qualities is nearly impossible.

Rest is where strength is rebuilt, creativity rekindles, and enjoyment blossoms. This is your encouragement to slow down. Take a nap in the dappled sunlight in a wildflower meadow. Make herbal tea and sit at a rain-streaked window as a storm rolls past. Read a trashy novel for the pleasure of it, not worrying about learning anything useful. Wander barefoot through the fall leaves, building piles of them to fall into. Nap again.

Society wants you to believe that your worth is tied up in your accomplishments—how much money you've made, your title, how famous you are. It is not. You are worthy because you are alive. You are deserving of respect, kindness, and dignity simply because you exist—nothing more and nothing less. You do not need to prove anything. You are deserving because you are alive. You are worthy—and you demonstrate this by the depth in which you live. The more you are present to your existence, the more you share meaningful moments with others, the more love you give...the more you demonstrate how worthy you are.

Rest is a necessity—you are entitled to experience it. But, it is also a gift we give ourselves. To permit ourselves to reclaim our rest is to honor that divine spark within. It's to affirm our worth as humans and not machines. As the Dalai Lama said, "We are human beings, not human doings." Take as much time as you need to explore your rest. Life is unfolding whether we rush through it or if we allow ourselves to pause and enjoy the journey.

So, close your eyes. Let the earth hold you as you sink deeper into your renewal. When you are ready to rise again, you will feel the power you've accumulated through this act of rest. You are deserving of this solace. Let yourself recover; whenever you're ready, the world will still be waiting for you. You will be prepared to reengage from a softer and kinder place, for you will have reconnected with your fuller self.

RITUAL:

Dedicate an entire day to rest. Turn off your phone, avoid any work, and engage in activities that nourish you—whether it's reading, napping, taking long walks, or soaking in a bath. Notice how your body and mind feel when you give yourself permission to rest fully without any guilt. When the day concludes, give thanks for the solace it brought, knowing that rest is your birthright and a path to deeper connection with your truest self.

JOURNAL PROMPTS:

- How do I currently respond to burnout or exhaustion? How could I allow myself more time to rest without feeling guilty or unproductive?
- Reflect on a time when I fully allowed myself to rest and recover. How did that period of recovery impact my energy, creativity, or emotional balance?

XXIII. REST AND RECOVER

GUIDED MEDITATION:

Allow yourself to lie down and close your eyes. Breathe deeply and feel the surface beneath your back. Envision that you are lying in a sun-drenched meadow. Soft grasses cradle you; wildflowers surround you. Butterflies and dragonflies flit overhead. Ladybugs tickle your nose. Feel the mighty willow trees swaying nearby. Feel their searching roots in the soil beneath you, reaching for water. Envision those roots forming a cradle for the earth and grasses that support you.

Allow yourself to feel held, nestled, by the surrounding environment. You are safe. You are well. Let yourself fully give over and be healed. There is nothing to do here, nothing to achieve or be. You are allowed to simply rest. For so long, you have striven and worked to take care of others. Now, this is just time for you. Let go of seeking and just be. Rest, finally, rest.

Give over and let the ground carry your burdens. You have done well. You have worked so hard. Now, in this meadow, all that is asked of you is to give over and sleep. Let the grasses and tree roots provide you nourishment. Allow them to draw forward whatever energies you need for healing. Just rest now. Reclaim your right to be at peace and rest.

MANTRA:

"I honor my need to rest."

XXIV. PAY ATTENTION TO YOUR DREAMS

Your eyelids have grown so heavy that you no longer have the strength to keep them lifted. You relax into the leaf-strewn hollow between twisting elm roots. The air is rich with the scent of decay and fecund soil—the breeze through the canopy overhead provides a calming rhythm of *ratatatatatat*. The earth holds you like a loved one welcoming you home. Nestled here, you surrender your connection to the waking world. You enter a liminal space where the boundary between what is solid and what is imagined is blurred.

A sleek, dark lynx prowls nearby; she is your guardian tonight. Her glowing eyes silently watch, ensuring that only friendly spirits pass through to your dreamscape. Golden tendrils of spirit rise from your body, lifting and spiraling into the air. Your consciousness is leaving your physical form and traversing the veil to another world. These delicate threads of light weave a bridge between the seen and unseen, the solid and the ephemeral. Your sentience transitions into a place with its own language, its own truth—no more real or fake than the more gravity-bound world you left.

The world of dreams is a sacred place. Though modern science assures us that dreaming is just the byproduct of the brain clearing out information while we sleep, cultures across the globe have taken the power of dreams more seriously. In the United States, even an organization as humorless as the Central Intelligence Agency has studied dreams and discovered that tangible, verifiable information can be gathered from them—impossible to know information has been gleaned by adept dreamers.

Dreams are sometimes just the ramblings of our sleeping mind, but they can also be voyages to other worlds (or even parts of our own world) and places to communicate with forces that are usually more silent (ancestors, spirit guides, interdimensional forces, or deities, for example). The dream world can provide warnings about events currently happening or which will be occurring in the future. We can slip beyond the limits of time, space, and human language to garner understanding and insight.

Throughout my life, I have had precognitive dreams—dreams where I will live experiences well before they occur in waking life. Usually, the moments are very mundane: sitting at a desk, eating lunch, walking into a building. Frequently, I won't remember them until the moment arrives during "real life." I will be in the midst of a conversation with another person when, suddenly, a feeling of déjà vu overtakes me. For the next few seconds, I can recall who will walk in or what will transpire next.

Additionally, I have awoken from a deep slumber in a panic only to discover some sort of natural disaster happened at that precise time somewhere across the globe. I have had ailing loved ones come to visit me in dreams, often waking me up, and then discovered on the subsequent day that it was at the exact moment their spirit passed out of their body and transitioned from this life. I have had spirit guides in human and animal form teach me and instruct me on my spiritual development and well-being in dreams.

These types of experiences are not uncommon; I know many others who experience similar on a regular basis. There are even those who have cultivated the ability for lucid dreaming—where they can actively choose where they go and what they do while in a dream state, something that has happened to me several times. Regardless of whether or not you actively seek to manipulate your dreams, it is crucial that you begin to become aware of what you're dreaming. Important information and insights may be arriving for you on a nightly basis, and you may be entirely oblivious to it.

I would highly recommend creating a dream journal to set next to your bed. As soon as you awake in the morning (or in the middle of the night), roll over and write down what you can remember of your dreams. They will fade fast, so try to be as prompt as possible. If you want to take this a step further, you can set an alarm to wake you in the middle of the night, when intuitive dreaming is at its peak, to set down those more intense dreams before your conscious mind wipes them from your memory.

This desire to remember and understand our dreams goes back to the dawn of recorded history. Ancient Egyptians had entire career paths that could be dedicated to the study and interpretation of dreams. Dreaming was seen as a place where the gods could deliver messages—entire temple complexes were

XXIV. PAY ATTENTION TO YOUR DREAMS

built to foster dream incubation. Aboriginal Australians talk of something called "Dreamtime"—an eternal, spiritual realm that can be traversed like the waking world. They believe that the waking world was dreamt into existence and that in sleep, we can reconnect with the spirit that created the universe, both past and present. In India, the term *maya* is used to describe how the waking world is also a dream, an illusion, and that the dreams experienced in sleep are no more or less real.

What if you began treating your dreams with a similar reverence? What if you imagined your nightly sleep routine as a ceremony, an opportunity to connect with your deepest self and the universe at large? What if you explored the symbolism and imagery of your dreams and held them as actual happenings that occurred in another realm, on another level, but still held wisdom for you in the here and now?

Dreams connect differently to the flow of time and logic, but they are no less real. They may sometimes seem chaotic or nonsensical, but that doesn't deprive them of an intuitive meaning. Messages are woven into the undulating and writhing fabric of dreamscape—they are there for you to parse out and comprehend. The more you unlock the hidden doors in your consciousness, the more full and vibrant life becomes. The more you pay attention to your dreams, the more deeply you'll be tapped into warnings, omens, forces affecting your life and the lives of others, and instructions for your well-being. There have been many times when I have resolved disagreements and conflicts with others in dream space when such a reconciliation was impossible in waking life—and these dreams can provide immense solace. I frequently get to visit with loved ones who are no longer on this Earth or in my life—providing me with understanding and peace regarding their departure. Dreams can be attuned to larger, universal events, reminding us that we are all interconnected.

Just as the dark lynx watches over you as your dream, you can likewise invite protective forces to guard your dream space. Envision ancestors or guardian spirits standing sentinel around your bed as you pass from wakefulness. Imagine a glass dome of protection surrounding you, only allowing in forces that benefit you. Place amethyst or smoky quartz crystals at the corners of your bed with the intention that your spirit stays safe as you venture into the other world.

Everything that arises in dreams is part of your personal mythology. They are revealing parts of you that you may or may not wish to see. It is a mystical space where you get to explore more facets of your psyche than you typically get to in waking life. Trust in your dreams—even the ones that leave you feeling uneasy. Treat dream space as sacred, as a place that holds keys to part of you that you never knew existed.

Dreams do not just occur at night—life itself is a dream. One day, you will awaken from this dream of life into another reality. Just as the waking world holds lessons, so too does your dreamworld. So, dream boldly. Dream deeply. And listen.

RITUAL:

Place a dedicated dream journal and pen by your bedside. Each night, before you sleep, take a moment to ask for guidance or insights from your dreams and whisper an intention for your mind to remember them. In the morning, as soon as you wake, record any impressions, symbols, or feelings from your dreams. After two weeks, review your journal and see if any themes, symbols, or insights arise. If you feel ready to go deeper, explore tools for lucid dreaming and begin incorporating them into your daily life.

JOURNAL PROMPTS:

- What recurring dreams or symbols have shown up in my life? What messages might they be trying to communicate to me about my subconscious desires or fears?
- What are some times where my dream world intersected with the waking world? What did I observe from the crossover?

GUIDED MEDITATION:

Explore this meditation once you are in bed for the night. Before lying down, sit upright and take a few centering breaths. Feel the air enter and leave your body in a slow, steady rhythm. Part by part, scan your physical body and invite each area to loosen and surrender any lingering tension from your day.

Take as much time as you need, but once you are ready, bring your mind's eye to the base of your throat. In this hollow space called the suprasternal notch, between your collarbones and above your sternum, let your focus rest. This is the space where dreaming lives. Centering your mind, envision a pulsing light here, surrounded by mist. Envision yourself entering this mist and dwelling in the shimmering light.

Now, lie down and keep your focus here. Ask that you remain somewhat present and alert as you enter the world of dreams. Ask that you remember your

XXIV. PAY ATTENTION TO YOUR DREAMS

dreams in as vivid detail as possible and that you recognize that you are dreaming while the visions are occurring. Keep your focus here, in the throat, as you gently doze, nodding off to sleep. Try to keep your neck straight—and if it's helpful, you can bend your knees and place your feet on the bed beneath you to prevent you from sinking too quickly into the dream state. Take your time and breathe.

MANTRA:

"I listen to the wisdom of my dreams."

XXV. TRUST YOUR INTUITION

With your eyesight obscured by a veil tied around your head, you step forward bravely. Your sensory vision is not needed here; instead, you trust an inner guidance. You are confident that your footfalls will avoid upturned roots and sharp stones. You believe that your subtle awareness will guide you swiftly and safely toward your destination ahead.

Though fear threatens to lift your stomach into your throat, you swallow and keep it at bay. You know you can do this. You breathe deeply and reach out with your awareness, feeling the space around you with your mind. Whispers from the earth reach up through the soles of your bare feet; the hum of the trees whispers in your ears. The trails of light left by the fireflies trace across your skin as the insects flit about in their mating dances.

The flutter in your chest and the twinge in your core are guides that speak in a language older than words. There is a language of symbols and sensations native to your bones, heart, and spirit. Feel the moon pulling you from overhead —his soft, silvery light encouraging you to trust yourself. Hear the plants rustle with secret knowledge. Walk forward, step by step, guided by instinct, by a quiet voice that says: *this way*.

Learning to trust your intuition and let go of logical knowing can feel risky or even intimidating. Who am I to be so bold, to trust something that feels so ephemeral, so fleeting? While these feelings of incredulity are valid, you have already been navigating by instinct throughout your life. When you've made that split-second decision based on a twinge in your gut, that was intuition. When you followed your heart down a course that was completely illogical but brought you great joy, that too was you following a deeper knowing.

Intuition is always existing underneath the surface—but in order to access it, you must trust that it is there and it's real. In Dr. Dean Radin's book on studying psychic phenomena in a laboratory setting, *Real Magic*, he demonstrates through data that the ability to experience metaphysical experiences is directly predicated by your willingness to believe they are possible. If you hold staunchly to the notion that nothing is possible beyond the recognized laws of physics, then you will see no effects from focused energy, intuition, or mindful attention. But, if you are open to the possibility that they can exist, then a consistent and quantifiable shift can be scientifically measured.

You are able to know things beyond the scope of your physical senses. Both Princeton University and the Central Intelligence Agency of the United States studied intuition for decades and reliably confirmed that it does, indeed, exist. You are able to uncover information about events, happenings, intentions, and even future events if you open and quiet your consciousness. The CIA used psychics to garner intelligence about foreign adversaries. Though certain individuals have a much higher success rate than the average, they found that anyone can tap into a transpersonal intelligence that exists outside their body and influence events.

Even if you want to think of intuition in practical terms, recognize that the body senses and interprets far more information than your logical mind will ever receive. Only a tiny portion of our brain is connected to verbal centers. The amygdala, for example, which governs the flight and fight response in the body (the stress response) is one such—it does not connect to the parts of the brain that can articulate its findings in words. This means that your mind is processing and making decisions in response to stimuli that it cannot communicate to you. If you are only relying on the thoughts that you are able to articulate in words, you are ignoring the vast majority of your brain's processing power. This is why we must pay attention to feelings, sensations, and images that arise from the subconscious; we must observe that pull in our guts or twisting in our hearts. Our body knows far more than it can communicate to us.

Begin noticing the slight tension in your shoulders when something feels off. Observe the excitement in your belly when you feel inspired about the path ahead. Heed the sinking in your chest when a questionable opportunity presents itself. These are all messages from your intuition guiding you.

When you feel that twinge, that pull, that feeling about a person, a place, or a decision—listen. Many cultures throughout history have revered this ability to receive information from a deeper place. Indigenous cultures have believed that animal spirits, ancestors, and even the land itself can communicate through

XXV. TRUST YOUR INTUITION

visions and sensations—that individuals should be trained to feel their presence and draw upon them to provide healing and guidance. The ancient Greeks looked to the oracle at Delphi for guidance, trusting the intuitive messages they received were divine truths. Cultures across the globe have used entheogenic substances (aka plant medicine) to bypass the logical mind and tap into a transpersonal experience of visions, symbols, and knowing. Author Jules Evans, who researched plant medicine for his book *The Art of Losing Control*, shares that he received historically verifiable information about his ancestors (names, dates, and status as being slave owners) through a journey with ayahuasca.

Intuition is a part of the natural world and is shared with animals, plants, and all living creatures. Think of the birds or butterflies who instinctively migrate thousands of miles across the earth or the deer who senses a predator before it is visible. Perhaps you have sensed a person watching you from a distance—hair stands up on the back of your neck, or you get the general sensation of being watched. We don't know why; we simply just know. We are sensing something beyond the scope of our conscious awareness. We are born with this gift, but it has not been encouraged to develop due to living in a society that delights in the mechanical and the mundane. One day, science will come to understand the reasoning behind extra-sensory happenings; but, right now, there is such a prejudice that even when research is done to conclusively prove their existence, no journals will publish their findings. We must reclaim this intuitive knowing for our own—we must accept it as our birthright as humans on this planet.

Our modern world often feels like it is lacking magic. It has become so prosaic—we are hyper-fixated on data, logic, discernible and dissectible happenings. So much so that we have lost all sense of mystery, majesty, mysticism, and awe. We are encouraged to plan every detail, predict every outcome, to make sure we obey all rules—there is no room for whimsy. This has led many to lives that exists in shades of greige—a life that has lost all sparkle and wonderment. No wonder so many people are so depressed, anxious, and suffering from mental afflictions—we have been cut off from that which gives life meaning!

We must re-wild ourselves, reconnect with our primal selves from a time before we learned civility. We must open to the ecstatic, the uncontrolled, the untamed. We must trust that we always knew, deep down. We must surrender to the unknown and embrace the potential for infinite possibilities. We must have faith—not in something external—but in ourselves. We need to pause, to listen, and to open to the quieter whispers that are always around us.

Trust that once this intuitive side to ourselves is cultivated, life will change in beautiful and dramatic ways. We will live with less fear and more confidence because we have tapped into this cosmic knowing that gives us resiliency and faith. We will dwell in a deeper wisdom, a sight beyond sight, that comes from within. We will be more free.

So, the next time you feel that nudge, that whisper, that inexplicable knowing, trust it. Honor it. Flow with it. Accept that you are being guided by something ancient and wise—a part of you that has always been waiting to be acknowledged. Your intuition will guide you step by step to wherever it is you need to go. Give over to the process. Know that you are not lost—you are, now and always, on the path you were meant to walk. Shut your eyes and take the next step. Let spirit walk with you.

RITUAL:

When the opportunity arises today, make a decision based entirely on intuition. Whether it's for something small, like choosing what to eat for dinner, or something more significant, like deciding whether to accept an invitation—let your gut feeling guide you. Take a few centering breaths and invite your inner knowing to surface. Ask for a sign to reveal itself to you—or ask for a way forward to become apparent. You may suddenly notice a symbol or sign nearby; perhaps a particular pathway will glow or flicker. You could also consult with a divination tool like a pendulum, tarot or oracle cards, runes, Omikuji sticks, mala beads, etc. Afterward, reflect on how it felt to trust your deeper knowing and how the decision unfolded.

JOURNAL PROMPTS:

- How often do I trust my intuition when making decisions, and when do I tend to ignore it? How has following my gut led to both positive and negative outcomes in the past?
- Reflect on a time when I acted on my intuition rather than logic. What was the outcome, and what did I learn about the power of intuitive guidance?

GUIDED MEDITATION:

Allow your gaze to soften inward as you breathe. Notice the state of your body, your mind, your breath. Allow yourself to be with whatever is and savor the

XXV. TRUST YOUR INTUITION

sensation of being you right now. There is nowhere else you need to be, nothing you need to do...just be here.

After you feel yourself settle in, breathe all the way down to the bottom of your pelvis. Feel your base, your connection with the earth below you. As this space opens and expands, your mind's eye can rise a bit higher. Come up to the space beneath your navel. Have you ever had a feeling in your gut that something is wrong? The belly is a seat of your intuition. It tells you when a situation is wrong or when you should be choosing differently. Allow it to teach you. What does it have to say?

Once you've listened to what it has to share with you, you can let your focus rise higher to the heart. Neural cells exist in the belly and, too, in the heart. What wisdom does it have to share? What unheard insights are lingering here, waiting for you to pay attention? Spend some time listening to the whispers of your heart and really knowing what they have to say.

Finally, bring your focus higher, to the space between and slightly above your eyebrows. Allow yourself to dwell here, seeing without eyesight. Envision the world around you while your eyes remain closed. When we can see through our third eye, we see things as they truly are rather than as how they wish to be seen. We can see people and events for their inner truth rather than their outer glamour.

Spend as much time here as you wish. Then, when you feel like you've reached a point of completion, find a ribbon of light connecting the navel, heart, and third eye. See how they operate as one. Feel the flow between them as you continue to breathe and reflect.

MANTRA:

"I surrender to my inner knowing."

XXVI. LISTEN FOR YOUR GUIDES

The sky is an expanse of cerulean fading to navy; the sun has just set behind the horizon. You have sat at the river's edge for hours, praying and asking for your spirit guides to reveal themselves, imploring them to offer you insights. The gentle ripple of the water and the soft hiss of the wind through the reeds have been your companions as you've sought out this divine guidance. A quiet tingle of anticipation fills the air—you know that a heartfelt request for wisdom and growth never goes unanswered. You patiently wait and continue your chant.

A rustle in the undergrowth nearby alerts you to the presence of an arriving creature. A squat, spiked porcupine waddles out, its spines shining in the fading light. You watch its approach with curiosity and a sense of wonder—could this creature be the guide you've been praying for? You feel a familiar pulling in your chest, telling you *yes*. You are not alone; an unseen force walks beside you.

The creature comes within a few hand spans. She sits, studies you with black, glistening eyes and then lets out an adorable squeal. She seems pleased to have met you here. A sense of delight breaks like a wave across your heart; this is the sign you've been looking for. Everything is going to be alright. You feel a connection between your spirit and hers. She continues to chirp and squeal; as she speaks, images flash into your mind unbidden. Shapes and colors rise in your consciousness. Spectral shapes manifest like mist above the water before you. Are they real or imagined? Who knows? But a sense of peace, a feeling of knowing, settles into you. And the answers to your questions begin to sink into your heart. What you have sought has come. Perhaps these moments are orchestrated by your ancestors, by divine beings, or even by the earth. Immense gratitude rises within you and wets your eyes —how wonderful it feels to be in communion with forces greater than yourself.

The small, spiky creature continues to chatter on as you observe the dancing shapes, absorbing their wisdom like sand during a rainstorm—soaking it in.

We all have soul contracts with various guides and guardians who have agreed to help us on the path of our soul's development. They are always waiting, just out of sight and earshot, but eager to lend some wisdom and assistance to help us in furthering our maturation. It's essential we take time to ask for their intercession—and then stay open to their wisdom. These guides take many forms—some may be plant or animal spirits, others may be ancestors. We have connections with divine beings, deities, our higher selves. Our future iterations can reach through time to offer us insights, loved ones who have left this earth can cross the veil and offer their perspectives.

In day-to-day life, these guides reveal their wisdom through the aptly overheard words of a stranger, a book or video that jumps out at you, or an unexpected challenge that makes us pause and reassess. Sometimes, it's through more subtle means like a nudge, a whisper, or an inner knowing that takes more alertness to hear or feel. The key to observing these bits of guidance is threefold: slow down, listen more, and be open to receiving.

Meditation is a reliable tool for quieting the mind and opening to extrasensory awareness. Subtle voices can be heard much more clearly once we have found silence to be comforting and stillness to be a friend. Journaling or automatic writing (allowing yourself to write without intentionally scribing in anything particular) can be valuable tools to reveal deeper truths your conscious mind is unaware of. Making abstract art can also reveal intuitive wisdom, visually seeing what is happening beneath the surface of thought. When we paint, dance, sing, or write, we make ourselves into a vessel through which higher vibrations can flow.

Some people enjoy turning to esoteric tools like a spread of Tarot cards, a pendulum for divination, the casting of rune stones, or even utilizing an oracle deck—like *Forty-Eight Gateways to the Ecstatic Self*. Allowing the universe to present messages or images through these means can make discerning the meaning easier. Depending on my needs, I have turned to each of these various practices at different times. In fact, that desire for a visual representation of the topics that I focus on in my spiritual development led to the creation of this oracle deck and guidebook.

Another way individuals can pierce the veil between realms is through mediumship and channeling. In these instances, the practitioner opens up to guides communicating more directly by using their body as a mouthpiece. Many have

XXVI. LISTEN FOR YOUR GUIDES

found great insight and healing through the wisdom of a higher source taking residence in the body of a seeker. Some can access these guides while awake, others while asleep. Dreaming can be a great source of receiving wisdom from forces larger than our conscious self.

Yet another way to access divine wisdom is through entheogenic substances, also known as plant medicines—ayahuasca, San Pedro, peyote, psilocybin, etc. These master plants have long served as portals to unseen realms—they have been used for many millennia with deep respect and reverence by the cultures that hold them. While expert guidance is highly suggested when approaching these psychedelic tools, they can dissolve the boundaries between worlds and allow direct communication with spirit guides. These sacred medicines have the power to reveal truths deep within, offering clarity, healing, and profound revelations.

When I faced a major transition in my life—a time when I felt an immense change was imminent—I explored plant medicine for the first time in a 12-day retreat with a well-respected shaman. Those days and nights spent in prayer and contemplation, with the assistance of mother ayahuasca and father San Pedro, were some of the most clarifying and transformative experiences of my life. Not only was I able to connect anew with my beloved grandmother, who had died years before, but I was brought to different worlds, initiated into profound sacred teachings, and even experienced my own death and rebirth—an experience that realigned me with my life's purpose and my forgotten power. I was able to freely forgive the people who had wronged me—offering them love and unconditional reprieve from my animosity. I understood that their betrayals were fundamental stepping stones on my developmental path. I experienced love as a tangible force that transcended the barriers of life and death, time and space.

It doesn't matter how you access your guides or in what forms they come. The truth remains that you are never alone, that wisdom is always available to you if only you open yourself to receive it. We are so much greater than these limited, isolated bodies that we typically think of ourselves as being. Instead, we are tied to a vast net of energies, entities, and experiences always waiting for us to call upon them. At every moment of your journey, your guides are walking with you and waiting for you to call upon them. All you need to do is ask—quiet your mind, open your heart, and listen.

Trust in their presence; trust in the wisdom that dwells within you. Know that you can develop the skills to discern even the quietest or subtlest message. Know that you are never alone. You are precisely where you need to be, walking in the direction you need to go. Even if it feels like a misstep, a roadblock, or a wrong road—these too are part of your path. Trust in the unseen forces guiding you to your highest good.

Listen, dear voyager. Your guides are calling.

RITUAL:

Set aside at least 15 minutes in a quiet space where you won't be interrupted. Light some candles, burn some incense in offering. Sit comfortably with your palms turned upward in a gesture of receptivity, close your eyes, and ask your guides—whether spiritual, ancestral, or intuitive—to share a message with you. As often or whenever you need, say aloud, "May I receive the highest and clearest wisdom available for my highest good in life." Pay attention to any thoughts, feelings, or images that arise. Notice if anything unusual manifests in the candle's flame or the incense's smoke. When you have asked enough times and have received a satisfactory answer—and keep asking until you do—write down your experience.

If you want to take this a step further and it aligns with your values, consider attending a facilitated experience utilizing plant medicine (ayahuasca, peyote, psilocybin, etc.) and record your experiences in a journal. They are powerful tools for opening portals where our advisors and guides can directly converse with us.

JOURNAL PROMPTS:

- What spiritual or ancestral guides have I felt connected to, either in my dreams or in moments of deep reflection? How do I receive their messages?
- Reflect on a time when I felt guided by something greater than myself. How did that guidance impact my decisions or outlook on life?

GUIDED MEDITATION:

Before beginning this meditation, align yourself to the cardinal directions. Starting in the east, envision a being of light manifesting at about an arm's length away from you. Then, turn to the south and envision the same.

You can imagine a line of brilliant light arcing from one to the other, the

XXVI. LISTEN FOR YOUR GUIDES

beginning of a circle surrounding you. Progress to the west and finally to the north; allow the circle to complete itself. Envision that each being of light is the manifestation of truth, conscious energy, protection, and love.

In this circle of guardianship, silently or out loud, ask for your other guides to reveal themselves. Close your eyes, breathe deeply, and sense any arriving entities. Some may be loved ones who passed over in recent years; some may be ancestors from generations back. Some may be animal spirits; some may be astral beings from other realms. They are all here to support you and guide you on your journey toward cosmic reunification, remembering your divine truth.

Feel their presence; drink it in as you would the energy of a good hug from a devoted friend. Sense if they are communicating to you through symbols, images, scents, or memories. Perhaps even words arise unbidden in your mind or ring in your ears.

With each breath, invite them closer, sensing their wisdom and protection surrounding you. Ask a question or present an issue you need guidance on. Trust that your guides are with you, offering support, insight, and love as you move through life. Accept whatever comes and know that if no answers arose today, they will come in time. Sometimes, the greatest guidance comes by simply letting go and allowing life to reveal the answers one moment at a time.

MANTRA:

"I am guided. I hear the wisdom of spirit."

XXVII

PRACTICE COMPASSION
FOR SELF AND OTHERS

XXVII. PRACTICE COMPASSION FOR SELF AND OTHERS

The path has been full of pitfalls and challenges. Despite walking it as best as you were able, you often find yourself complaining that you should have traversed it better. You could have packed better supplies, found faster routes to reach your destination, and been in better shape for the trek. There is always an impressive list of ways you could have improved, ways other people would have handled the ordeals on the adventure better.

It's time to stop with the self-critique. Pause here and breathe, just where you are. Stand in the middle of the glen as rain drops softly on your shoulders and wrap your arms around yourself. Affirm that you are exquisite, just as you are. Everything has worked out precisely as it needed to. You did enough.

Instead of chastising yourself for not being perfect—how about you start being more compassionate with yourself? Instead of rigidly evaluating where you've been or even where you are presently, what if you simply accept? What if you notice the array of beautiful wildflowers surrounding you? What if you notice the zipping of the hummingbirds from blossom to blossom? Many cultures believe they are a blessing and a good omen. What if you saw the gentle drizzle landing on your shoulders as a portent of change, a sign of growth? What if, instead of complaining, you felt gratitude in your heart and extended gentleness toward yourself?

One of the great mantras I repeat to myself is: *I am doing what I can, and that is enough.*

Our culture is obsessed with improvement. We are always supposed to be better, faster, smarter, and winning at life. What if we stopped this relentless pursuit of perfectionism and had compassion for our follies, weaknesses, and humanness instead? What if we embraced our flaws and mistakes not as detractors but as part of the beautiful whole? What if we saw the perfection in the imperfections?

Practicing compassion is learning to soften when the world is teaching us to harden. Compassion asks us to embrace what hurts and mindfully sit with the discomfort without trying to fix it. It asks us to open when we want to close and choose love when our instinct is to hate. This experience of cultivating compassion is most often difficult to apply to ourselves—which is why it must begin there.

From the time we are young, we are told to notice peers who are more popular, beautiful, talented, or athletic. We are encouraged to measure ourselves against them—and we almost always come up wanting (because there will *always* be people who are more talented, glamorous, strong, etc.). This pursuit of perfection can leave us feeling perpetually lacking, distant from ourselves, and even self-hating. We can find ourselves in a relentless cycle of self-criticism and self-loathing. Compassion begins with acknowledging that cycle of self-abuse, pausing, and choosing differently.

Another mantra I repeat to myself: *My goal is not to be the best; I am just striving to do my best in this moment.*

We are all works in progress—we will all be ever-evolving, having room to grow. Perfection is never reachable when there is "something else" that can be addressed—and there always will be. Additionally, every failure, misstep, and errant choice can be seen as a blessing when viewed as an opportunity for growth, cultivating humility, and self-learning. No roadblock comes without valuable lessons; no detour from the path is ever really a delay. Everything that befalls our route is fertilizer for our growth and self-understanding. The winding path is itself the goal—not the destination.

Ask yourself: Would I be so harsh and critical to a loved one if they made similar mistakes as I have? Likely not. Just as flowers grow in the rain, we grow through our missteps. Compassion allows us to embrace the fullness of ourselves—our light and shadows. It invites us to see all parts of ourselves as integral to our wholeness.

It's critical that we begin the exploration of compassion with ourselves because, after all, we are only able to offer others that which we have genuinely cultivated for ourselves. If you try to offer kindness and forgiveness in difficult situations, but you would belittle yourself if you were in their stead, then your soothing words will ring hollow. How we treat others is a reflection of our rela-

XXVII. PRACTICE COMPASSION FOR SELF AND OTHERS

tionship with ourselves. So, by cultivating greater compassion for ourselves, we will be better able to authentically extend it when facing others' shortcomings.

The world is filled with people doing their best with the tools they're given. Most individuals are navigating hidden struggles that we know nothing about. We live in a culture that demands perfection and is only too happy to mock or berate those who fall short. Especially since the advent of the internet and online trolling, the blatant cruelty of humans toward one another is staggering. It's easy to judge—it's easy to write someone off as being "good" or "bad," angelic or wicked, often based on a single interaction. Genuine compassion invites us to go deeper: to see people's intentions and then assume that, if we lived their lives, we would probably behave similarly.

One of the great gifts I received during my years of training and working as a professional actor was the experience of entirely inhabiting another person's point of view. It's often said in acting training that you cannot fully play a character if you are judging them. We must fully embrace their vantages (as reprehensible as they may seem to the audience) and realize that had we lived their life (had their parents, endured their hardships, etc.), we would likely be making similar choices. Another mantra I love to repeat: *But for the grace of God, there go I.*

This ability to fully take on another person's point of view without judgment is a tool that lends tremendous compassion. Often, I will strive to imagine how someone I vehemently disagree with might be correct. What if I forced myself to see the world through their lens and adopt their vantages as my own? While this may not make me change my beliefs, it grants me empathy for them and helps me understand how they came to feel the way they do. It makes me realize that I could readily espouse similar views had things been different in my life.

This makes it easier for me to love them. Sometimes, I will sit in a room of strangers—or, better yet, a room filled with people who have opposing views to my own—and strive to feel love for them. I will focus on the center of my chest, summon up the feeling of loving compassion, and feel it extend away from my body and fill the space. I will look at each person and try to feel that sensation connect with their hearts. This is similar to a centuries-old Buddhist practice called *metta*—loving-kindness meditation. In that practice, you begin by wishing love and peace to yourself. Then, you grow it to include loved ones, strangers, and finally, people who have harmed us.

It is also similar to a Tibetan practice called *tonglen*. In this practice, practitioners send blessings and good wishes first to loved ones, then to all beings, and finally to those with whom they have difficult relationships or view as enemies. The purpose is to cultivate compassion for all beings and to invite healing and transformation for all involved, even those who cause harm. By blessing those who have instigated pain, we are inviting them to heal so that their own suffering abates, they cause no further suffering to others, and so the energetic cords linking us to them (through our animosity) are dissolved.

These are profound acts of radical compassion—imagine how changed our world would be if we blessed our enemies and tried to understand their suffering rather than what we see typically happening online and in the media. Imagine what a kinder, more tolerant world we would live in if we practiced compassion this way. Compassion is learning to see the whole of someone, not just the bits we either admire or despise. Compassion allows us to see the complexity, the contradiction, and—eventually—the divinity in all beings. It's about seeing that each person is striving to find their path in the rain and are stumbling just as much as we are.

When we adopt these skills, we become softer, gentler, and more tender. Our own (and other's) insecurities and foibles seem less daunting. We are no longer as intimidated by our or another's shortcomings—they are simply a part of life, a part of the human experience. It allows us to be braver and bolder in life because we realize everyone is doing the best they can with what they have available to them. This doesn't excuse other people's—or our own—carelessness or callousness, nor does it mean that we don't erect protective boundaries regarding what we behaviors we will tolerate, but it makes it easier to work with. The world, as a whole, turns into a kinder and more comfortable place to be when we employ empathy.

The Dalai Lama often speaks about compassion as the key not just to individual healing but to healing the world. When we hold greater compassion for ourselves, it becomes easier to show up authentically, with less judgment and more understanding. We become like a stone tossed into a pond—sending out ripples of kindness to everyone we encounter. Compassion is a reminder that we are all on this journey of soul together, connected in a vast web of existence, each doing the best we can. We realize that each sentient creature is worthy of love, belonging, respect, and dignity.

As the rain continues to fall, you find yourself dancing in the meadow. You are dancing not because everything has suddenly become perfect—you dance because it is. It exists. And that is enough. We don't need the ideal sunset or flower garden to find joy. This moment is enough. We are enough. The flowers bloom, the hummingbirds flit, and you are experiencing your exquisite humanity in its entirety.

How lucky we are to be here, right where we are.

XXVII. PRACTICE COMPASSION FOR SELF AND OTHERS

RITUAL:

For one day, make a conscious effort to offer kindness and compassion to everyone you encounter. This could be through kind words, a smile, or simply listening with an open heart. At the end of the day, take a quiet moment in your sacred space. Light a candle, close your eyes, and place a hand over your heart. Reflect on the kindness you extended today, and with the same tenderness, write down three things you genuinely appreciate about yourself. Let this practice deepen your connection to both your own heart and the hearts of those around you.

JOURNAL PROMPTS:

- Where do I struggle most with showing compassion—toward myself or toward others? How can I cultivate more understanding and empathy in those areas?
- Reflect on a time when I received compassion from someone else. How did that act of kindness shift my emotional state, and how can I pay it forward?

GUIDED MEDITATION:

Sit comfortably and close your eyes. Begin by focusing on your breath. As you inhale, imagine filling the center of your chest with warmth and compassion. Envision a warm, rose or gold-colored light swirling inside.

This heart-center, located near the bottom of the sternum, is the seat of compassion, love, forgiveness, and wisdom. Dive into this space here. Feel it pulse and shine brighter. With each successive inhale, breathe in more warmth and compassion, letting it fill your ribcage, expanding wider and wider.

When you feel like you have contained as much as you are able, dive deeper and seek out the root of this loving compassion. Go further into the heart-center. Allow this positive energy to nourish you at a core level. Bathe in it. Swirl in it. After many breaths of marinating in compassion, feel free to dedicate the merits of this practice to anyone or anything that you sense also needs similar energy in their life. It could be a specific person, a group, an animal, a population in general, or even all sentient life.

As you exhale, now send that compassion outward, offering forgiveness for any mistakes or imperfections. Visualize the warmth of compassion surrounding them, easing their burdens and filling them with peace. Let this practice remind you that compassion is a boundless force, flowing from you and returning to you in endless waves of love and understanding.

MANTRA:

"I extend compassion to myself and everyone I meet."

XXVIII. EMBRACE NEW IDENTITIES

You dared to descend into the damp caves seeking something...but you don't know what. All you know is that it's time for a change. Winding down the steep incline, ducking under stalactites, you found your way to a placid, underground pool. Softly luminescing rocks light the cavern, and you settle at the water's edge. Around you, color-changing chameleons lounge—each a slightly different shade to match its environs.

A strange figure stares back at you from the slivery lake—it's not the person you've always known. They are someone new, someone evolving and vaster than you remembered yourself being. A subtle current in this subterranean water causes small ripples—and as the water shifts, it reveals angles and parts of yourself that you've never seen prior. It's as if the lake is showing you versions of yourself that you didn't know existed. Like the chameleons adapting to their environments, you, too, are constantly conversing with your surroundings, subtly shifting minute by minute, day by day.

You are becoming who you were meant to be. You are not stagnant, locked in time as one earlier iteration of yourself. You are not bound by past identities or labels. Here, in this fluid space of possibilities, you can step into a new version of you. You are encouraged to become your most expansive, authentic, and joyful self. What you are growing into might exceed your imaginings—you might be becoming something far more magnificent than you dared hope. The possibilities are limitless as to what you could be.

Allow the reflection in the water to continue to change and morph—envision them becoming whomever your heart longs to imagine. Allow yourself to see the new facets emerging. You are not bound by the person you were yesterday—you are not confined to the roles you played, the labels you've worn, or the expectations others have placed upon you. Take a breath and feel your potential expand—you are becoming vaster and more aligned with your values and longings.

The reflection in the water is not singular; it is multitudes. Today, you may feel called to embrace your artistic side—striving to bring beauty from the depths of your soul. Tomorrow, you may don the mantle of the healer—using your gifts to comfort others. Each identity is a doorway, and you are standing at the thresholds, ready to step through whichever one resonates with your soul at this moment. You can become many things—it's up to you to choose how many or how few identities you wish to explore. Within you are many aspects, talents, and ways to express yourself.

Growing up, we are taught to figure out who we want to be in the world and diligently work to become that person. We identify if we want to be a lawyer or a nurse, a high achiever or a more meandering type of person. Seldom are we encouraged to try on many roles and shift between them—to not latch onto any too tightly. The drag artist RuPaul says, "We are all born naked, and the rest is drag," meaning that none of us are actually the roles we play... We are (for all intents and purposes) just playing dress up. Whether you are a congressperson or a trash collector...none of those identities are you. They are just costumes you wear. Many of the struggles people face come from over-identifying with their donned identities and the roles they play. If we can maintain a light-heartedness and awareness of the silliness when it comes to any particular identity, we can adapt and change to circumstances more easily and effortlessly. We won't be weighed down by what has been—we can step into what is new with an open heart and relaxed gate.

How often do you run into someone who takes their role in life too seriously—they have taken on their career, appearance, or pedigree as being who they are. They are often supercilious and obnoxious to be around. In contrast, you've likely also met those who have figured out this is all a great game—they can be, say, or do whatever inspires them because they know not to take anything too seriously. Those individuals are a delight and joy to spend time with. How many young adults have you encountered who are laser-focused on becoming one specific thing and missing out on all the opportunities that surround them because they do not align with the strict vision they maintain as to who they are becoming?

We are all things. We contain multitudes. We must open to the vast array of identities we could be and be willing to change things up when they are no longer serving us so we can expand into the most whole versions of ourselves. If

XXVIII. EMBRACE NEW IDENTITIES

we heed society's suggestion that we should pick one identity and cling to it—that choice will eventually become a type of cage. It will box us in and limit the joy we are capable of experiencing.

Each of us is so much more than any single identity. We dwell in a world of limitless possibilities—why give that up for only one experience, one vantage, when so many more are available? What if you permitted yourself to become whomever your heart desires, even for a little while? Society will try to tell you it's better to stick in your lane and be safe, but who does this serve? Not ourselves—only our corporate overlords who want us to remain predictable and quantifiable. What if you reclaimed all the colors you prohibited yourself from coloring with—what if you expanded your palate to include the whole rainbow?

In doing so, you become a spark of the divine, a shard of the cosmic Oversoul expressing itself in all its brilliance. This world was created because of your initial question of "What would it be like to live in a world where ___ were true?" Through this pondering, an entire galaxy manifested to explore the answers. You are a part of that—you are a shard of that cosmic being who once posited that question and then took fleshy existence to see the results. You are that creator who dreamt up a world to live within—to explore a myriad of possibilities, vantages, and identities. You came here to try different tastes, sights, and sounds—you incarnated to explore what your heart desired.

So often, we are not afraid of what we aren't; we fear all the fantastic things we could be. We stand in terror of our own expansive brilliance. But what if you were capable of having a more dazzling life than you can presently fathom? What if all this abundance, bliss, and laughter were waiting for you, if only you were ready to step out of your box and try something new? What if this new version of you were far happier, more authentic, deeply aligned, and mightily powerful? Who are you to deny that fullness, to avoid that radiance? As you grow and explore new ways of being, you grant others permission to do the same through the example you set. You become a beacon of light that encourages other people to explore their vastness and step into their truths.

So, look into the water. See the shimmering and shining possibilities of who you might become. Surrender the fears of being "too much" or "too brilliant." Embrace the chance that you may be braver than you think, wiser than you know, and more beautiful than you could imagine. This life is a canvas; you are painting your identity with new strokes daily. Be bold and reach for all the colors. Dare to experiment. You can always try a new shade if the one you opted for proves unappealing. Embrace the fluidity of your identity and let yourself be amazed by what emerges.

Who says you must stay the same? Be like the chameleon and adapt to what colors enliven you. Each day, become someone new—become increasingly aligned with your highest self. Embrace the journey and know you are forever growing, evolving, and becoming.

RITUAL:

Choose a physical item—a piece of clothing, a piece of jewelry, or another personal object—that represents the new identity you wish to embrace. It could be a hat that symbolizes confidence, a ring that symbolizes commitment, or even a scarf that makes you feel more vibrant and expressive. Sit, holding that item in front of your heart, and instill your intention for intentional growth and development into the object. Wear or carry this item for a full day (or longer), allowing yourself to embody the qualities of this new identity whenever you interact with the item.

JOURNAL PROMPTS:

- What part of my identity is evolving right now, and how can I embrace it fully without fear or hesitation?
- Reflect on a past transition or shift in identity. How did I navigate that change, and what did I learn about myself in the process?

GUIDED MEDITATION:

Close your eyes and allow yourself to soften. Imagine yourself deep underground in a subterranean cavern. Torches shine from the walls, and water drips from stalactites in soothing, rhythmic drops. Before you, set into the rough-hewn rock, are a series of archways set in a semi-circle. Through each opening is an alternative life path you could take.

One represents the path you are walking right now, the identity you have cultivated, and the roles you have chosen to play. Another represents the antithesis of your current life, something still you but far afield from the ways you currently live and express yourself. The others lead toward the myriad of other identities that are possible for you.

Which do you choose? Do you wish to go through one archway and see where it leads for a while? You can always come back to this cavern and choose another. Go ahead, explore. Scout the different options that life has available to you. Step into a new identity, a new role, a new way of being. We are all all things. Why limit yourself?

Find the most full, free, and fun expression of you. This life is meant to be enjoyed. Try whatever calls to your spirit!

MANTRA:

"I am effortlessly evolving into my highest self."

XXIX. LET PARTS OF YOU DIE

Sit here with me, close to the fire's glow. Feel yourself sink into my quiet embrace as the night sky envelops us. This part of the journey is oftentimes the hardest. Allow the warmth of the flames to penetrate your skin and soothe the growing chill within. Let the whispers of the wind crackling the trees' branches be an invitation to let go of what is no longer serving you. Because, really, it's long past time—you've been holding onto these parts for far too long, and they are only holding you back.

This is a sacred moment—this is where old parts of ourselves fall away like embers drifting into the night. Now is the time to release, to allow what has outlived its course to burn away and make space for something new to rise from the ashes. So, close your eyes. Take a deep breath. And set those parts of you free.

Letting go of who we have been sometimes feels impossible. If we are not those things that have come to define us, then who are we? Will we cease to exist if we abandon those old stories, those outdated ideations, those self-limiting beliefs? Even if the parts that we now recognize need to die have caused us a tremendous amount of pain...sometimes that pain feels so familiar, so integral to who we are that we cannot fathom existing without them.

But we must let go of what is not serving us—it is depleting our life-force, slowly draining us of vitality. If we don't let the soul-diminishing attributes go, they may, in truth, kill us. We see nature constantly releasing what no longer serves, whether it's the gentle shedding of leaves in the autumn to make room for new growth in the spring or the more violent gnawing off of an infected limb so the rest of the body can survive. We have to sever what is rotting and move on.

Nothing resists this cycle. The fox doesn't lament the loss of her winter coat when the cold sets in. The flowers do not fight the frost as they wither back into the earth. Everything yields to the cycle of life and death, knowing that in surrendering, new life is always waiting with the turning of the wheel.

The great secret in life is realizing that nothing truly ever dies—it just transmutes and changes form. From matter to energy—and then back to matter. From flesh to spirit—and then back to flesh. The lilies burst forth from their roots in the spring, though they seemed gone and the landscape desolate of their presence. We, too, will live and die many times within this lifespan before we finally leave our bodies and transition back into unembodied consciousness, pure spirit. Nearly every culture on Earth has mused on the cyclical nature of time, life, and nature. All life forms grow, wither, and then grow again.

But modern culture is so afraid of diminution and decay. We are enthralled by this notion of perpetual growth, perpetual youth. We are told that our economies should always be booming and our society should be constantly expanding. However, the only organisms in the natural world that behave this way are cancerous tumors. Cancer cells, unchecked, grow relentlessly until they consume all. Everything else accepts that there is a time to let go, to return to nothingness, and then come again. Why should we resist this natural order?

Can you accept that parts of you are waiting to be released? Aspects of yourself have withered and are ready to die. Can you let them go? Can you send them off with gratitude and a blessing—thanking them for what they've taught you and then setting them free? Can you accept that it's time for you to diminish so that someday soon, you may grow again? Can you accept that death is a part of life? To live is to die—to die is to live. You cannot have one without the other.

What stories, what identities, what old wounds are you holding onto? Lay them down here, by the fire. Offer them to the flames. See the burning not as a destruction but as a transformation. Just as the fallen leaves fertilize the forest floor, you will be nourished and more alive from allowing these things to release and decay. Trust in the process.

Why do we fear the death of old habits when we know they are inhibiting us? Why do we dread the ending of relationships when we know that we've outgrown them? Why do we cling so tightly to dreams that we know can never come to be? What if we saw death not as an end but as a rebirth—we are creating room for what will rise anew? What if we saw that, by giving up what is no longer really serving us, we are creating space for something more beautiful, more aligned with what we are becoming?

Throughout nature, we see the rhythm of expansion and contraction. From

XXIX. LET PARTS OF YOU DIE

the phases of the moon to the cycles of the tide, nothing grows without rest; nothing arrives without first departing. Can we do similar? Can we accept that things will come and go in a balanced cadence—and by only welcoming new things without surrendering the old, we are inviting imbalance? We are becoming increasingly heavier because we are unwilling to let go in equal measure.

Think of the people who hold tightly to identities that are no longer tethered to their realities. Have you met a forty-five-year-old man at a bar who still talks about his winning pass during sophomore year football? Have you encountered the fading beauty queen who still acts like everyone should kowtow her former glamour and ignore her egregious behavior in the present? These people haven't moved on. Have you, perhaps, held onto outdated stories about yourself? How about that third-grade teacher who called you "stupid?" Or that first romantic partner who told you you weren't that funny or lovable? Where have you been holding onto limited and outdated narratives? Do you recognize it's time to let them go?

While clinging to labels may be comfortable, these stories do not reflect our growing underrating of ourselves—they do not encompass the majesty and magnificence we are discovering as we harmonize with our luminous souls. By remaining under their dominion, we stunt our growth. We rob ourselves of the possibility of becoming something new, something more aligned with our burgeoning truth.

Who are you today, and how much of that self-perception is rooted in who you were in the past? Are you still embracing identities formed in young adulthood or childhood that no longer accurately reflect you? What parts of you are ready to release back into the void, to return to the world of spirit?

Look up at the sky and watch the stars shimmer in their ancient and distant dance. Watch this arriving comet blaze through the darkness—an omen of your own transformation. It appears for only a short while and then is gone—a harbinger of change. This is the cycle of life: birth, life, death, and rebirth. It is as old as time and as constant as the stars. And you are a part of it.

Release what you no longer need. Let those parts die with grace and tenderness. Sit here with me beside the fire. Lean in—allow me to comfort you as you let go. Whisper your goodbyes to whatever is ready to fall away. And with the warmth of the fire, the coolness of the night, and the vastness of the sky above, allow yourself to be transformed.

You are not alone. The earth, the sky, the fire—they are here with you, holding you in this sacred cycle. For what is fire but the transformation of physical matter into light? That is what you are doing: transforming the gross into the sublime. You are transmuting solid waste into light. Let these parts of you die. Then, pick up the ashes, smear them on your forehead, and be ready to rise again.

RITUAL:

Write a heartfelt goodbye letter to a part of your identity that no longer serves you. Describe why it's time to release this aspect of yourself and reflect on how it shaped you in the past. Acknowledge the lessons it brought, but affirm your readiness to let it go.

Once the letter is complete, enact the following steps to ritualize the letting go process:

1. Tear the Letter: Begin by tearing the letter into pieces, symbolizing the dismantling of this part of your identity.

2. Burn the Pieces: Take the torn paper and set it aflame, watching as the fire scorches your outdated stories, transforming them into light.

3. Dissolve in Water: Add the ashes to a glass of water, stirring until they dissolve, seeing this as the final dissolution of your former identity.

4. Return to the Earth: Dig a small hole in the ground and pour the darkened water into it, allowing this part of you to return to source.

As you pour, silently thank this part of yourself for its presence, and express your openness to what will arise in its absence.

JOURNAL PROMPTS:

- What parts of my personality, habits, or relationships no longer serve me? How can I release them in a way that feels compassionate and intentional?
- Reflect on a time when I had to let go of something or someone to move forward in life. What did I learn from that process of releasing, and how can I apply it to my current situation?

GUIDED MEDITATION:

Take a few deep, soothing breaths. Feel yourself loosening the knots within. Feel yourself thawing the parts of yourself that have been held rigid and crystallized.

XXIX. LET PARTS OF YOU DIE

You are becoming something new, and in so doing, you must surrender what has been.

As you loosen and melt, envision before you a dagger with a three-sided blade like an elongated pyramid. It glimmers and gleams in a dark metal that looks almost like an oil slick. This is the knife that removes negative psychic energy and cuts the cords that are holding you locked in place. You can either pick it up to use on yourself or envision a beneficent psychic surgeon who appears before you. Either way, home in on the areas in your energetic field that need removal, the parts of you that need to die.

Gently, with love, envision the dagger plunging into those parts and cutting them free. Allow yourself to be excavated. Become hollowed out and, through that act of letting go, become hallowed. Carve out empty spaces where joy, life, and freedom can now flow. Surrender the density to become a vessel for divine energy. Scan through your energetic body and remove any areas that no longer serve you. And as they, one by one, disappear, quietly whisper, "Thank you."

Take as much time as you need with this visual.

MANTRA:

"I surrender what no longer serves me."

XXX. GET COMFORTABLE WITH CHAOS

The sky is being torn apart, and you seek shelter in the stillness at the eye of the storm. All about you, the wind peels bark from branches, trees get tossed about as if they were weightless. The heavens roar in agony as the rain pelts you from the sides. Destruction and dissolution are all around you—everything that felt familiar is being rent asunder in the hurricane.

Across the way, a wise and old elephant has stumbled into the clearing beside you. His eyes are frightened, but his spirit is confident—he has weathered many storms in his long life. He is optimistic that he will make it through this one, too. He invites you to remember that, while tumult and transition are scary, we can usually endure. Can we relax into the chaos and allow it to billow around us without our anxiety rising into terror? Can we permit the world to disintegrate while still retaining some modicum of tranquility and acceptance? The fire may sputter and even go out, the roots may be pulled from the earth—yet we will still survive.

Can we find comfort even amidst chaos? If we can achieve this, we will have attained a mighty skill in life.

Our minds love predictability—the human brain is often described as being a pattern recognition machine. We find great comfort in predicting probable outcomes, garnering a sense of control over knowing how events are likely to proceed. But, all too often, life blows in an unexpected gale that upends our models and predictions, and we are left reeling with uncertainty. We are unable to prognosticate what comes next—we are incapable of discerning the subsequent iteration in the pattern.

We get so comfortable with order, structure, and harmony that chaos can feel foreign and deeply unsettling. One of the goals of spiritual development is to achieve a state of poise and equanimity no matter what arises. Whether painful or pleasurable, whether anticipated or entirely unexpected, we greet arriving events with graciousness, relaxation, and ease. It is a quality that many of the greatest souls—the saints, the seekers, the sages—have in common: they gracefully accept whatever comes.

The truth is that none of us are strangers to chaos. It greets us in small doses daily: an unexpected flat tire while on the way to an important meeting, a stranger who reveals information that upends your sense of reality, a loved one's unexpected medical diagnosis. If we can train ourselves to greet the smaller bits of unplanned happenings with grace and equanimity, then it makes the larger things more manageable.

If we examine the etymology of the word, we find its origin in the Ancient Greek *khaos*, which means "gaping void," an abyss of infinite potential. Chaos isn't just disorder or confusion—it's the absence of the order we took for granted, a yawning expanse where structures we rely upon disappear entirely. It is an upending of reality, a renegotiation of life itself. It is the thing that humans dread almost more than any other.

However, within this total dissolution also comes a tremendous opportunity. When the forest is cleared away by fire or tsunami, it leaves in its wake a fertile ground for new woods to grow. When destruction takes away what is familiar, it creates the space and opportunity for something new and more aligned with our values to take its place. When our home is destroyed, we can build it back with attributes we longed for and without the ones that frustrated us.

On several occasions, my life dissolved. Over the course of one notable summer, nearly everything that defined my world dissolved. I gave up my career as a professional actor—something I had been seeking for over a decade, something I had wanted since I was a child. It left my identity feeling raw and unformed—after all, if I wasn't an actor, who was I? I had based so much of my sense of purpose around that pursuit.

Only a few weeks later, the man I had taken as my spiritual teacher, my guru, unceremoniously cut all ties with me via email. For eight years, he had taught me about spirituality and meditation. He had promised to walk the path with me for however long I needed or until I achieved liberation. This man I saw almost as a personal savior left me standing at the roadside with no explanation and no discussion about what went wrong. Countless hours of volunteer work, traveling across the globe to be near him, and years of my time given to his community were wiped away with the press of a "send" button.

Also during this time, I moved cities and quit my day job, I lost my home, and I had to find a new career field. I was reeling; I felt like a person trying to escape a submerged car wreck—unable to discern which way to swim, up or down, with the threat of drowning looming large. Everything I thought I knew about how spirituality worked, who I was, the roles I played were dismantled. But, in the aftermath, something amazing happened.

I moved in with my partner and started building a life centered around our shared love, our relationship. I began the path toward a new career, one much more aligned with me and my values—eventually leading to the founding of *Ecstatic Self*, my YouTube Channel and coaching practice. I began to discover a spirituality that was native to me and not adopted from some foreign culture. Although the life I lost was undoubtedly wonderful in many respects, it was also unable to contain the expansiveness of my growing soul. When the dust settled and the skies cleared, I found myself in a new environment that was much more aligned with me, my values, and the man I was becoming. I stepped into a new world that was far better than the one I left, one filled with unimaginable joys.

In the void of chaos, we are offered the profound gift of rethinking what we thought we knew. When our certainty is upended, we are given the choice of either clinging to what was or opening to what is new. We can try to piece our old world back together, or we can surrender to the unknown and trust in divine guidance. Usually, the destruction comes because our old way of being is too small to contain the vastness of who we are becoming—we had to break the shell that was holding us captive so we could grow beyond it.

What often feels like disorder is frequently the precursor to creation. It is the fabric of reality reorganizing itself to birth something new. In chaos, we are forced to surrender our illusions around control and certainty—to trust in a greater intelligence that knows better than we do ourselves what is required next for our well-being. Accepting chaos is a shouted "yes" to the adventure of being alive.

Chaos is the sacred void from which all things emerge. When life feels like it is falling apart, when everything you thought you knew is proved false, when nothing seems to make sense...congratulations. You have reached a new burst in your personal development. You have outgrown the old and are awaiting the new. You are experiencing a reshaping of reality; your life is being reoriented to something truer.

To turn again to the ancient Greeks, the philosopher Heraclitus discussed *logos*—a deep intelligence—operating beneath the surface of life's tumult, guiding us through the flux of *khaos*. Though the path through the storm is seldom obvious while it is unfolding before us, it makes much better sense in retrospect. Looking back, we understand why the destruction had to occur—why the old had to be wiped away. Often, we can even arrive at a state of tremendous gratitude once we see how the old ways were limiting us from realizing our highest potential and greatest joy.

So, close your eyes. Accept the rain pelting you in gusts; breathe in the terror of the land being torn asunder. Feel the swirling storm around you and find the stillness in your center. Beneath the wildness, there is a deep and unshakable peace. It's always there, waiting for you to tap into it. The more you find it in the midst of chaos, the more resilient you become. In time, you will no longer fear the storm—but rush out to greet it with open arms, dancing barefoot in the rain. For you will recognize it as a blessing, a teacher, and a force for transformation and growth.

We are not here to control life but to ride its waves. Trust that you are where you need to be, that events are unfolding to lift you to your highest good. Allow the old to be stripped away; allow the new growth to come. You stand in the eye of the storm and feel the peace well up within you. After all, you are not just surviving; you are thriving—not in spite of the chaos but because of it.

RITUAL:

Explore the notion of allowing chaos to play a role in your day tomorrow. Begin in the morning by asking the universe to bring the unexpected into your life. Then, as you go about your day, let go of your usual routine and do things in an atypical order. Instead of brushing your teeth first, take a shower. If you usually go to the gym before work, try going afterward. Whatever you typically do, switch it up—bike instead of walk, turn right instead of left, take the stairs instead of the elevator. Notice what happens when you invite more randomness, chance, and the unknown into your life.

At the end of your day, take a moment to reflect. What surprises did chaos bring? Were there any chance encounters or serendipitous moments? Thank the universe for the opportunity to step into divine flow, experiencing what it feels like to release control and invite in the unexpected.

JOURNAL PROMPTS:

- How do I typically respond to chaos or unpredictability in my life? What can I learn from moments when things don't go as planned?

XXX. GET COMFORTABLE WITH CHAOS

- Reflect on a time when chaos led to unexpected growth or opportunity. How did embracing the uncertainty open doors that I hadn't considered before?

GUIDED MEDITATION:

Close your eyes and take a few deep breaths. Visualize yourself standing in the middle of a swirling storm—hail, rain, and debris swirling all around you. The wind pulls at your clothes and tugs you in all directions. You feel in danger of being blown away. It feels overwhelming—will you be able to survive, you wonder?

You bring your focus down into your legs and envision roots growing out of you and into the ground beneath. You feel yourself becoming both sturdier and more flexible. Like a willow tree: rooted but able to move any way required, bend with however the winds demand. You feel a profound stillness at your center. No matter what happens, you will endure. You can change and shift however is required while remaining rooted into your truth. Regardless of how chaotic the storm becomes, you remain calm and centered.

Allow yourself to stand tall in this chaos, trusting that you are safe while the storm blows. Knowing that at some point the winds will calm and sunlight will again return. Feel the power and resilience within you, knowing that you can remain steady even when life feels at its most turbulent.

MANTRA:

"I dance with chaos and find my flow."

XXXI. ENJOY SIMPLICITY

Oooooffhh.... Take a deep sigh and settle into your hammock. The breeze is blowing so pleasantly, and the light from the setting sun is golden...could you conceive of anything more perfect? Society wants us to believe that happiness is found in high achievement—in glittering awards and sparkling job titles—but you know the truth. Happiness is found in the simple things: a creamy cup of coffee, a forested vista at twilight, a sleepy sloth smiling graciously beside you. Enjoying simplicity does not make you simple—it permits you to experience profundity. You are dwelling in the presence and majesty of this magnificent world. You are seeing the dazzling beauty present in how a blade of grass grows, in how the fingers of a loved one tenderly caresses your cheek.

Notice the warmth of the evening air, the quiet and the stillness of the arriving night. Hear the faint rustle of the animals in the undergrowth like whispers of old friends reuniting. Everything you need, everything that matters, is already here. Sense the grains in the wooden floorboards beneath your toes. Feel the prickle of humidity beading sweat on your skin. All is well.

We dwell in a world that relentlessly urges us to go faster, achieve more, and fill each moment. Even in childhood, many of us were whisked from soccer practice to dance rehearsal to study group. After eight hours of schooling, we were often sent home with three or four hours of additional homework. Seldom nowadays is there an unscheduled childhood where the wisdom of trees and ladybugs is considered as potent of teachers as a classroom setting.

We took those overly-filled youthful years and developed them into an adulthood where we force ourselves to always be "on." We develop complex workout routines and elaborate plans for elevating our career status. We over-plan, underlive, and frequently experience periods of fatigue if not complete burnout. But nature teaches us a different way. The sloth hanging lazily from the eaves, the slow spiral of the Milky Way on a dark and cloudless night, the calm flow of a river—none of these hurry. There is a quiet wisdom in slowness and simplicity. It's not how much we can achieve but how deeply we can live.

During my collegiate years and young adulthood, I used to pride myself on how few hours I slept. I kept such a rigorous schedule and had so much to accomplish that I could only spare three to five hours a night for rest. I wore this self-deprecation like a badge of honor. "Look at how much I am accomplishing; observe how hard-working I am!" I seemed to shout. But, in hindsight, I wasn't running toward something but away from it. I was avoiding doing the soulful work of sitting with my emotions and allowing myself to have meaningful experiences of connection with others. I was trying to outpace my humanity by becoming something beyond human. I wanted to make my life immensely complex and impressive so that I would finally feel sufficient within myself.

Years later, I can now proudly say that I have a very simple life. I get up before sunrise and meditate for an hour. I walk the dogs, go to the gym, cook, and then work through the afternoon and into the early evening. At night, I spend time with my beautiful spouse and walk the dogs again. There is minimal variation from day to day—the progression of event and routine s is quite basic. I seldom attend glamorous events—I don't cultivate relationships with the rich, famous, or influential. I have a quiet, simple life...and I am happier than I have ever been.

Take a moment with me to take a deep breath. Inhale...and let it go, allowing the air to merge with the atmosphere around you. As you breathe in again, realize that the air entering your lungs was once exhaled by those around you and transformed through the leaves of plants. As you breathe out, let go of whatever you no longer need to carry.

Realize that through breathing this way, you are offering parts of yourself to the world and accepting parts of the world into you. You are blurring the boundaries between what is yours and everyone else's. Notice how simple and natural this process of sharing is. Notice how the rhythm of your breath aligns with the rhythm of the earth—the inhale and exhale of tides, the rising and falling from day to night. You are part of it, and it is part of you. Nothing else matters right now. All there is is this—there is no rush. Happiness is found here, in the simple act of being.

A story I love to share is that of the fisherman and the businessman.

One day, a well-heeled businessman stumbles across a tiny fishing village on a beautiful coast. He notices a shabby-looking fisherman sitting lazily in a rowboat, almost napping. His line is in the water, and he doesn't seem too busy with the pursuit of catching fish.

The businessman calls out and says, "Hey, fisherman! It doesn't look like you are catching much. Let me offer you some suggestions." He then proceeds to try to explain to the fisherman ways he could work harder and improve his efficiency.

The relaxed man interrupts and asks, "Now, why would I want to do that?"

"Well, then you could buy a bigger boat and catch more fish," the businessman replies.

"And what good is that?"

"Then you can sell your fish to the local village and make more money."

"And after that?"

"Then you can buy more boats and hire a crew to work for you."

"And what will that get me?"

"Well, then you could expand and sell up and down the coast...eventually making enough money that you can afford to retire."

"And what will I do then?" the fisherman asks with a smile.

"Then," the businessman replies, also smiling, "you can spend all your time living in a cottage by the sea and fishing whenever you want for the pleasure of it."

...There's no need to explain what the fisherman said next because it's self-evident. He already had everything the businessman was chasing.

We unflaggingly sprint on these hamster wheels, hoping that by being frenzied enough, we will eventually find a state of peace. This is self-defeating logic. Calm, quiet, and repose are available to us here and now if we willingly choose to simplify.

And, yes, I am aware that we have bills to pay, obligations to meet, and people we need to care for. Those explanations for enduring the hustle are all well and good—but many of us continually make choices to opt into a hectic life, choosing complexity over simplicity. It is possible to step off the hamster wheel. It is possible to make life choices that permit you more time for yourself...but it often requires bucking the trends that culture tells us we need to pursue. It may mean spending less and saving more; it may mean moving to a different location that can better accommodate your lifestyle; or it may mean shifting friend groups who better align with what you're coming to value.

Simplicity isn't necessarily about having less; it's about appreciating more. Do you really need those new shoes when the ones you already own are serving you well? Do you really need another dinner at that Michelin-star restaurant—when an equally satisfying meal is available down the street for a fifth of the price? Simplicity is about noticing and valuing what is already around you. It is about finding gratitude for the blessings that are already present in abundance.

Our minds struggle with this, however. That granite countertop you paid many thousands of dollars to install in your kitchen initially seems so beautiful—but after a few months, you hardly notice it anymore. This is called "hedonistic adaptation"—our mind always returns to baseline after the newness of a stimulus wears off. That body you worked so hard to cultivate—even after you hit your goal weight, it will eventually start seeming very ordinary to you. It will no longer feel so attractive or noteworthy. This is why taking time to slow down and truly appreciate what is around us is critical.

So, notice the sound of the birds in the trees. Savor that sip of tea. Revel in the sensations of the cool breeze on your skin. These are the moments that fill your soul and nourish your heart. They are the essence of life, the foundations upon which true happiness is built.

The founder of Taoism, Lao Tzu, wrote, "Nature does not hurry, yet everything is accomplished." The seasons turn without haste, the flowers bloom in their own time, and the river flows unhurriedly toward the sea. There's no rush or urgency. Can you allow yourself the same grace—to slowly and methodically move into being, simply and directly?

Surrender the need for complexity. Give into the presence that is always surrounding you. Marvel at the beauty that envelops you in this moment—the golds and pinks of the sky painted by a master artisan. The warmth of the cup in your hands. Simplicity reminds us that life isn't a race to be won but a journey to be savored. By slowing down, we make space for what is essential: sharing love, connecting with others, and experiencing joy.

Sit back and relax. Let the world move at its own pace as you dwell here. There is no rush. There is nothing more you need to do. Everything is already here—in the stillness, in the quiet, in the simplicity of being.

RITUAL:

Choose one area of your life (your wardrobe, a room, your daily routine, etc.) and simplify it. Declutter or remove excess items, focusing only on what truly brings you joy and utility. Create a moment to appreciate the simplicity, perhaps by enjoying a cup of tea or spending time in the newly simplified space, feeling the peace that comes with less.

XXXI. ENJOY SIMPLICITY

JOURNAL PROMPTS:

- What simple pleasures in my life am I currently overlooking? How can I bring more awareness to the joy that comes from living simply?
- Reflect on a time when a simple, easy to overlook moment brought me greater peace. How can I create more of those moments in my daily life?

GUIDED MEDITATION:

Find a comfortable spot where you can sit and observe your surroundings. Allow your eyes to remain softly open, and begin by taking a few deep breaths, settling into your body. Slowly, let your gaze wander, noticing the small, simple details around you. Just enjoy the delight in being where you are, the perfection of this moment. Savor it; drink it in. Really sense the perfection in whatever is around you.

There's no need to focus on anything in particular—just let your attention drift naturally. Maybe you notice the texture of the leaves on a tree, the way sunlight filters through the branches or the patterns of shadows on the ground. Gently observe without judgment, without needing to change anything.

As you continue to look around, allow yourself to feel a sense of appreciation for the simplicity of what is before you. The world is perfect in its quiet, gentle existence. With each breath, feel the peacefulness that comes from simply being present with your surroundings. No need to strive or change anything—just observe the beauty in what already is. Let the simplicity of this moment bring you a sense of calm and gratitude.

MANTRA:

"I find beauty in the simple things."

XXXII. DEVELOP HELPFUL ROUTINES

Kneel in the dirt and press your bare fingers into the dark soil. Smell the fecund earth filled with the potential for life, rich with nourishment. You pick out a single seed from the pouch on your belt and tenderly place it into the velvety loam, pile a small mound above it, and offer a silent prayer for its growth and resiliency. You ask that the earth will protect it, help it grow, and eventually bear fruit that will ripen and grace your table.

Then, you kneel again and repeat this process, creating a long line of soon-to-be seedlings. Each little cap of soil marks where the green tendrils will burst forth, reaching for sunshine. Though the labor has been long and sometimes monotonous—you experience a profound sense of pride. One seed at a time, you have planted your future. You have engaged in a regular practice that will one day grow into the food that nourishes you.

You stand and stretch your arms heavenward, taking in the sights around you. Though it took many weeks, you have created something extraordinary. You have planted the potential for a tranquil garden that will one day bloom with flowers, vegetables, and an assortment of new life. Imagine the rainbow of blossoming sights that will arise from your actions. You have laid the groundwork for not only a place you can find comfort, but where countless other creatures will come to call home.

Just as we plant seeds in a garden, we also build the loom on which our life will be strung, one action at a time. One choice after another, we lay the patterns that will form the warp and weft of the fabric of our lives. Just as a tapestry is formed one stitch at a time, we are also formed by individual decisions that coalesce into the design of our lives. You are creating your life each and every day by what you choose to invest your time in and how you decide to spend your life-force.

You are the creator of your destiny, and what is the fate you wish to cultivate for yourself? Small, insignificant things add up over time. Take for example something as simple as brushing and flossing your teeth. Though it doesn't seem terribly life-altering in that moment, after months of opting into the experience of oral hygiene, you will have a much better health outcome than a person who opted out. And when you reach the later stages of life and still have your teeth (and have avoided painful oral surgeries), your mouth will thank you.

Choosing to exercise this afternoon doesn't seem like such a radical idea... but if you opt into doing it nearly every day, in a few months, you will start to have a very different experience of your body than someone who doesn't. We look at the people who age most gracefully, and they are, universally, people who move their bodies regularly. It's a small action in the grand scheme of things, but it adds up to a vastly different quality of life in a relatively short span of time.

What are the routines that you are either enacting or forsaking—and how are they making you feel? Are you choosing to prioritize your rest by getting to sleep at an early hour, ensuring 8-hours of quality slumber? Are you choosing to eat nourishing, home-cooked meals over soulless fast food? Are you taking time to meditate, walk barefoot in nature, or connect in real life with friends and loved ones?

It's relatively easy to predict a person's future—look at the choices they are making now, and it will reveal the likely outcome of their arriving days. Similarly, you can discern much of a person's past by looking closely at the state of their mind and body today.

What is the legacy you want to leave behind? What do you want to be known for? Achieving anything of worth takes regular, steady engagement with a specific task, skill, talent, or desire. The effects of one, lone day of extraordinary effort is quickly surpassed by a moderate effort applied over many months. Going back to the image of the garden, tending your plot of land cannot be accomplished with one massive action undertaken all at once—it requires a daily investment of time and energy to weed the beds, fertilize the crops, and prune the overgrowths. For a bountiful harvest, you must water both your crops and your intentions daily.

I often say that you can have almost any life you want—you just have to be willing to put in the hours and pay the price to achieve it. Have you identified

XXXII. DEVELOP HELPFUL ROUTINES

your goals and committed to daily efforts to realize those dreams? Have you set a schedule that assists you in cultivating these routines so that you become the person you desire?

We are gifted only so many hours and days on this planet; the average lifespan is a mere 4,000 weeks. Time will slip by faster than we could anticipate. If there's something you'd like to achieve, it's best if you start taking meaningful strides in that direction now. And if you fear there is insufficient time to reach your goals, have faith. It is seldom too late to change your life. I have witnessed people who decided to begin cultivating a yoga practice in their late eighties and go from being practically immobile to doing handstands within a few, short years. Studies show that the most productive decade of a human life is their sixties; the second-most productive decade is their seventies.

Start today. Identify your goals and engage in meaningful daily work to bring them to fruition. You do not need to spend hours daily manifesting your longed-for outcomes, but some small daily engagement is recommended. Once the practice becomes habitual, it will feel much more effortless to keep it going. The hardest part is getting started. "An object at rest tends to stay at rest; an object in motion tends to stay in motion," says Newton's first law of motion. Studies show that, depending on the skill you wish to acquire, forming a new habit can take anywhere from 18 to 254 days—with an average of 66. Yes, it will take time —but all good things do.

Begin by noticing how your current routines make you feel—are they serving you? Is it time to reassess? Remember that not every routine is meant to stay with us forever—we go through seasons, just like nature. It may be time to shed old habits and adopt new ones. Remain open to re-evaluating your plans and surrender what is not aligning with your needs.

Your days oughtn't feel overly complicated or filled with endless tasks and to-do lists. The simplest routines often become the most sustainable and enjoyable over time. The beauty of routines lies in their consistency, not their intensity. Avoid striving for perfection—aim instead for progress. The goal is to live a balanced life filled with joy and well-being.

Each act you undertake is a gift you're giving your future self. Choose what aligns with your deepest desires and highest good. Plant the seeds today that will nourish your tomorrows. Embrace being the gardener of your life—and know that, in time, your efforts will yield a harvest beyond your reckoning.

RITUAL:

On the night of a new moon, write a brief description or draw a picture of the habit or routine you wish to develop. Light a candle and burn your paper in its flame, and as the smoke rises, visualize yourself fully embodying this new routine. Then, take a string or ribbon and tie it around your finger or wrist, knotting your intention in place. As you do so, say aloud something like: *"With this string, I commit my intention into action. Each day, I will diligently work to cultivate the skills I desire."* Practice the habit each day, keeping the string in place until the full moon.

JOURNAL PROMPTS:

- What daily habits or routines have helped me feel more grounded and focused? How can I integrate more structure into my life in a way that feels supportive rather than restrictive?
- Reflect on a time when I felt lost or overwhelmed. What routines or practices brought me back to a place of stability, and how can I reintroduce or enhance them?

GUIDED MEDITATION:

Close your eyes and allow yourself to soften. Envision yourself standing in a lush but overgrown garden. Wisteria climbs over balustrades, bamboo spreads and claims land veraciously, and fruit trees are overgrown and in need of pruning. Take a deep breath, and as you exhale, feel your feet connect with the land beneath you, sensing what it needs. Where do you need to prune? Where do you need to plant? Where do you need to deracinate and relocate some beautiful but misplaced plants?

Keeping rooted into this awareness, begin to move through the garden, taking it in. Notice what parts are flourishing and which are floundering due to neglect. Envision that the perfect tools are nearby for the tasks at hand: sheers, trowels, rakes, and watering cans. Kneel and get to work. Dig where needs digging, cut where needs cutting, tie tendrils to stakes, merry vines to trellises.

The work is joyful and fulfilling, and notice how, little by little, the garden begins to return to full glory. You are the steward of this sanctuary, and you are helping it thrive. Envision yourself planting seeds that represent the future you wish to cultivate. Water them and tend them carefully. Watch how they, in your mind's eye, begin to sprout and grow into the magnificent plants that are your destiny.

XXXII. DEVELOP HELPFUL ROUTINES

Find a cozy spot to sit and admire your handiwork. This, too, is perfect. You have achieved something remarkable. You are a magnificent work in progress, and all it takes is a bit of daily effort to help you fulfill that potential.

MANTRA:

"I effortlessly adopt new, helpful habits."

XXXIII. SEE YOURSELF THROUGH ANOTHER'S EYES

As you continue down the tree-lined path, you notice something peculiar. Out of the corner of your eyes, you catch glimpses, flashes of a person moving, matching you stride for stride. Curious to understand better who or what this being is, you step from the well-worn road and into the woods proper. Nestled within the dense trees, flashes of light shine out from unexpected places. Examining further, you discern floating shapes suspended from branches, tucked beneath roots, tied to tree trunks. Mirrors. In every direction, mirrors have been placed, many suspended far out of reach of human hands.

What sort of giant placed them here, and for what purpose? As you step toward them, you realize that none of the mirrors are reflecting you in precisely the same way. In one, you are taller and grander—you have a majestic aura around you that makes you seem royal. In another, you are shorter and squatter—making you look like someone who lifts heavy objects for a living. A third mirror reflects you hollow-eyed and scared. A fourth makes you appear aggressive and domineering.

As you step past one then another, you realize that there is no fixed version of you. You are a different person depending on which frame you are looking into. Some make you seem competent and suave, others make you seem anxious and dull. You begin to wonder if there ever has been a concrete "you"—or have you always flickered between these myriad perceptions and opinions? Have you always been many things coexisting in one body?

You pause in an open hollow amidst the trees and close your eyes. Does this really represent all the different ways the world sees you? Are any of these reflections your truth? You sit down, breathe deeply, and turn your focus within —questing inside to find the answer to the question: "Who am I, really?"

In this world, perception is everything. You could walk into a room with people seated behind a table, prepared to judge and rate you—and they could laud your brilliance and poise. You could walk into a different room while wearing the same clothes and saying the same words—and they could chastise your incompetence and dullness. I saw this happen routinely when I worked as an executive coach for some of the world's top companies. In interview settings, one panelist's perception hardly matched another's, despite the interviewee maintaining the same presence and competency in relaying information. I saw it, too, when I worked as an actor—the same monologue could deliver rapture or reproach depending on whom was sitting behind the audition table.

No two people see us the same way. This is why it is so critical we cultivate a network of friends and colleagues who think we are kind, good, talented people. Because...they are correct. We could, in contrast, find a collection of individuals who believe we are little better than cockroaches. And they, too, would be correct. Reality is subjective—and what people see in another person reveals more about themselves, the vantage through which they are looking, than it does about the object of their attention. It is critical we find loving, supportive people to provide a buffer of love while we navigate this fraught-filled world. This isn't about surrounding ourselves with sycophants and enablers. We want people who will lovingly challenge us to fulfill our potential and hold us accountable. This is about cutting out the naysayers, doubters, and one-sided critics.

Acknowledging that there is a vast discrepancy in outlook is helpful in examining our own biases. Because none of us are objective—we all see what we want to see.

For example, a common struggle for men who lift weights is a condition colloquially called "bigorexia." Though the average onlooker would see their bodies and say something like, "Oh wow, you're jacked"—the guys pumping iron at the gym only see their insufficiencies. They look in the mirror and still see the scrawny teenager that they were—they compare themselves with the even-more-fit fitness junkies they see on social media. These muscle heads will turn to you and say, in all earnestness, "Nah, I am a little guy. Really, I am not big at all." They're not downplaying—that is genuinely how they see themselves.

Many of us have also witnessed the opposite—a rail-thin person spending hours on the stair master who genuinely believes themself to be overweight. Or perhaps you've seen the super talented front-line worker who believes themself to be lacking competence because someone, some time ago, said that they were

XXXIII. SEE YOURSELF THROUGH ANOTHER'S EYES

"stupid." For none of these people are their vantages accurately reflecting their truths.

This goes back to why it's so crucial that we surround ourselves with voices that affirm our worth in a grounded, honest way. But, going one step beyond this, we should also regularly engage in seeing ourselves from a point of view that is different from our own.

What if you imagined yourself as your most beloved friend sees you? Perhaps your hard edges are now dulled—your kindness and generosity shine brighter. Maybe you are suddenly funnier than you typically think of yourself as being. Perhaps you become awed at your loyalty and willingness to show up whenever needed—qualities that typically go unobserved within yourself.

Or, instead, you view yourself from the vantage of your lover. Notice how much more attractive and seductive you are. Notice how those laugh lines (that usually draw your disdain in the mirror) are unnoticeable. Notice how much nicer your body proportions look, how caring and sensitive you seem. Your lover undoubtedly sees you in more flattering terms than you see yourself.

Another option: how would a talented coach or advisor see you? Yes, they look at you with compassion and understanding—and, at the same time, they hold you accountable for your areas of growth. They support you and challenge you to face the things you typically prefer to ignore. Where are the areas you are giving yourself a pass? Are there places where you're falling short—or even causing unintended harm? Maybe you thought you were being proactive but, from another perspective, you weren't doing nearly enough. Perhaps you were even callous and selfish when you thought you were just reinforcing your boundaries.

Our actions can feel justified to ourselves, but we can come across as cruel, unforgiving, or ill-intentioned to others. Rare is the person who thinks that they are intentionally coming across as a narcissist; from their point of view, they are totally justified. Outsiders see differently, however. What are the ways that you've been more self-centered, uncaring, or cruel than you thought you were being? Stepping into another's vantage can help you reassess and perhaps make different choices so you can do less harm. It's always good to consider how we could improve and do better.

Undergoing this exercise regularly digs us out of our entrenched perspectives. It forces us to see ourselves in a new and surprising way. Because no one perspective is correct. The way you see yourself is not the totality of who you are —it is but a tiny facet. So, what if there were ways you could hold yourself accountable to improve more rather than letting yourself slide? What if you allowed yourself to believe that you are more talented, powerful, kind, and worthy than you presently think? What if you've been misguided in your self-perception this whole time?

Adopting a more flexible point of view regarding ourselves also makes it easier for us to become less intransigent regarding others. What if that person you wrote off as being "terrible" actually wasn't? What if you were able to adopt a vaster vantage that allowed you to see them from other angles, seeing the struggles and shortcomings that make them act that way? What if that celebrity you view as "faultless" and aspirational suddenly becomes more humanized and fallible because you see them from other points of view and realize that they, too, are making mistakes and figuring life out as they go along.

Opening up our field of view makes us kinder and softer—but also more resilient. In doing so, we learn to appreciate that nothing is ever just "one way." There are multiple options for seeing every happening, experience, and person. And if we can extend the grace to ourselves to perhaps be different than we supposed, then we should also be able to open that up to others.

So, as you wander through this landscape of magical mirrors, take whatever time you need to see yourself in each. Then, keep or discard what you learn about who you are—hold fast to the affirming and jettison the detracting. Know that you are all things—you contain multitudes. Let the parts that matter most to you shine at the forefront and worry less about needing to make everything congruent. You will always have facets of your disposition that disagree with the rest of you. And that is perfect. We are never just one thing; we are a beautiful kaleidoscope of shifting contours, colors, and designs.

Become more than just the dominant story you tell about yourself. Extend the grace of being a complex and contradictory being to everyone that you meet. And trust that there are always new angles from which to see others and situations. In expanding your perspective, you also expand your heart. And that, in turn, makes everything better.

RITUAL:

Invite a close friend or loved one to write a letter describing how they see you—your strengths, qualities, unique attributes, and areas for growth. Take time to reflect on their words, noticing the ways their perspective may differ from your own self-image. What new truths can you embrace about yourself? Allow their

XXXIII. SEE YOURSELF THROUGH ANOTHER'S EYES

insights to reveal facets you may have overlooked, and integrate these affirmations into how you perceive your own worth and potential.

JOURNAL PROMPTS:

- How do I think others perceive me? How might their perspective differ from how I see myself, and what can I learn from their viewpoint?
- Reflect on a time when someone gave me feedback that challenged my self-image. How did their perspective help me grow, and how can I continue to use others' insights for personal development?

GUIDED MEDITATION:

Breathe deep and sink deeply within. Release into the fertile landscape of your inner life. Envision yourself standing on the shore of a forked river that carves the land up into three banks. On one bank, you stand, feet firmly rooted into the loamy earth. On the bank to your right is someone who loves you immensely—either real or imagined. On the bank to your left is someone who wants to help you grow—again, either real or imagined. They look at you with kindness, and you gaze back at them.

Now, leave your body where it is, but switch places with the person on the right. This person who loves you so deeply, what does it feel like to gaze out at you from behind their eyes? How do they see you differently? Does their image of you look different than how you see yourself? What feelings arise within? Do you see anything you did not anticipate? Feel their admiration and kindness as if it's your own. Let this perspective fill you with love and acceptance, helping you see the beauty and strength that others see in you.

Now, switch to the person on the left bank. This person wants to see you be your best self. What do they notice? Not areas of critique but invitations for growth. Where do they see you're already excelling and wishing you to go even further? Can you see the radiant potential that they envision for you? Accept the belief they have in you as your own; you are wonderful and capable of even more.

Now, come back to your own perspective carrying with you all the positive vibes that you have garnered from the other sides of the river. Notice how it feels to be inside you now. Feel free to envision other mentors and champions and see yourself from their perspectives.

MANTRA:

"I see my light reflected back in others."

XXXIV. FIND A TEACHER IN EVERYONE

You've wandered far, alone in the wilderness. But now, for the first time in a long while, you've stumbled upon a group of other soul-searchers. Here, in the depths of the forest, far from places that have been known and well-traveled, you come across a band of others who are also on a quest for their ecstatic, joy-filled selves. They lounge, laughing and exchanging stories as their dinner roasts on a spit above the campfire. They hear you approach and turn to smile at your arrival. "Come, join us!" they shout. Eager for their company, you sit on a fallen log beside them and join in on the conversation.

You realize how wise and soulful each person is. Every individual gathered here has stories and insights worth sharing—they, too, have been wandering this forest of soul for quite some time, venturing through the portals of self-understanding. As the meal is served and the plates are passed around, you find yourself learning more than you ever anticipated. Each nugget of wisdom, each blossom of insight, is eagerly accepted and stored for future use. Through examples of what to do or not do, they are illuminating paths that you have not yet trod—or shining perspectives on landscapes you've already traversed. Either way, you are learning and growing through their wisdom.

Yes, these travelers are mightily gifted in understanding the human condition. But it makes you wonder: *How many others have also had wisdom to impart, but I was too busy or dismissive to hear them? How often have I walked past someone with a great deal of meaningful insight to offer?*

Nearly everyone we encounter has something to share that we can learn. From the grandest to the humblest, each person has had travails, successes, and surprises that can illuminate our own journey. Not only people but animals, too. The land itself can proffer insights about life and how we live it.

Some of my most excellent teachers have been trees—a view that has been affirmed by numerous spiritual traditions across time. The Druidic Celts revered the oak as a source of divine wisdom—in fact, their written script, *Ogham*, used different trees as represented by letters to convey spiritual teachings. In Shinto, the indigenous religion of Japan, ancient trees are seen as manifestations of gods, and shrines are built around them to honor these spirits. The indigenous Tibetan Bön tradition reveres old trees as living guides—capable of conveying messages and wisdom to those who can attune to them. Taoists believe the flow of life energy, or *qi*, moves through trees similarly to how it flows through human beings, and trees are often seen as models for harmonizing with this energy.

Numerous are the times where I've sat before an old tree and felt it become a part of me. I have felt its roots extending into the earth, mirroring the branches overhead. In one lesson, I learned about reciprocity in energy—that to extend upward, we must first move downward in a commensurate amount to the highest we wish to ascend.

Other forms of nature, too, routinely grant me wisdom. Standing on a beach and observing the uncountable grains of sand around me, I reflect on my smallness and the temporality of reality. Standing on a cliff, I may better understand expansiveness and eternity. The undulation of a body of water may key me into insights around surrender and letting go.

Moreover, as we come to sense and resonate with the energy or spirit inherent to each sentient creature (which includes plants and even landforms when viewed from an animist perspective), they can begin to speak to our hearts. Sensations, visions, symbols, and emotions can be transmitted to us directly from the source with which we are engaging.

How often have you written off people, places, or things because you thought they had nothing to teach you? Some of my greatest teachers have been those who have demonstrated deplorable behavior—they have become living, tangible examples of what I do not wish to be. That reckless driver who cut you off might be there to teach you about patience and slowing down. That arrogant boss who is unconcerned with the effects of their selfishness may be here to help you rediscover altruism and conscientiousness for others. What if you revered everything that crossed your path as a potential wisdom-holder, as someone who might hold a critical piece of information that you require for this stage of your development? That person who offered you an unexpected compliment might be helping you to remember that even a small gesture of kindness can make a big impact. Even the parrot repeating the words and phrases he has heard reminds

XXXIV. FIND A TEACHER IN EVERYONE

you that the words we speak and the stories we tell have power, even if we think no one is listening.

As we sit by this fire, beneath the glowing blanket of stars, we open ourselves to the great teachers around us. The travelers, the animals, the trees, the earth—all of them are our guides. They all impart a lesson that we need to accept. As we learn to treat the world with reverence and to receive wisdom from any and all sources, something within us shifts. We become more open, more compassionate, and kinder. We are more patient with ourselves and the wider world. We come to see that every being is both a teacher and a student—a wisdom holder and a novice. We are all walking the path of self-discovery and learning if...*and this is key*...if we choose to see it as such. If we choose to see this world as a place of learning and growth—a place to evolve and expand—then the lessons are endless.

Strive to find a teacher in everyone. Learn from their stories, actions, and presence. Each encounter provides insights about yourself and your place in this dazzling universe. Learn that the journey is endless—and we are all doing the best we can with the information we have. And after this encounter tonight, perhaps you'll know just a tad more than you did before.

RITUAL:

For the next week, approach every conversation and interaction with the intention to learn something valuable. Imagine each person you meet as a teacher sent to reveal a specific lesson for your journey. Whether they inspire, challenge, or surprise you, observe closely and note any qualities they embody that stand out to you—whether they are examples of kindness, resilience, patience, or, perhaps, reminders of behaviors you'd rather avoid. At the end of each day, take a few minutes to journal about the insights you gathered, considering how these lessons can guide your own growth and understanding.

JOURNAL PROMPTS:

- Who are the unexpected teachers in my life—people, experiences, or challenges that have taught me valuable lessons? What did I learn from them, and how can I be more open to seeing the world as my classroom?

- Reflect on a time when a difficult situation became an opportunity for learning. How did I find wisdom in unexpected places, and how can I embrace that mindset in my current life?

GUIDED MEDITATION:

Breathe deeply and feel yourself relax. Soften into an internal space where you can envision yourself in a vibrant forest of massive trees. Smell the fecund air; feel the rich soil beneath your toes. Gaze at the mother tree nearest to you, this ancient sentinel and guardian of the forest. What does she have to say? What wisdom does she have to impart? She has stood, rooted here, for many ages. What can you learn from her?

Observe the fox whose den is made amongst her roots; notice the spark of intelligence in his eyes. What does he have to say? What lessons can he offer? Begin to walk through the forest and notice how all the flora and fauna are longing to teach you. From the tiny crocuses that push up through the earth in early spring to the mighty condor and his massive wings...there are lessons with everyone and everything.

Perhaps you also encounter other humans in this sacred abode, fellow travelers with stories to share and wisdom to impart. Can you envision a life where everyone and everything is here to impart something deep and meaningful to you? With each inhale, you absorb these lessons, and with each exhale, you release any preconceived judgments or biases.

Recognize that every person, no matter how different they may seem, has something valuable to teach you. Stay with this awareness for a few moments, feeling gratitude for the wisdom that is all around you.

MANTRA:

"Everything is my teacher."

XXXV. LET YOUR BODY MOVE YOU

As the moon rises, a powerful urge overtakes you to run, to move, to let the muscles of your body strain with the force of exertion. You pick yourself up from the damp moss of the sodden ground and run—sprint at full speed. Into the darkness, you let your intuition guide you around stones and over fallen tree limbs. You reach a thick, ropey vine and clasp it with both hands, swinging into the night.

You land with a quiet thud and begin your galloping once more. Dodging bushes and briars, leaping over rivulets, you outpace your shadow. A fox runs beside you, racing as if this were a game. Your spirit is light and free—a gleeful shriek of delight escapes your chest. You feel feral and unfettered. This is the primal hunt; you are searching for moonbeams.

Soon, this gallop through the dark woods begins to feel like a dance. The trees are your partners; together, you spin through the abyss. You cannot help yourself—you laugh heartily in merriment. You feel so alive—as if this is what you were born for: to frolic, to flit, to fly. You are a creature of the night, and the shadows give you wings. Your body attunes you to the secret wisdom within you; your truer nature is revealed. You are a thinking animal—a beautifully embodied being. You have fully come home to your physical self.

We live in such an analytical, data-driven world that has crowned the head as being supreme. We are taught that all knowledge comes through thinking, and we have written off any primal intelligence that can come from allowing our physical forms to dictate our course.

Not only is there wisdom in the body, but profound discoveries can be unearthed by letting it move you. It really doesn't even matter so much what form the movement takes—by allowing ourselves to return to being creatures that climb, crawl, and swing, an earthy knowingness arises from our depths.

Perhaps you've uncovered a form of mindful movement like tai chi, qi gong, or hatha yoga. These breath-connected, life-force-driven body shapes and movement patterns can unlock an understanding of how your soul functions. Or maybe you've uncovered the wisdom that comes through ecstatic dance. You've removed your shoes and let your body undulate and shake in the ways it feels called, unconcerned with outside viewership, revealing hidden aspects of yourself and guiding you back into a state of harmony.

If you enjoy a slower pace, you may have found walking to be a revelation. Slowly progressing forward, one step at a time, has led you into deep unfolding of your truer self. Instead, maybe you've preferred a rougher form of movement—martial arts, wrestling, rugby. Perhaps the experience of violence or sport has stripped away pretense and revealed a more raw and visceral understanding of your animal body.

The body understands and can teach so much—but often, those lessons are locked in place by the rigidity and stillness we maintain. When we let our bodies explore, move, and do the things they feel called to do, an explosion of insights can occur.

Have you been taking time to let your body move you? Have you let it whisper its secrets through the swaying of your arms, the sprinting of your legs? Have your soft footfalls in a balletic dance revealed something of your deeper truths?

Perhaps, instead, you've uncovered how the vibrations of your vocal cords can unlock secrets of your identity. Who we are is deeply connected with the use of our voices—and when we sing, important parts of ourselves can shine forth. Recently, I began exploring singing lessons again for the first time in over a decade. In so doing, I came to understand myself in a new and more profound way; parts of my identity were revealed to me through the thawing of tension in my throat. When we sing, we unveil who we really are. When we dance, we expose our spirit.

This is a call for you to reconnect with your physical form, not just in stillness but in wild, ecstatic movement. Go for a run, row a kayak, somersault through a field of daisies, catch and throw a ball, hike a mountain. Do whatever calls to your heart—but realize the wisdom that is inherent in your physical form.

The Ancient Greek philosopher Socrates said, "Many people's minds are so invaded by forgetfulness, despondency, irritability, and insanity because of their poor physical condition that their knowledge is actually driven out of them." A saying that has survived in Greece into modern times is Νους υγιής εν σώματι υγιή—which means: a healthy mind is in a healthy body. Through developing our physical forms, we can cultivate selves that are more well.

There is a thrill that comes from really using your body. Running further than you did previously, lifting something heavier. There is a deep sense of pride and accomplishment that comes from seeing yourself achieve something with this body that you once thought was impossible. "To be healthy without trying to run faster and longer, or harden one's muscles, is to squander a chance to be more than one is; to miss the unique joy of striving, however painful," says another Ancient Greek wise man, Xenophon.

In today's world, too many people see fitness in the body as being unimportant in regard to cultivating the mind. How often do you see a scientist or political pundit with a developed and fit body? It is uncommon. There are, in fact, several groups within the modern world who see the development and use of one's physical form as a waste of time and distraction from more useful, mental pursuits. Some in our society have gone so far as to think any person with a well-cultivated body is likely to be a "dumb jock" or lacking any great insights. This is odd, given the knowledge that neural cells exist outside of our brains—our bodies can think, so to cultivate them is to nourish the power of our minds.

How have we come so far in disregarding the majesty and wisdom inherent in our physical forms? It's time we reclaim our bodies as sacred vessels for cultivating a well-rounded and healthy consciousness. So take time to push beyond your limits—sweat, strain, move. Learn the insights that your body can reveal to you.

For myself, I spend approximately three to five hours a day engaged in some sort of exercise. My morning begins and evening ends with a lengthy walk around the city with my pups. In the late mornings, I go to the gym for approximately two hours. I will stretch, do tai chi, lift weights, and ride a stationary bike during this time. My goal is to open, strengthen, and sweat. By doing these things, my mind feels more relaxed, facile, and focused during the rest of my day. My husband and I often talk about our exercise time as a form of meditation —without it, I would become more tense and anxious.

So, leap, spin, dance, push, pull, yank on something. Lift something heavy and put it back down. Run with wild abandon down a forested trail. Swim against the current and push your body to its limit. Let your body become your teacher—allow it to reveal its inherent wisdom. By doing so, you will better come to understand yourself and your place in the world. You will feel good and grateful for the form you inhabit. Take time each day to move your body—and let your body move you.

RITUAL:

For the next week, dedicate yourself to exploring a different type of movement each day. Allow yourself to play with variety, selecting from practices like yoga, hiking, ecstatic dance, tai chi, kickboxing, weightlifting, or simply letting your body move freely in nature. At the end of each session, take a few minutes to reflect on how that movement affected you physically, emotionally, and energetically. Did it bring release, joy, or newfound strength? Notice how each form of movement invites you to connect with different aspects of yourself, and allow the body's wisdom to reveal new insights.

JOURNAL PROMPTS:

- How does my body feel when it's free to move without constraint or judgment? What movements feel most natural to me, and how can I incorporate more spontaneous movement into my life?
- Reflect on a time when moving my body brought emotional or spiritual healing. How did it help me release tension or connect with deeper parts of myself?

GUIDED MEDITATION:

Take off your shoes and step onto the grass. Close your eyes and feel the fresh air on your skin, the sunlight on your face, the dirt under your toes. Let your body begin to sway, moving in concert with the stimulus from the world around you. Feel yourself undulating, swinging, breathing.

Allow your body to move in any way it feels called. Rise onto your toes, sink down onto your knees, and roll around on the earth. Notice what feelings arise within you—can those be expressed in your movements as well?

Take several breaths and enjoy the sensations of being an embodied individual. Let your body move naturally, without any force or direction, allowing it to express itself freely. Trust your body's wisdom and let it guide you through this

XXXV. LET YOUR BODY MOVE YOU

meditative dance. Stay with this gentle movement, connecting deeply with the rhythm of your own body.

When you feel like it's reached its natural conclusion, sit cross-legged and observe what shook loose within. What has changed inside? What lessons has your body revealed?

MANTRA:

"I trust my body's wisdom."

XXXVI. RECONNECT WITH THE NATURAL WORLD

When you close your eyes, you see yourself wandering concrete mazes, treading over tarred asphalt streets. Glass and steel loom down at you; blazing LED screens scream electronic advertisements that poke at your inadequacies, encouraging you to mindlessly purchase and consume. The artificial ground hums with the thrum of the relentless chase, billions of souls pursuing contented-less fame and fleeting status. And... Isn't it all so exhausting? Don't you feel pulled thin and hollow?

Now, you open your eyes. Wiggle your toes in the soft, loamy soil. Breathe in the sweet, life-filled air rich with honeysuckle and plum blossoms and the unmistakable tang of photosynthesizing green leaves. As you step, the ground quiets your footfalls with grasses and ferns bending under your weight. The sky glows richly in hues of azure fading to fuchsia as the sun drops low and heavy toward the distant horizon. You reach your arms wide and touch the craggy surface of the nearby ancient elm. This mother tree has stood guard over this forest for centuries—feel her trunk pulsing with sentience.

This is where you belong; this is your home. Rooted into this natural world, you come alive again. The constructed world of our modern era of artificiality and plastic everything has removed us from our earthy abode. We have become divorced from the sights, textures, and scents that remind us of our truth—that we are a part of something far greater than ourselves. We have forgotten that we are just one small part of a much larger conscious organism. The world of men forces us to feel small and disconnected; the world of trees reawakens our sense of vastness and immortality.

Notice the raccoon following in your wake. She is a master at slipping between the world of humans and the organic world. She can navigate city streets, obtain what she needs from the refuse and scraps that we leave behind, and then return to her den in a hollow tree in the forest. She invites you to be like her—to engage with this manufactured reality but also to be able to escape it.

The call has come to reconnect with the natural world. It's time to say goodbye to paved streets and wander barefoot through mossy terrain. The call of the mud, of the mycelial matrix within the soil stretching in all directions and uniting everything—including you—is reaching for your heart. It is time to abandon the synthetic and reunite with the organic.

Studies show that when we spend time outside, our sleep improves, our blood pressure lowers, and the chance of chronic disease gets reduced. The verdant world also improves mental health, reduces the effects of overstimulation, and can even help combat anxiety and depression. Ideally, we should aim to spend at least two hours outdoors over the course of the week—broken into 30-minute increments or longer. Doing so will lead to vast improvements in our day-to-day well-being and increase our resiliency to stress.

But, more than the measurable health benefits, time in nature reunites us with deeper parts of ourselves that have been lost in the modern era. Before the age of industrialization, humans lived in constant contact with the natural world. It held a space of deep reverence and magic for us and not just because scientific understanding hadn't yet risen to contemporary levels. No, in spending regular time engrossed with the flow of the seasons, the rhythm from day to night, the process by which things grow and evolve...we became rooted in a sense of awe and extra-sensory knowing.

Earth-based cultures across the globe have revered the unspoken wisdom that can be transmitted from plants and landmasses to people. They talk about a communicable sentience that exists within lifeforms that aren't human—that the plants, animals, oceans, storm clouds, and mountains can speak to us. The Celts would meditate with mother trees and whisper to wild animals, learning secrets that allowed them to have incredibly elevated qualities of life without our modern innovations. The indigenous communities of the Americas speak of a pre-colonial age where humans lived in harmony with the spirits of the natural world, where a joyful and balanced life was the norm—far distant from that found in the suburban abodes of modern man.

When we return to the earth, when we come back to the water, we reencounter our connection to spirit. We step back into our mystical totality. We become part of something much grander than our limited selves; we adopt an

XXXVI. RECONNECT WITH THE NATURAL WORLD

understanding of a reality that is timeless, inclusive, and organic. One of the self-chosen names that the people of India use for their spiritual beliefs is *Sanatana Dharma*—which translates to "eternal truth." The idea is that if you become very quiet and attune your observations to the world around you as well as the space within, cosmic truths will arise—truths that can be found by any person, anywhere, at any time.

That is our "ecstatic inner self" I have referenced many times on our journey together. We come to feel the flows of light, these rivers of sentience that move through our body and extend into the ground, the sky, and the beings that surround us. We are not, in fact, separate. *You and I are one.* I know that is a phrase that has developed semantic satiation (a loss of meaning due to its overuse), but it is nonetheless true. You and I are not independent entities—we are the same soul-stuff broken into different bodies. We are the same cosmic Oversoul incarnated into separate physical forms.

Take a grove of aspen trees, for example. They look like hundreds or thousands of separate beings dwelling together, but they are not. In fact, they are one organism joined at the roots—what happens to one happens to all. You and I are not so different. When I offer you blessings, aid, and assistance—I also benefit myself. When I intentionally cause you harm or suffering—I likewise mar myself. Injuring you would be no different than were I cutting my own arm. And this is true, too, of all the life forms around us. The plants, the animals, even the planet itself.

Our modern world has a very narrow view of what qualifies as sentient—it wasn't even until recent decades that animals were given this designation. The philosopher René Descartes notoriously threw a cat out of a window to prove that animals were unable to experience emotions—he also mutilated dogs for the same purpose. As late as the 1960s, it wasn't uncommon for American families to euthanize their household pets in preparation for a trip abroad—their opinion was they could just obtain a new one when they returned. Much has changed since then. Recent research shows that birds have sophisticated languages that can indicate cardinal directions, level of approaching threat, and type of nearby predator. These are languages that must be taught, given that young chicks are found to misspeak and receive correction from adults. It's been wonderful to see the language shift in humans regarding how they more often now regard their furry wards as "children" rather than "property."

Few have gone further to extend that relationship designation to plants. It is interesting, however, that recent research has demonstrated that plants do, in fact, communicate with one another. If a tree is felled by a natural disaster or a woodsman's axe, the surrounding trees may reach out through their roots to share nutrients and water with the surviving stump, causing it to continue living for additional centuries. Through the underground network, trees are able to share biochemical markers, effectively sharing information.

In her book, *To Speak for the Trees*, scientist Diana Beresford says, "In humans, the tryptophan-tryptamine pathways generate all the neurons in the mind. [...] Such pathways exist in plants—in some more than others, in trees most of all. Plants contain the sucrose version of serotonin; [...] serotonin is a neuro-generator. By proving that the tryptophan-tryptamine pathways exist in trees, I proved that trees possess all the same chemicals as we have in our brains. Trees have the neural ability to listen and think; they have all the component parts necessary to have a mind or consciousness [...] and perhaps even dream."

Even when acknowledging the sentience in living creatures, we still tend to hold the landscape itself as being unthinking. We see rocks as inert, waterways as merely conduits for living beings. But cultures across time have revered the consciousness present in weather patterns, in fire, in rivers and streams. Hills are known to be wise, old masters. The forest as an entirety has a life unto its own.

I, myself, was awakened one morning by the call of a faraway mountain asking me to come pay my respects. I have seen fully embodied spirits float in the currents of a waterfall, maintaining minutes-long conversations with me and revealing profound insights. Though I wasn't raised with the view that the earth harbored sentient life that wasn't attached to a cellular body, I have come to revere it. Just because the heartbeat of a cliffside is far slower than we can measure, just because the tide moves in rhythms that don't easily feel tied to a living pulse, doesn't mean they don't exist.

It's time to redefine what nature means to us. It's time to challenge our assumptions that the world outside our door is dull, inert, and lacking the spark of awareness. When we come home to nature, we return to the fullness of ourselves. We are part of the natural world, and it is part of us. By severing ourselves from our connections to the clouds, the sea, the fields—we have become partial people. We have amputated our limbs and wonder why we feel desolate.

So, take off your socks and shoes and stand barefoot in the dirt. Roll across a grassy meadow like a child playing games. Pause your walk to smell the roses growing in their beds. Speak to the rain and ask what it has to teach you. Treat that honeybee that mistakenly flew into your home as a cherished guest and gently usher them back outside.

Reclaim your connection to the natural world and reunite with the totality of your soul.

XXXVI. RECONNECT WITH THE NATURAL WORLD

RITUAL:

Take off your shoes and place your bare feet on the earth—whether it's grass, soil, or sand. Spend at least 15 minutes walking or standing barefoot, allowing yourself to feel the connection between your body and the earth's energy. As you do this, focus on the sensations in your feet and how the earth supports and nourishes you. Reflect on how this simple practice of grounding can help you feel more centered and connected with the natural world and yourself.

JOURNAL PROMPTS:

- In what ways have I disconnected from nature in my daily life? How can I create more moments of connection with the earth, even in small ways?
- Reflect on a memory of being in nature that filled me with peace or wonder. How can I recapture that feeling in my current environment, no matter where I am?

GUIDED MEDITATION:

Breathe deep and envision yourself seated in a deep forest. Moss grows on trees, and a brook babbles nearby. Breathe deep and let the sounds and smells of nature sink into you. Feel the tree roots reaching through the soil and sense the small plants swaying in the breeze. Somatically know where everything is and how you are a part of this. Feel the pollen on your skin. Breathe in the fresh scent of pine and cedar.

    You are fully alive here. You belong here. You become part of something so much bigger than just your limited self—your periphery fades, and you merge into a large ecosystem. You become part of a whole. Do you feel how alive you are? How simultaneously grounded and buoyant? Allow yourself to notice the details through all five of your senses. Feel yourself merging with the sentience of the plant and animal life nearby. You are part of them; they are part of you.

    Find the oneness. Allow your limited sense of self to dissolve.

MANTRA:

"I am one with the natural world."

XXXVII. FIND MOMENTS OF RETREAT

The call of the rushing waterfall has pulled you forward. Climbing along slippery, precariously sharp row of rocks, you've somehow managed to maintain your footing. You've edged along the long line of algae-covered stepping stones toward the torrent of water. As the mist from the fall sprays your body, making it glisten with a million shining prisms, you have to lean into the cliff face and then take a small leap into a hidden alcove nestled behind the sheet of rushing water.

Standing erect, you notice how the walls are scratched with ancient symbols and archaic runes. The interior is softly lit like a starry night from thousands of glow worms clinging to the cavern's roof. In awe, you settle into a seated position and allow the thrum of the pounding waterfall to reverberate through your bones. The cascading noises lull you into a trance-like state—you sense you could sit here contentedly for ages. Every aspect of this space seems designed to pull your focus inward, away from the ever-changing world and into the constancy of your own heart.

Retreats have been utilized by nearly every spiritual tradition to unite us more deeply with our soulful selves. From the vision quests practiced in indigenous American societies—where seekers are sent off alone for days with no food or water and asked to stay within a ring of stones, seeking wisdom from spirit—to silent Buddhist retreats—where an aspirant might seek refuge in a cave or a monastery for days, weeks, or even years contemplating the nature of mind—time spent in isolation has been practiced. Christianity has the example of the

Desert Fathers, who emulated Christ's 40 days of fasting in the desert. Sufis have retreats from the world that focus on mindfulness and dancing.

The world is loud and constantly demanding our attention. Even if we strive diligently to detach from technology, the cacophony of life is impossible to fully block out. It is a modern challenge, but even slower-paced, agrarian societies found that retreats and stillness were necessary to achieve balance and self-mastery. How much more do we need it now due to the relentless and hectic pace of contemporary life?

When was the last time you chose to take a step back from your life and reevaluate? When was the last time you opted out of phone calls, text messages, work and familial obligations, and your social life—choosing to embrace quiet instead? Have you taken a week, a weekend, or even an afternoon to simply unplug from the busyness of the world? This retreat could be done in a seaside beach house, a cabin in the woods, or the structured environment of an ashram or mindfulness center.

A retreat is more than stepping away from the world—it's a conscious choice to step back into yourself. To realize that the world outside is merely a reflection of the world within. As you sit in stillness and quiet, focusing on your breath, a candle, a mountain, or a depiction of divine energy, something quietly begins to arise within you. A pulsing, a knowing. It is an expression of the sacred power that dwells within all beings—an energy usually buried under life's hecticness and chaos.

The world is very good at training our focus to remain outside ourselves. There is always something interesting to observe, some gossip to share, some insight to glean. It requires a concerted effort to turn that flow of awareness inward toward our inner selves. This practice is known as *pratyahara* in Sanskrit —the withdrawal of senses. In Patanjali's *Yoga Sutras*, it is considered the fifth amongst the eight limbs of traditional practice. Giving yourself the space of days or weeks to allow the thought-waves of the mind to subside so focus can root into the present moment may be necessary because it is often such a foreign concept to many people.

Once our awareness has become firmly focused on the space we occupy, the contours of our life-force begin to be revealed. In ancient Egypt, it was called *sekhem*; in China, it is called *qi*. Indians termed it *kundalini* or *prana*, Polynesians named it *mana*, and the Iroquois said it was *orenda*. It is the force that animates and unites all things, that fills the knowable and unknowable universe, that binds us all together. Have you given yourself the opportunity to experience it?

When we take time in retreat, we emerge with a better understanding of the functions of our minds—the running from our aversion, the pulling toward our cravings, the entrapment from our delusions. We become better acquainted with the present moment and less pulled toward the future or pushed into the past. We feel lighter and more aligned with our truths; perhaps we receive divine guidance from our guides or ancestors.

I spent seven years living in an ashram—which, in itself, could very well be considered a retreat—and we would routinely undergo day- or weekend-long intensives focused on silence and meditation. Through this concerted, daily effort, my experience of my sense of self totally revolutionized—I shed so many of my self-limiting beliefs and personal hangups due to the ongoing restructuring of my mind. I am not confident I would have had the same profound shift in my sense of selfhood with only brief or interment attempts to focus within.

But we don't need to give up all our possessions, take vows of poverty, or move into a monastery to experience the benefit of retreat. A weekend spent in quiet reflection by the ocean, a day hike with no other intention than to listen to the wind through the trees, or even a solitary morning spent in meditation can be immensely beneficial. These deliberate acts of stepping away from the routine of life can have tremendous effects on the soul.

So, find your retreat. Whether it's in a glow worm-lit cave hidden behind a waterfall, a beach hut, a park bench, or your own bedroom—commit to some time away from your obligations and pursuits, allowing yourself to simply be. Because, really, that is the focus of a retreat—to stop doing and start being. To let go of all the demands of our mortal life and attune ourselves to the endless expanse of our spirits. When the time comes to step back into and reengage with the world, you will carry all that wisdom and insight with you. You will be more present, more joy-filled, and more aligned with your sacred knowledge of self. You will remember that you are a spirit living a human life, and what a gift it is to be here today, to walk the path before you now.

RITUAL:

Dedicate a day or afternoon to a personal retreat. Disconnect from your usual routines and devices, creating space for stillness and reflection. Choose activities that deeply nourish you—meditate, journal, read, or simply sit in silence. If possible, find a natural setting that feels peaceful. Allow this time to be free from expectations, where you focus solely on being rather than doing. At the end, reflect on how stepping away from daily life has refilled your inner reserves and what insights or clarity have emerged in the quiet.

JOURNAL PROMPTS:

- Where can I find small pockets of retreat in my daily life? What environments or activities help me recharge and reflect, even if I can't take a full vacation or escape?
- Reflect on a time when stepping away from a stressful situation brought me clarity and peace. How can I incorporate more moments of retreat into my daily routine?

GUIDED MEDITATION:

Close your eyes and take a few deep breaths. Imagine a place where you feel completely at peace—a sanctuary that is yours alone. It could be anything: a massive crystal geode shimmering with light, a serene Shinto temple nestled in the mountains, a futuristic alien structure bathed in silver and blue light, or a floating cloud tower high above the earth. I often envision a lodge hidden deep within a wintery forest, a river rock fireplace with a merry log set ablaze, books lining the walls and tea boiling on the stove.

See the details of your space emerge—the colors, the textures, the sounds. This is your personal retreat, a sacred space where you can come to rest, recharge, and reconnect with yourself. Take your time to explore this space. Walk around, touch the walls, and feel the ground beneath your feet. Then, when you are ready, find your cozy spot. Settle in and take several deep breaths.

Feel yourself fall into deep time here. Let yourself find peace in this sacred abode that is yours, deeply yours. This is a space you can return to and dwell in whenever you need it, a refuge that exists within you. Spend a few moments here, simply being, and whenever you are ready, gently return your awareness to the present, knowing that your sacred space is always within reach.

MANTRA:

"I am creating sacred space for me."

XXXVIII. SEEK MEANINGFUL COMMUNITY

From a distance, you hear laughter and camaraderie emanating through the trees. Voices are chortling and guffawing as a spritely dulcimer quietly plays. A group has gathered nearby, enjoying some genial revelry this sultry evening.

As you step closer, the voices become more distinct—a dozen or so, you figure, have gathered. Sparks of firelight shine through the silhouetted trees, backlit by the nearly-set sun. You deliberately increase the noise your steps make so as not to make it seem like you are trying to sneak up on them. The voices quiet as they anticipate your approach. Stepping through the final ring of trees surrounding the clearing where they gather, smiles and campfire smoke greet you. They throw open their arms and welcome you into their midst.

Slaps on the back, firm handshakes of welcome, food and drink passed into your outreached hands—what a hearty greeting. Within moments, you are settled amongst them near their fire, enjoying the dulcet tones the musician strikes, feasting on some stewed meats and preserved jellies on homemade bread. Though you have just met the group of individuals, it feels as if you perhaps knew them before—they feel innately familiar to you. Maybe it's because they are fellow soul journeyers exploring the forty-eight portals as you are. Perhaps it's because you all have that spark of adventure gleaming in your eyes. Whatever the reason, you feel a sense of deep belonging—and how excellent that is. It's been a long while since you've felt like you genuinely belonged somewhere, that you met a group with whom you felt enough of an affinity to sit and stay a while.

Socialization is so essential for us humans—we evolved as pack animals. For millions of years, we hunted, sang, ate, and thrived in bands and tribes. Generation after generation, we have become hardwired to appreciate community and camaraderie. More than appreciate, we have come to find it entirely necessary. Survival is much more assured when you're within the safety of a group. Together, you can collectively farm and hunt, you can drive off predators, you can tend to your sick more deftly, and you can specialize in different trades and abilities. All alone, the likelihood of starvation, injury, and all sorts of life-endangering events skyrocket. We are hardwired to seek out others with whom we can share our lives, our dreams, and our hopes for better days.

In the modern world, we are facing a crisis different from any our ancestors faced. Many of us now work in remote environments, cut off from face-to-face contact with peers. We live lives where most of our social interactions are mediated through computer screens. If you wished, you could utilize technology so that you never have to interact with another human—you could have everything dropped off outside your door. While reducing the in-person exposure to other people creates a reduced risk of rejection, since they never get to see our totality, we also end up only ever partially meeting our social needs.

We require skin-to-skin contact to thrive—we need to see people's microexpressions, observe subtle changes in posture, and smell their pheromones. We need to touch and be touched. Without these meaningful interactions, our neural pathways aren't fully stimulated—and, also, our fears and anxiety climb. There is a direct correlation between the percentage of our lives that is lived in virtual environments and our overall sense of satisfaction and well-being. The rates of depression, anxiety, and mental health issues associated with being overly engaged in online social environments are startling—nearly one out of two people have self-reported being affected detrimentally. A staggering 30% of Millennials say they often feel lonely—27% say they have no close friends.[1]

The more we hide ourselves, the more disconnected we feel. I firmly believe that were we to spend intimate time, body to body, in deep connection with people who care about us, we would be markedly healthier and happier as a society. This sense of hiding also extends to our choice of clothing. Most cultures would have some sort of communal nudity—whether in a bathing facility or for group athletics. The fact that we have kept our bodies hidden has led to mass feelings of body dysmorphia and lingering anxiety around insufficiency. We haven't bared ourselves to our friends and neighbors, so we don't know what is real...we are blinded by what we see online, which is a poor

---

1. Ballard, J. (2019, July 30). *Millennials are the loneliest generation.* YouGov. https://today.yougov.com/society/articles/24577-loneliness-friendship-new-friends-poll-survey

XXXVIII. SEEK MEANINGFUL COMMUNITY

substitute for the flesh and blood knowledge that comes through real-life encounters.

In order to flourish, we need to surround ourselves with individuals who are willing to give and receive in equal measure. There is a term called "mutuality," which means that we feel like we have something to offer our intimate relationships that is roughly proportional to what we receive in return. For our neural pathways to be sufficiently nourished, we must feel like there is a commensurate level of benefit received between the parties and an equal amount of sharing of valuable goods or ideas.

Additionally, we must feel like our shared company accepts us enthusiastically and without reservations. Ideally, the care and concern shared amongst the group should feel unconditional—that no matter what we share or disclose, our group will enthusiastically support us. No matter if this is regarding our past history, future goals, or our identities or orientations, we must feel like our tribe will accept us no matter what. Without this unconditional mutual appreciation, there will never be a space where we will fully be able to experience trust, which is the bedrock for meaningful relationships.

Lastly, the communities we enter must have a high crossover in shared interests. If your great passion in life is esoteric philosophy and that is your predominant topic in which to engage in conversation, you would be hard-pressed to find meaningful connections with those whose primary interests are pop culture or fashion. Neither interest is right or wrong—but there is minimal crossover between them. When we are younger, we are willing to accept a lower level of mutual interests because other factors override its necessity—namely, proximity to the other party, frequency of interactions, and a shared history of trauma. If you encounter the same people daily, you will likely strike up a friendship with them out of convenience.

The same goes for ease of access—if you are already sharing similar spaces, co-creating together is an easy thing to orchestrate. In regard to past trauma—growing up is an inherently traumatic event; it's impossible to escape childhood and adolescence unscathed. When people go through tremendously challenging circumstances together and survive, a sort of "brothers in arms" mentality arises. You survived the trenches together—you looked out for one another in dangerous situations—that creates a unique bond that is unlikely to be found again in adult gatherings.

We must actively put ourselves in situations where we can frequently run into others with a high crossover of mutual interests so that our social network can develop. These relationships must be easily accessible; otherwise, they will be difficult to take root. Driving an hour to spend time with a friend you've known for a decade is a much smaller hurdle to leap than doing similar for someone you are just coming to know.

It is further essential to recognize that we require relationships of varying levels of intimacy. We need those bosom companions with whom we can tell long-held secrets that we will maybe only whisper to three others over the course of our lifetime. We need friends with whom we can go to festivals and social engagements. We need those casual acquaintances who know our partners' names but probably not our parents' or siblings'. We also need more acquaintances that we are merely social with—people you say hello to at the gym or the grocery store. By building this social network of varying intimacy, we get our social needs met at a variety of levels.

Most critical of all is the person or persons we choose as our primary life partner(s)—since they will exert the most significant influence on who we are and who we will become. Ideally, we choose to spend time with those who inspire us and help us tap into our better qualities—that we like the people we become when we spend time with them. They should help us aspire to be our best selves. In the words of investor Warren Buffet, "You want to associate with people who are the kind of person you'd like to be. You'll move in that direction. And the most important person by far in that respect is your spouse. I can't overemphasize how important that is."

How many people do we know who settle in their relationships? They choose lackluster individuals because they just happen to be in proximity, they have a fear of love or intimacy, or they think a mediocre person is all that they are worth. So many people settle for less than they really want because they are afraid of being lonely or they are scared that nothing better is out there for them. These are, of course, fallacies; we are all deserving of mutually stimulating and inspiring relationships of all varieties.

It can be daunting to imagine cutting out the people in our lives who are not serving our well-being. We have shared history and invested time in nurturing our bond. But we must be brave and realize that each relationship has a season: some linger for weeks, others years, others still, decades. Sometimes, we have grown and no longer share any commonality—or perhaps we realize that there never was mutuality and that the relationship had always been primarily one-sided. Whatever the reason, we must lovingly release those who are no longer serving our well-being and create space for more life-giving relationships.

A quote I return to again and again is from author Richard Bach: "The space for what you want is already filled with what you settled for instead." You could have fabulously nurturing and enthusiastic relationships where everyone benefits—or you could have connections that are merely "*meh*." The choice is up to

XXXVIII. SEEK MEANINGFUL COMMUNITY

you. But this is your call to find those who light up your soul, make you giggle in ecstasy, and inspire you to achieve your highest self.

So, wander into the woods and meet those kindred spirits who sing your songs and dance your dances. Find those with whom you spark one another's hearts alight. The journey is long, yet at the same time too brief—and there is just not enough time for poor traveling companions. Or, in the words of an unknown writer, "You can pack for every occasion, but a good friend will always be the best thing you could bring!"

RITUAL:

Reach out to someone or a group with whom you feel aligned but may not have connected deeply yet. Alternatively, join a new community or group that resonates with your interests, whether online or in person. Set the intention to truly engage—listen, share, and show up as your authentic self. Notice how it feels to interact with others who inspire you, and reflect on how these connections might enrich and support your journey.

JOURNAL PROMPTS:

- Who are the people in my life that I feel truly connected to? How can I strengthen those relationships and seek out more opportunities for meaningful connection?
- Reflect on a time when I felt a deep sense of belonging in a community. What made that experience so powerful, and how can I cultivate similar connections now?

GUIDED MEDITATION:

Close your eyes and breathe deeply. Visualize yourself surrounded by a circle of people who love and support you—whether they are people who are presently in your life, have yet to arrive, or have long departed. As you inhale, feel their presence, their warmth, and their kindness. With each exhale, send out gratitude and love to each person in the circle.

Imagine the energy of the group flowing between you, creating a sense of connection and belonging. Envision a web of light connecting you and each member of the tribe. Feel yourself belonging to each of them and them to you. Feel how you support one another, love one another, and belong to one another. Feel how good it is to dwell with your pack, your tribe. Feel the love and joy that flows between you. Feel the safety and encouragement that wells up here.

Stay with this feeling, knowing that you are part of a community that gives you the support and nourishment that you need. Realize how you are never truly alone; there are others who always have your back.

MANTRA:

"I am enmeshed in wonderful, nourishing relationships."

XXXIX. BECOME NOTHING

Staring into the starlit bay, nestled amongst the reeds and cattails, you watch in awe as the luminescent jellyfish glide through the waters. Like sails opening and closing, their bodies move through the brine in a cosmic dance. Staring into them, they feel so ephemeral that they could almost be nonexistent. Like ghosts or cosmic specters, alien in their appearance, they make you question the solidity of everything. What is real—what isn't? What does it mean to exist?

Your vision shifts, and you find yourself floating through outer space, weightless and unbound. Your edges blur into the dark expanse. Soon, you no longer remember your name, your gender, your body. You are just a force drifting on the cosmic winds of nothingness. You are like the jellyfish—barely viable, almost not there.

There is a sort of freedom that you find in this nothingness. There's nothing you need to be, nothing you need to achieve. You can fully give up control, finally. You simply glide along on the waters of existence—weightless, boundless, free. You are merely existing—and that's enough.

From a young age, most of us are trained to become "something." One of the first questions we get asked is: *What do you want to be when you grow up?* We receive praise from our teachers for our hard work and diligent efforts—and our sense of worth gets tied to accomplishment. We get sold a story that tells us, to have value, we must achieve fame, success, wealth, and recognition. We are told we ought to "leave our mark" and "strive to be remembered." But for and by whom? What does that really mean? Why does achieving a level of notoriety supposedly make someone's life worthwhile? As a child, we do not yet have the awareness to push back against these bold assertions that our life's worth is demarcated by our achievements—but we ought to have done so.

As we get older, these messages only intensify. We find ourselves competing against our peers for positions in social groups and in college applications. We fight to become valedictorian, to get scholarships, to garner competitive internships, to graduate *summa cum laude*. We fight for the illustrious job titles, six-figure salaries, and corner offices. Before we know it, we've structured our lives around ambition, proving our significance, and pursuing perceived status.

For some of us, this clamor for "more" follows us all the way to the grave—just look at the number of business leaders and politicians who are unable to step away from their roles because they have no identity outside of their jobs or cannot bear the loss in social status. They will likely die while commuting to yet another lunch meeting. Look at the billionaires who still greedily strive for more money, though they have so much that they could not spend it in a hundred lifetimes.

Then, there are the others. There are those who wake up to the fact that this is all bullshit. They have given up the chase; they have found satisfaction with and within themselves. None of this really matters—it is all a great game. What the world thinks of us, what we have, or who we impress...it's all a facade; it's all a charade. While we may continue to fulfill our duties, work, achieve, and play the game...we recognize its shallowness. It is a cardboard facsimile of real life, not life itself. We understand that, while accomplishment can bring us flashes of satisfaction, it will seldom last. Studies show that after a long-sought-after achievement is reached, quality of life returns to baseline shortly thereafter.

The pursuit of success is not the key to lasting fulfillment. No matter what you achieve, it will eventually be paved over by someone else's accomplishments. No matter how high of a hurdle you've jumped, another person will come along who can jump higher. No matter how deep of an impression you carve, your mark will be blasted away by the sands of time.

Think of this: how many people from fifty years ago can you remember with depth and nuance? Not just their name, but what they achieved? How about from a century ago? Far fewer? And a millennia ago? Your list is probably running thin.

No matter what you achieve—you will be forgotten. Even if you become as famous as Marilyn Monroe or Cleopatra...even they, too, will eventually fade into the mists of time. There is no escaping your own insignificance. Fifty years past your death, who will recall the intricacies of your life? Perhaps a few close friends and family, but even their memories will fade. Likely, a century after you're gone, there won't be a soul who remembers you were ever here.

XXXIX. BECOME NOTHING

Breathe deep and accept this truth. You don't need to be remembered—you don't need to have achieved lasting significance. That is not how the worth of your life is measured. Instead, it is appraised based on the love you shared while you were here, the people you touched, the joy in which you lived, and how you made the world just a little bit better than how you found it.

There is freedom in embracing the smallness of your life, of surrendering the need to be "important" in the grand scheme of things. By stepping into your own insignificance, you move into a place of radical freedom. By not needing to be seen or remembered, you free yourself to just enjoy the moment at hand. Unburdened by expectations, you can find the joy of simply being. You can just enjoy the walk in a field of wildflowers, not because it leads to something greater, but because it brings you happiness.

Have you ever stood on a cliff or on a beach at the edge of a continent and felt how tiny you are compared to everything else? Perhaps you looked at an expanse of sand nearby and realized how vast and uncountable it is—and how there are more stars in this universe than grains of sand beneath your feet. Around those stars, there are an unknowable number of life-inhabited planets—and they have incalculable numbers of sentient beings. On this planet alone, there are 500 quadrillion beetles in residence at any given time—that's 500 followed by 15 zeroes. Think of how insignificant you are, your lone life, in comparison with all of those thinking, breathing creatures roaming this green Earth.

There is power in realizing your insignificance. There is a freedom in acknowledging your temporality and terminality. The irony is that by accepting your smallness, you grow in size. By accepting how tiny your worth is in the grand scheme of things, you end up embracing how you are intrinsically part of everything. In realizing that there's nothing to achieve, you realize that you have already gained everything. By giving up, you win. By letting go, you find yourself.

When you allow yourself to be nothing, you find the exquisite beauty in simply being. Life then becomes less onerous—you don't take things as seriously as you used to. You dress up in your costume for work, but you realize you are only playing a role. You are no longer the character—you are the actor. You feel lighter and less burdened because you know that nothing matters—this is all a great dance, a cosmic game. It is the universe experiencing itself by incarnating aspects of its consciousness into independent bodies that believe themselves to be unique and important...but really, they are just small shards of the Oversoul that have forgotten their truth.

In nothingness, there is immense beauty. The more you lean into this, the more light- and joy-filled you become. You lose the fear of not measuring up;

instead, you feel tremendous gratitude for the honor of living at all. Worth is not in what you achieve but in the profound experience of the richness in each breath. It's the cessation of pushing and pulling and simply floating along with the current—allowing divine providence to guide you.

Scientific research shows that cause and effect are not nearly as concrete as we once thought. Studies on the nature of light have demonstrated that past, present, and future are not as tight of an alignment as we tend to believe—in fact, they may occur simultaneously. That means that the belief that "if I do X, then Y will happen" is illusory. There is no direct line from present to future in the quantum world—there is no linear space. Therefore, no action you take really matters.

While this might sound terrifying, it is actually quite freeing. If nothing is real as we think of it—time, space, cause-and-effect included—then there's no need to chase after things that will fade, no need to worry if your achievements will be remembered. This is echoed in the teachings of many spiritual traditions. In Buddhism, the concept of *Śūnyatā*—or emptiness—teaches that everything is devoid of inherent existence. In India, the notion of *Maya*—the grand illusion—teaches us that this world is only a dream from which we will eventually wake.

Science shows us that particles exist in multiple states at once—how they show up depends entirely on when they're being observed and by whom. In quantum foam, all potentials simultaneously exist. Reality bends and shifts based on perception. Many scientists have embraced the notion of "simulation theory" to explain this: the idea that we are living in a computer program, akin to that in the cult classic film *The Matrix*. Neil deGrasse Tyson suggests there is about a 50% chance that this theory may, in fact, be true.

So, if everything is an illusion, why keep striving? Why fight so hard to become something? Your desire to be important and achieve is just part of the game, part of the dream. In Taoism, there is a saying: "Do nothing, and nothing will be left undone." We stop striving, stop trying to force life into a particular shape. Instead, we flow with its currents, knowing we are mere specks in a much larger painting. The universe needs nothing from us but to simply enjoy the ride.

You are not this body or mind—words repeated by spiritual masters throughout time. You are not your achievements nor your failures. You are not the labels you have chosen or others have stuck on you. You are nothing. And in that nothingness, you are everything. You are one with the stars, with the cosmos, with all beings that have ever been or will ever be. You are like the glowing jellyfish before you—both here and not. Existing and yet also ghostly.

So, allow your boundaries to blur—allow yourself to dissolve. And by becoming nothing, meld with the Oversoul, the source from which you sprang.

XXXIX. BECOME NOTHING

Practice becoming "the void"—a long-honored tradition in many meditation practices. This is a profound step in your journey toward liberation (whatever that means to you). By becoming nothing, you will discover your freedom.

RITUAL:

Visit a place that evokes a sense of vastness—a cliffside overlooking the ocean, a forest clearing under a starry sky, or a quiet mountain peak. Allow yourself to fully absorb the experience, letting the immensity of your surroundings sink in. Breathe deeply and notice the magnitude around you, each detail, each sound, filling you with awareness of the endlessness of life and how small and fleeting you are within it. Notice the innumerable grains of sand, the infinite stars—each a reminder of your own humble place in the grand scheme. Let the need to "be" or achieve dissolve into the scenery, into the dirt beneath your feet or the sky above. Reflect on how freeing it feels to simply exist without striving. Embrace this moment of nothingness, letting go of all definitions and boundaries. Relax into the vastness around you.

JOURNAL PROMPTS:

- How does the idea of "becoming nothing" make me feel? What fears or resistance come up when I think about letting go of my identity and attachments?
- Reflect on a time when I felt insignificant in the vastness of the world. How did that experience shape my understanding of my place in the universe?

GUIDED MEDITATION:

Envision yourself standing on the edge of a massive body of water. It could be a lake, a river, an ocean...whatever calls to your soul. With each inhale, feel yourself pulling the energy of the water into you. On the exhale, allow yourself to surrender your limitations back to the gentle waves. Repeat this several times. Inhale the power of the massive water; exhale your limited self.

Over time, feel yourself give over to the large body of the water. Surrender to it. Merge with it. Feel your finite self as you dissolve into the briny sea. You become nothing, but in that dissolution, you also become the ocean, the sea, the river. By becoming nothing, you become so much more. You didn't need those rigid rules and self-definition. You are allowed to become the vastness of space, of time, of elemental forces. You are allowed to expand and meld into the void of nothingness that exists between all things.

Feel the peace that comes from being without definition, being in a state of formlessness. From the void we came, sentience floating in the nothingness of space. To the void, we shall return. Enjoy this brief return to the nothingness that we all are.

MANTRA:

"In nothingness, I find everything."

XL. BECOME ONE WITH EVERYTHING

You've reached the mountaintop and now take your deepest breath yet. Your head is light from the thin air and the exertion of the climb, but the view is worth it. All around you, the world extends in opalescent, shining beauty. The setting sun flickers off the ridges and crevasses, the ravines and ponds—an eerie, fragile beauty overawes your heart. You spread your arms wide in exultation as eagles circle overhead.

The boundaries between you and the world are thinning—you feel less substantial up here, as if you were made of air. Your skin feels permeable, as if your consciousness were leaking out, spreading through the vista surrounding you. You become part of the land, the sky, the mountains. You become one with every living thing: the billy goats, the mountain lions, the caterpillars, the tufts of dandelions growing from the rooks. You feel a pulse rippling through your body—not from your heart or lungs, but from life itself. You are connected with the world's heartbeat—it is you, and you are it. You are everything—the eagles that ride the currents of air overhead, the wildflowers blooming near your feet, the stones nestled against one another.

Maybe you're just lightheaded from the altitude, but it feels more than that. You feel transcendent; this is easily one of the most resounding spiritual experiences of your life. You take another deep breath and pull this awe-filled sensation into your bones. You lock it in place so it will stay with you forever, this feeling of oneness. As the sun dips further, you are reminded of the need to begin your descent. With a cracked-open heart, you start your climb down, carrying with you this ecstatic moment where you expanded past your physical limits and reunited with the cosmic all.

On an average day, we walk through the world with a feeling of separateness. You are you, and I am I. We are differentiated individuals living independent lives. You go home to your TV shows and your macaroni and cheese dinner—I retreat to my books and record player and make a smoothie. We live our lives as two completely unique entities. But there are moments—cracks in the usual flow of reality—that remind us that this is not actually so. You are me, and I am you. We are co-currently experiencing separate realities, but we are—in truth—a single consciousness in individual bodies.

We progress through our days thinking that our thoughts and physical forms are our own and that we are isolated beings distinct from the world around us. But this is the grand illusion of the human experience. We are not separate from everyone and everything else; we are a shard of the cosmic Oversoul placed in different selves. But you, me, the man down the street, the woman in the coffee shop, the dog in the backyard yonder, the cat lounging in the window, the grass under our feet...we are all one. They, too, are shards of cosmic consciousness incarnated into physical form. We are all united in the great web of life that ties together everything.

Many spiritual traditions understand this notion of non-dualism. The Taoist sages taught that the Tao is all things, flowing like water, moving as one. The Zen Buddhist masters spoke of the emptiness—*śūnyatā*—not as a void or absence but as the ultimate fullness of being one with everything. In that oneness, there is no you or me; there is only life. One spirit expressing itself through countless forms. The *rishis*, or seers from India, discussed the experience of *brahman*—the ultimate reality or universal consciousness present within every living creature. This means that every being is part of this divine essence—everything is *brahman*.

When we allow ourselves to dissolve and surrender our limited sense of self (or ego), we merge back into the flow of consciousness. Our sense of self extends to include all beings, all things, all places, and all times. This is what it means to become one with everything—everything becomes an extension of ourselves. In this state, there is only divine unity.

When you stand outside and look toward the horizon, observe how every cloud and landform in the distance is a part of you. Each bird, each land animal, each person—they are you too. You are the sky. You are the mountains. You are the rivers sliding through the earth's surface. You are the eagles soaring through the heavens, carried by the winds that shake the trees and bend the grasses below, which are also you.

If you want to ponder the notion of our sameness in less mystical terms...

XL. BECOME ONE WITH EVERYTHING

consider how our bodies share the same molecules. When we sit in the same room, we continually inhale and exhale air, exchanging oxygen, hydrogen, nitrogen, and an assortment of other elements with each other. Those molecules, once part of my body, have been released and are now becoming part of yours.

The water you drink has passed through countless other creatures before it reached your lips. In fact, all of the atoms that make you up have been recycled over billions of years—and they first came into existence when they were forged in the bellies of distant stars. You are quite literally made of starlight...and so is everything else.

The atoms of your bones were once carried by the wind, rain, and rivers. Every breath you take contains parts of ancient forests, oceans, and animals long passed. By embracing this truth, the boundaries between what is yours and mine begin to fade. None of these parts that make up our bodies are actually ours—they are simply on loan for us for a period of time before they get passed along. I am made of you; you are made of me. We are made of everything that has ever been.

When we embrace these ideas, it becomes more challenging to hold onto our notions of separateness or something being "mine." Everything is shared between us—everything is "ours" for only a limited moment in existence. There is no need to hold onto the false notion of separateness. By opening to this notion of oneness, everything can become sacred. Because, in this state of connection, everything is God, and everything is you. The love you give is the love you receive. The kindness you show others is the kindness you give yourself.

This is why the ancient mystics—whether Taoist sages, Buddhist monks, or indigenous shamans—spoke of the oneness as a paramount spiritual understanding. In order to truly live, we must become one with the whole. We must surrender to the greater flow of life. You are not only a drop of water falling through the sky, you are the ocean it merges into.

A long time ago, in an age before time or memory, you were not a lone individual—you were everything. You were the Oversoul, the collective consciousness. You dwelled in bliss, floating in the nothingness that exists outside of time and space. That is, until a thought arose: *What would it be like to experience X or Y?* With that idea, parts of yourself spun off and began to form a physical reality. You became galaxies, universes, stars. You created laws that this reality had to operate by: gravity, the constancy of the speed of light, Newtonian physics, etc. You took physical form to become everything that exits on the worlds of your invention—each tree, every animal, and—on this world—all the human beings. You, the great consciousness, fractured yourself into countless forms, each to have its own journey, forgetting its cosmic truth.

Even though you now experience life as a singular being, you have never been separate from the whole. You have never lost your connection to all other things because you *are* those things. You are not just the person reading this; you are the air you breathe, the ground you stand on, and the people nearby you. We chose to forget our divine nature so that we could fully go on this adventure. By not knowing our immense power and truth, we get to experience the profundity of smallness and isolation. We get to believe that the stories we experience are real—which is a great deal more fun than remembering the whole time that this is all a dream. Losing yourself in the story is what makes watching a movie or reading a book enjoyable. It would take away much of the pleasure if you were perpetually reminded of its falsity. We chose temporary amnesia so we could fully partake in the richness of this constructed world. It allows the lessons to be real, the discoveries to be true, and the soulful evolution back to full awareness to be profound and well-earned.

And then, we go from lifetime to lifetime, incarnating into different bodies, genders, races, and species based on the actions of our previous lifetimes and the lessons we desire to learn. That is until we reach a point where partaking in the illusion is no longer desirable, and our souls crave reunification with their larger self. Then, we begin the ascendant journey of rediscovering and remembering who we truly are. But the forced forgetting was important—it allowed us to undertake this adventure. Now, however, you are starting to recognize that this "reality" is just a dream.

Throughout time, great sages, saints, and mystics have directly experienced this oneness and shared their findings with their students and disciples. As you continue to grow in your awareness, you will be able to feel this truth for yourself—it is available to anyone with the desire to seek it out. You are the creator and the creation, the dreamer and the dream. Once you understand this, the boundaries between you and the world dissolve. You stop seeing others as separate from yourself and begin to act from a place of unity, compassion, and love.

You are God incarnate, and you always have been. It's time to remember your cosmic truth—you are one with everything. So, stand on the mountaintop, with the wind blowing your hair, and feel your boundaries dissolve. Let yourself expand into the sky, into the earth, into the rivers, and into the stars. Allow yourself to dissolve back into the Oversoul from which you incarnated—one with everything in creation.

For you are everything, and everything is you.

XL. BECOME ONE WITH EVERYTHING

RITUAL:

Choose a day where you consciously decide to view every person, every animal, and every object you encounter as another version of yourself. They are "you" in a different body, experiencing life from a different vantage point. Observe how this changes your interactions, your thoughts, and your feelings of interconnectedness with the world around you. As you move through the day, reflect on the beauty of this unity and how deeply you are connected to all that is.

JOURNAL PROMPTS:

- When have I felt most connected to the world around me, as if the boundaries between myself and others dissolved? What triggered that sense of oneness, and how can I invite it into my life more often?
- Reflect on a time when I felt deeply connected to nature or another person. How did that connection shift my perspective on individuality and interconnectedness?

GUIDED MEDITATION:

Envision yourself perched on the very peak of a mountain. The world extends before you in all directions. From this vantage, you can see herds of buffalo as specks below. Eagles fly in the distance. The canopy of mighty trees looks almost like ankle-high vegetation from up here. As you observe the space, allow the edges of you to dissolve. Feel yourself expanding to become as vast as the sky overhead, stretching from horizon to horizon.

As you do, feel yourself encompassing all things before and beneath you. You become part of the valleys, the gorges, the waterfalls. The herds of buffalo and packs of wolves are also you. The fish in the streams are you. The hawks hunting prey are you. Feel how you become the sky, the land, and the stars beyond. Feel how you grow to fill all corners of creation, taking up all the space in heaven and earth.

You are in all things, and all things are in you. All is one. You have become everything. Rest here, feeling your expansive self for as long as you wish.

MANTRA:

"I am one with everything."

XLI. RECONCILE YOUR MASCULINE AND FEMININE

You find yourself wading at the convergence point of two rivers. To your right flows the river of masculinity—fierce, pounding, relentless in its surging. To your left, the feminine—softer, more tranquil, sounding like the tinkling of bells. They flow together into one swirling, undulating stream that encompasses all things. You stand with one leg planted in each current, your toes gripping the mud and silt that lines the bottom of the waterway. Not far ahead, herons hunt for fish; they are said to be creatures that exist in two worlds simultaneously like messengers from the beyond. You know what it is like to have also always dwelt in two worlds—the solid and the amorphous, the living and the dead, and the masculine and the feminine. You are a being of spirit and flesh—and you are all things. You have come to accept that two currents twine their way through you and always have.

Most people love encampments—they enjoy being firmly rooted in one perspective, bulwarked behind one side. They like the certainty of claiming the righteousness of their views and the wrongness of the other side's. In fact, people are very fond of "other-izing" people. We claim the opposite gender, the opposing team, the foreign opponent as different from us as can be imagined, so we can more fervently root into our own limited perspectives.

But we have always been all things, all of us. We have always held the good and the bad, right and wrong, light and dark, positive and negative within us. By failing to acknowledge that we contain multitudes, we disconnect ourselves from our totality, from the richness of life that is our birthright.

It's time to observe the ways in which you have been limiting the totality of your experience of life because you have become too entrenched in tying yourself to just the feminine or the masculine. The call has arrived for you to reconfigure your understanding and relationship to the genders and to realize that they are both a part of you.

Regardless of if you identify as cisgendered, transgendered, or gender-fluid, and irrespective of if you identify as heterosexual, homosexual, pansexual, asexual, or otherwise, you still encompass aspects of both genders within you. The modern world is so caught up on labels; we like to demarcate and define everything. We want to specify that "This is for girls" and "That is for boys"—we like to say, "This is a masculine attribute, and that is a feminine one." But, really, what are these? These are subjective understandings of a very fluid thing that is defined by cultural context, societal conventions, and current trends.

Blue is not an objectively masculine color, nor is pink feminine—there have been cultures across time that have believed quite the opposite. Men are not the natural hunters and protectors of the family unit—throughout the animal kingdom, we see numerous of examples where the females are the primary food providers, such as with lions. Elephant herds are matriarchal—the females are the social leaders dictating what the men do. Women are not inherently more creative or loving. Men do not necessarily have better endurance or are more well-suited for manual labor. It is well known that women often have higher pain tolerance than men, yet men are usually flagged as being the "strong ones."

So much of our understanding of gender is learned. So much of what we call "masculine" and "feminine" is a collection of attributes that have been brought together by forbearers with a distinct interest in creating dynamics of control. They are not objectively true traits; they are imposed categories.

By staunchly labeling something as only being masculine, we have cut men off from the totality of their experience. They have denied their emotions, their need for closeness and physical contact with other men, and their desire to be creative and nurturing. By limiting women to "feminine" characteristics, we have routinely asked them to surrender their power, deny their intelligence, and refrain from fulfilling their ambitions because their reactions are deemed "not ladylike."

By subscribing to these limited and faulty notions, we have prevented ourselves from experiencing everything that makes us complete, dynamic, and energized human beings. It's time to strip away the labels, deny the categories, and reclaim ourselves as being fully and authentically human. It's time to reintegrate the parts of ourselves that we have severed because they did not conform to societally approved notions of who we were allowed to be.

How, over the course of your life, have you felt more connected with one river or another? Were you taught that strength lies in stoicism and that tender-

XLI. RECONCILE YOUR MASCULINE AND FEMININE

ness is a sign of weakness? Or, were you told that your softness was a necessity and, were you to strive for anything beyond nurturing and care, then you were stepping beyond your purview? The journey toward reconciliation requires you to face the parts of yourself that you've been taught to fear. Perhaps you've learned to associate masculine energy with aggression, control, domination, or icy detachment. Maybe you've come to see femininity as vulnerable, too frail and emotional, being less valuable than masculinity. It's time to surrender these limiting concepts and embrace something much more expansive.

Let go of being confined to labels of what masculine and feminine mean—redefine your identity in whatever ways make sense to you, what makes your heart shine brighter. Throw away the rule book and embrace the notion of there being no correct or incorrect way to embody masculinity or femininity. Realize that all options, all expressions, and all perspectives are open to you. Stand in the currents and realize that the rivers were never that different, that separate, to begin with—they are both water. They are both flowing. They are much more alike than they differ.

Spiritual traditions worldwide have revered those who have broken past the barriers of traditional gender assumptions. Two-Spirit individuals in the indigenous American traditions are those who are seen to have both the masculine and feminine energies embodied within them fully, and they are given special roles as spiritual leaders, mediators, and teachers. In India, the *Hijra* community, which includes those who identify as transgender, intersex, or gender nonconforming, is seen as magical, with the ability to grant luck, encourage fertility, or cast curses to those who scorn them. In the Lugbara tribe of Eastern Africa, gender-nonconforming people serve as spiritual functionaries, mediums, and intermediaries. The Hawaiian mahi is associated with shamanic and healing roles.

Further, many spiritual traditions view the creation of the cosmos, the turning of spirit into physical form, as the result of the union of masculine and feminine energies. Whether this is *Shiva* and *Shakti* in Indian tantric traditions, Ardhanarishvara, the half-man, half-woman Hindu deity, *Vajrakilaya* in the Tibetan Buddhist tradition, or the depictions of *lingams* (penises) and *yonis* (vaginas) in Cambodia—the notion of the masculine and feminine being united is constant.

How sacred is it, then, to observe that union within ourselves? Yes, we can find connection and balance in gender by those we partner with—but we more deeply find it internally. When you enter this union, you embrace your belief in your totality as being all things. You step further into the knowledge of your sacred connection with all forms of life. For, through our many incarnations, we have been all genders, races, and identity expressions. We are all things.

We need to look no further than nature to see that gender is more inclusive and more fluid than we tend to think. Green sea turtles, snakes, bearded dragons, and clownfish can all change sexes; lobsters can be one-half male and one-half female. Male seahorses carry the eggs of their offspring, nurturing them until they are born. Plants like dogwood, yellow poplar, magnolia, apple, cherry, and pear produce single flowers with both fully functional male and female parts. The Japanese cobra lily, pink tree, and striped maple can all change genders depending on specific needs or environmental changes.

Let's let go of our rigidly held beliefs around how to be masculine or feminine. Let's open up to the totality of human expression that is available to us. Let us embrace this notion that all life forms are sacred and deserving of respect, dignity, and love. Let us invite all parts of ourselves home to ourselves. And let us see ourselves as the beautifully sacred and kaleidoscopic beings that we are.

By embracing our gender inclusivity, we step closer to spirit. By demonstrating that we are all things, we encompass the nature of the divine—which generates and manifests all things in the physical world. Can we deconstruct our prejudice, release our fear, and become the totality of what we are capable of being? Can we see ourselves as complex, contradictory, and unabashedly beautiful?

When you accept this union, you will move through life more effortlessly and joyfully. You will be less afraid and more powerful. Moreover, you will uncover your true self—the self that is not defined by external expectations or limited by societal roles. You will be freer to express the fullness of who you are. So, step into both rivers. Wade in, waist deep, and swim in the conflating of two powers you once saw as opposite but now embrace as being the totality of you.

For you are all things; you always have been.

RITUAL:

Reflect on the qualities you associate with masculinity and femininity. Consider aspects like strength, sensitivity, decisiveness, nurturing, and courage. For one week, each day, choose one quality from both sides to consciously embody in your interactions, actions, and thoughts. As you express these energies, notice how they balance and enrich one another within you. Take time to meditate at the end of each day, reflecting on how each energy shaped your experience, strengthened your sense of self, and connected you to the wholeness within.

XLI. RECONCILE YOUR MASCULINE AND FEMININE

JOURNAL PROMPTS:

- What qualities do I associate with masculinity and femininity, and how have they shaped my understanding of myself? How can I bring more balance between these energies within me?
- Reflect on a time when I felt conflicted about expressing certain traits (e.g., sensitivity, strength). How can I begin to embrace both masculine and feminine aspects of myself without judgment?

GUIDED MEDITATION:

Breathe and envision yourself standing at the confluence of two rivers. The river to your left is gray, tranquil and burbling softly. The river to your right is brown, ferocious, and gushing in a hurry. Neither is right; neither is wrong. Accept them both as they are. Notice how they come together and flow together just a few paces ahead of you.

When you feel comfortable, wade into the water at their joining point. Feel how you are the river of ferocity and the river of tranquility. Feel how you are the river of adventure and the river of acceptance. Feel how you encompass the light and the dark, the fierce and the tender, the solemn and the boisterous. You are already all things. Notice how both currents swirl around you, mingling, becoming one. Notice how, no matter your gender or sex, you contain both streams. You are all things. No side is good or bad, holy or sinful, right or wrong. We are just wading in the water and accepting the flow of life as it comes.

Envision yourself as whole, complete, and perfect with all expressions of yourself, no matter how they arise. With each breath, find yourself finding peace with the competing forces within you, finding your internal equilibrium and balance amidst the flow and tide.

MANTRA:

"All sides of me are welcomed home."

XLII. EMBRACE JOY AS LIFE'S PURPOSE

For so long, you've wandered through a dense woodland almost entirely devoid of human habitat. But just ahead of you, nestled deep in this forest of soul-stuff, is a stone village with thatched roofs and cobblestone streets. The inhabitants of this little township have streamers hung between eaves, carts filled with baked goods, and celebration bells ringing through the streets. We've come upon the Canton of Joy—a place where souls who remember their purpose for incarnating can come to dwell.

You step between the outermost buildings, and the sounds of lutes and lyres make your feet dance a jig. Your spirit feels lighter, soaring even. People fill these narrow streets, laughing and cavorting. Their eyes and souls are alight with delight in living—they are joyous in their celebration of this day. You find that you are not the only one dancing; plenty of others have shed their inhibitions and frolic merrily, circling the town square arm-in-arm. Others are picking up their instruments and joining in on the songs; a fiddle adds its sharp chords and a hammered dulcimer offers its dulcet tones. A steel handpan supplies a percussive slap.

A woman passes you a handmade paper lantern with a lit flame within. She encourages you to make a wish and then set it free into the twilight sky. You close your eyes and breathe deeply—from the depths of your heart, a prayer arises: *Let me feel this joy throughout my days, wherever I may go.* You release it, and it floats skyward with dozens of others—wishes traveling off to the heavens. By your side, a dog barks happily. You reach down and scratch its ears; dogs are such joyful beings, you realize. They want so little but offer so much happiness. Perhaps you should drive to be like a Labrador retriever more often.

As you continue through the festival, you feel love, joy, and gratitude radiating off every person you pass. Each individual is brimming with the realization that this life is a gift and should be enthusiastically celebrated. Life is the festival—if we choose to see it that way. These people have figured out the puzzle; joy is our reason for being here. And each day brings something worth celebrating.

One of the questions that has haunted philosophers over the past many centuries is: what is our reason for being alive? What is the meaning of our existence? Answers to this query have been debated by mystics, religious figures, scientists, alchemists, and spiritual seekers across ages. But what if the answer were something quite simple? What if the reason we are here is simply for the joy of it?

Pause for a moment and consider this proposition. If, as the cosmic Oversoul, you chose to take physical form, to live, breathe, and feel...why? Why would you put yourself through the hassle? Could it be as simple as wanting to experience the joy of being alive? To momentarily give up all your unlimited power and experience what it would be like to live for a finite span of time? And, during those years, experience the rushes of ecstasy, the quiet moments of peace, the thrill of overcoming obstacles? Even the moments of confusion? Could it be possible that you wanted to feel all of it?

Philosopher Alan Watts proposed this very idea by sharing what he called the "dream machine" hypothesis. He invited people to posit: if you went to bed each night where you were allowed to dream yourself into any life you wished to experience for what felt like seventy-five years or more...what would you pick? Undoubtedly, you'd choose an existence where you got to experience every form of pleasure—you'd choose to be a beloved king, rockstar, famous artist, or talented athlete. When you woke up in the morning, you'd say, "Wow! Wasn't that fun?" And then, that next night, you'd probably pick something quite similar.

But after several nights of having these luxurious and comfortable lives, you might say, "Let's have a surprise. Let's have a dream which isn't under my control. I want something to happen to me without knowing what it's going to be." And after you woke up from that more chaotic life, you'd think, "That was a close shave, wasn't it? What an adventure, though!" And so, you'd go on dreaming lives that became riskier and risker, realizing that there were no inherently good or bad, right or wrong lives to live—because it is all a dream—and when you come out of it, you can laugh and reflect back on the experience from a safe distance. Eventually, you would dream the exact life you're having right

XLII. EMBRACE JOY AS LIFE'S PURPOSE

now...because this particular life is one amongst the infinite options that could be dreamt of when you went to bed.

From this perspective, all lives are lived for the joy and the adventure of it—the highs and lows, the ups and downs. Aren't the best adventures the ones with some hardships and strife? Aren't they the ones you barely make it through, but when you do, you laugh and say, "Let's do that again?"

You came here for the joy of it. You incarnated into this body, these circumstances, and this world for the experience—influenced, of course, by the choices in your previous lives, your "karma." By seeing the effects of your previous actions manifest in the life you have today, it teaches you about what really matters: how giving love begets more love, how causing pain hurts yourself most of all. If you study it from a level of removal from your current sensations of suffering, you can see that life is arranging itself for you to learn and grow and —ultimately—experience profound joy.

This physical universe is a playground for the soul. Anything you want to explore, you can—the possibilities are infinite. If you wish to create, travel, love, or simply be, the choice is yours. This world is your soul's dream—you have manifested this reality via your intentions and past decisions.

It's not just Alan Watts who holds this perspective—countless spiritual traditions argue that this physical realm is the manifestation of mental energy and that all souls are incarnations of divine consciousness who purposefully chose to forget their cosmic power so they could fully go on the adventure of mortal life. This world is an expression of your cosmic Oversoul choosing to live the life you have right now so it could experience the thrill of it.

When we get caught up in our limited, mortal vantages of life, everything takes on a gravitas, a seriousness. We feel weighted down by responsibilities and social expectations. We are unable to see that it was the pursuit of joy that brought us here in the first place. But when we reconnect with this higher-level perspective, we reconnect with the joy that is available to us. We chose this life for the joy of it. When we remember that, everything can shift. Yes, of course life brings challenges, but from the vantage of the Oversoul, these obstacles are just part of the grand adventure.

In the yogic tradition of India, *Ananda*—or bliss—is considered one of the most fundamental aspects of our soul, alongside truth and awareness. We can realize that joy is our true nature...once we get past the layers of obscurations that keep us from seeing who we really are (the divine incarnate). Taoism says similarly—that when we align ourselves with the *Tao*, joy flows naturally as part of our existence. Even the Christian mystic Meister Eckhart said, "God laughs and plays." Numerous spiritual traditions recognize this truth regarding joy as our purpose.

If you had met me several years ago, when I was a "serious spiritual seeker" living in an ashram, you would have found that I didn't hold joy in very high regard. I considered it a frivolous, fleeting thing that wasn't worth consideration. No, I aspired toward something more weighty and profound: enlightenment and liberation. The pursuit of joy was a lower goal for less serious aspirants. Fortunately, I've become less rigid and onerous in the intervening years. I've lightened up and learned that joy is not some flippant notion for people who do not take their spiritual lives seriously—it is essential. A good rule of thumb: if you want to know how well someone's spiritual practice is working for them, look for the lightness, tranquility, and joy with which they live. If they are heavy, angry, fearful, judgmental, or generally dour...then their path isn't enlivening their soul. Authentic and deep spirituality should make a person increasingly more ebullient, joy-filled, and easygoing. Measure someone's spiritual attainment by the graciousness, ease, and good humor with which they live.

So, this is your invitation to throw off the heaviness. Let go of the notion that life needs to be serious or hard. Surrender the idea that you must earn your joy. Joy is already yours—you just have to accept its presence. Come, dance with me. Laugh deeply from your belly. Love with wild abandon. See life as your festival, your playground, and your adventure.

You came here for the joy of it. Joy is your birthright.

RITUAL:

For one week, each morning, ask yourself, "What is one thing that would bring me joy today?" Commit to doing at least one small act each day that fills your heart with happiness, whether it's dancing, enjoying a favorite meal, spending time in nature, or connecting with a loved one. At the end of the week, take a few moments to reflect on how these joyful practices have impacted your mindset and well-being. Let this habit remind you that joy is always within reach.

JOURNAL PROMPTS:

- When was the last time I felt pure, unadulterated joy? What can I do to cultivate more of those moments in my everyday life?

XLII. EMBRACE JOY AS LIFE'S PURPOSE

- Reflect on the role joy has played in my personal journey. How has the pursuit of joy influenced my decisions, and what does joy mean to me as a life purpose?

GUIDED MEDITATION:

Breathe deep and allow yourself to sink within. Imagine yourself standing on the edge of a mystical, magical fair. Sparkles and orbs of light float about. Creatures of all different kinds move through the space: intelligent foxes, bipedal bears, well-manicured unicorns. Street vendors shout, hawking their wares, their potions, their talismans.

Enter the fair and feel the pulsing of nearby drums and fiddles moving through your body. Feel how electric and alive you are becoming. Allow your gaze to take in the sights and delight in all the novelties, wonderment, and awe-inspiring happenings. Smile at the absurdity of all of this—how could something this outrageous even exist? But then...why shouldn't it? Why cannot a mystical fair of assorted creatures exist here in your mind?

Delight in its silliness—and realize how sacred the joy that it sparks inside you is. Life doesn't need to be so serious; it can be playful, whimsical, color-filled, and sparkle-laden. It can be absurd, wondrous, and magical. Realize how joy is one of the reasons you are here—to enjoy this life. Reclaim your joy. Allow yourself to take in the sights, sounds, and smells...and relish it all. Enjoy being here now.

Let go of any feelings of self-consciousness or needing to be more solemn or sincere. Frolic amidst the frivolity and outrageousness. Life is meant to be savored and enjoyed. You are here to experience the wonders of existence. Take a few moments to bask in this realization. You are allowed to seek joy, to live in it fully, and to let it guide you in this life. Stay with this feeling for as long as you need, knowing that joy is always accessible to you.

MANTRA:

"Joy is the reason I am here."

XLIII. SEE WITH CHILD EYES

You settle into the tall grasses and inhale the scent deeply into your lungs. Like a range of colors on a painter's palate, the variety of scents stimulates something at your core. There is so much there to observe, so much that you usually miss.

Your eyes trace the contours of the stalks of grass, the leaves on the flowering bushes, and the insects climbing them. You pay close attention to a solitary ladybug traversing a magnolia blossom's breadth. Its shiny, dome-shaped body, its evenly dispersed arrangement of dark spots. Its white markings on its head look like large eyes. You watch it move with a type of grace you never noticed before. For some reason, this experience delights you, and you giggle. The forest around you takes on new depth, new complexity as you begin to see the things your eyes previously glossed over. The world becomes vibrant and magnificent—it truly feels like a magical place.

Steeped in awe, stand and walk forward on the path, fully alert to all the majesty surrounding you. You observe the owls hooting from the dark hollows of trees; you witness the unfurling of fern tips. You listen for the sparrows calling to one another in complex patterns. You've stepped into a realm where even the simplest things pulse with a quiet magnificence. The color of the leaves feels more vivid; the smell of the wild roses is almost intoxicating. Magic is all around you, woven into the fabric of existence and just waiting to be noticed. And, for the first time in what feels like forever, you actually see it. You feel that wonderment deep within your bones, in the beating of your heart.

When we were children, we observed the world around us with awe. Everything we encountered felt enchanted and nuanced—things to be studied deeply, seen from every angle, and profoundly understood. Our walks were filled with possibilities, wonderment, and potential for magic. Every corner we turned held the possibility of rich discovery. The whole world felt alive and fascinating, from the smallest pebble to the tallest tree.

As we aged, however, the childlike wonder faded. The world took on a sense of familiarity. We passed through our haunts unseeing the subtle changes and nuance. Eventually, the potential for magic disappeared. Everything began to feel routine and blasé. After all, we have more important things to draw our focus; we became serious people with important responsibilities. The daily demands of life slowly dull our senses, and the world that once felt extraordinary becomes quite plain.

Take a moment to consider: how often do you move through your day on autopilot? How frequently do you wind up at your destination without recollecting how you got there? When was the last time you purposefully chose to notice your surroundings and pay attention to what is there—rather than planning your next few hours in your head, replying to messages, or daydreaming? How often do we progress through not just physical landscapes but time itself—weeks, months, seasons—without really noticing much of it?

Living this way causes the vibrant, vital energy that is our life-force to slip through our fingers unnoticed. Little by little, we forsake that which gives life meaning and joy—choosing instead to focus on meetings, to-do lists, rehashing old conversations, or planning tomorrows. But what if we could return to this wonderment? What if we could pause, breathe, and see the world again freshly with childlike eyes?

The world's magic didn't go away; we just stopped noticing. We stopped listening to the buzzing of honeybees flitting from blossom to blossom. We ceased looking for the dew-covered geometric patterns of spider webs in the morning light. We have forgotten to witness the miracle of a dandelion pushing itself up through a crack in a concrete sidewalk, something that could be likened to a Herculean effort. The miracles are still there; we just have to choose to look outward and see them.

Inviting yourself to slow down and witness the world with awe is a tremendous gift. To see beauty in the mundane, the marvelous in the ordinary, is a supreme and ever-life-giving ability. To truly observe that bird, leaf, or stretch of sky is to bear witness to how much life is around you. You begin to see the beautiful and complex interweaving between people, places, and things. Like the mycelial matrix of fungi running beneath the surface of the land on which you stand, there is a web of connection between you and everything else that exists.

XLIII. SEE WITH CHILD EYES

It pulses in silvery, ephemeral strands, akin to hypha, when you train your eyes to notice. These are the fibers of magic you can touch at any moment, anywhere.

Notice the intricate veins on a leaf—and see how they replicate the tree's overall shape. The patterns of the branches reaching from the trunk into the sky mirror the branching of your veins and arteries running through your limbs. That acorn on the ground contains the full potential for the mighty oak that soars above you—isn't that amazing? That massive, ancient tree can fit within a seed roughly the same size as the first joint on your thumb.

Observe the blooming of the dahlia—can you count the dozens or hundreds of petals? Think of how it blossomed from a tiny bud to a flower the size of a dinner plate. It grows here, inviting pollinators to come and transmuting sunshine into food before it will eventually wither and drop to the ground in graceful surrender to the earth. Notice the clouds passing overhead and the ever-changing shapes that they make. They seem alive—and perhaps they are, for what defines sentience anyway? Many cultures believe that weather patterns, landforms, and bodies of water contain their own awareness—that spirit dwells in these things, too.

This view of seeing the world as alive, magical, and conscious is sometimes called animism. This is a belief system where all things have a spiritual essence and are animated with agency and free will. That the world around us is alive in a very real way—and we can interact with that sentience through our attention, intentions, prayers, and actions. It is an extrapolation of the notion that if everything is created from the same Oversoul, then everything is a manifestation of God incarnate. All things have the capacity for awareness and are deserving of respect and kind attention.

By adopting a vantage where we see each thing before us with awe and wonderment, not only are we honoring the divine within all things, but we are also enriching our experience of being on this globe. By choosing to see with childlike eyes, the world becomes more vibrant, meaning-filled, and endearing. By respecting the sentience and the potential for spirit within all things, it makes us feel less disconnected and alone on our journeys—for life, love, and support are surrounding us wherever our feet take us. It encourages us to live with curiosity and rediscover the joy of questioning how the world operates.

Children ask "why" about everything. Why is the sky blue? Why do flowers bloom in the spring? Why do birds migrate? They become curious about the world and thereby engage with it deeply. They become invested in not just moving through life but touching it, interacting with it. As adults, we usually stop asking these questions and just take things for granted. But what if we started asking again?

Notice the pencil on your desk—do you realize how amazing and awe-inspiring it is to have something as simple as this within arm's reach? Think of all the countless hands its components had to pass through before it could be fabricated and delivered to you. Tens of thousands of people were involved in its crafting—from the miners who dug up the metal that would come to form the band that holds the eraser (which then needed to be refined and shaped) to the machine operators who cut the trees and milled the wood. Chemists had to generate and manufacture the synthetic components that created the eraser. Then, it all had to be assembled, packaged, shipped, and distributed. Its very existence is an engineering and manufacturing marvel! When was the last time you paused to appreciate it in depth?

Imagine something even more complex—like the cell phone in your pocket. We often focus on what it can do for us, but do you appreciate the amount of mind-boggling innovations, experimentations, and mechanical wizardry that went into forming something so complex? Its various parts require worldwide sourcing of materials and labor to bring it to fruition. It's so complex and sophisticated that even a team of a thousand diligent workers could not create one on their own.

When was the last time you paused to marvel at the load-bearing ability of the glass-paneled skyscrapers towering overhead? Or how about the global supply chains that allow you to eat out at your favorite restaurant? Even a simple city sidewalk requires stone from various quarries ground into pebbles and sand shipped from distant places. How many hands touched these raw materials before they were mixed, poured, sculpted, and finally set by skilled laborers? When you stop to think about it, even the most ordinary things we take for granted embody an awe-inspiring level of human ingenuity and cooperation. Creating something as seemingly simple as a sidewalk would be almost impossible without modern tools and supply chains for a single person.

This ability to reconnect with wonder is a profound spiritual practice. It teaches us that this life isn't something just to be rushed through while pursuing our goals but something to be savored and deeply experienced. It encourages us to slow down, feel more, and bear witness to the profundity that exists in this world. There is so much to marvel at if we simply train our eyes.

So, cultivate your sense of childlike curiosity. Learn to see the world not as just an assemblage of non-sentient stuff but as a living, breathing ecosystem of interconnection. Strive to experience awe in each landscape you pass through, each path you trod. Ask yourself: What magic will I uncover today? Drink in the beauty that is always waiting to be noticed. Marvel at the immense honor of living in such a complex and sophisticated society that provides us these innovations to enjoy. And, most importantly, learn to open your eyes to truly see what wondrous sights are perpetually before you.

XLIII. SEE WITH CHILD EYES

RITUAL:

Take an "awe walk" with the intention of seeing the world through fresh, child-like eyes. As you walk, pay close attention to the small details around you—the colors, shapes, sounds, and textures. Reflect not only on the beauty of nature or human-made creations but also on the energy, effort, and resources that brought them into being. If you notice a tree, consider the years it took for it to grow to its full height and the intricate ecosystems it supports. When you pass a building, reflect on the hands that built it and the global resources that contributed to its materials.

JOURNAL PROMPTS:

- What parts of my life or surroundings have I become numb to or taken for granted? How can I begin to see the world with fresh eyes, as if experiencing everything for the first time?
- Reflect on a time when I saw something familiar in a new light. How did that shift in perspective bring a sense of wonder, and how can I invite more of those moments into my life?

GUIDED MEDITATION:

Close your eyes and imagine a time when the world was sparkling and new. Imagine the colors bolder, the light crisper. Reenter a time before becoming jaded, before becoming blasé, before feeling like you've seen it all before. With these fresh, childlike eyes, perceive the world around you — either literally or in your imagination. Either way, the goal is to simply be present. To see what you see and feel what you feel.

Try to move into a state of experiencing everything for the first time. Allow everything before you to become wondrous. Marvel at the shapes, the curves, the edges, the colors. Notice the textures and the subtle details that you've overlooked before. Drink in this existence as someone who can truly and deeply appreciate it. Feel as if the world is revealing its hidden beauty just for you.

Stay in this state of wonder, allowing yourself to feel a deep appreciation for the simple miracles of life. Linger here with this vision for as long as you'd like.

MANTRA:

"I dwell in awe and wonderment."

XLIV. HOLD PARADOXICAL TRUTHS

You've stepped out on a causeway so narrow that it feels less of a bridge and more of a tightrope. Nonetheless, you gather your courage and bravely step forward, one foot before the other. Striving not to look down into the murky water below, you train your gaze to the approaching cliff face. Behind you, the land was bathed in sunlight; ahead, it is covered in shadow. Halfway across now, you feel as if you were suspended verily between light and dark, past and future, safety and danger.

As the path approaches its narrowest section, you extend your arms out and envision a weight in each hand; you know about counterweights and balance. You are aware of how carrying a pole with a heavy mass on either end keeps you better centered. Stepping forward, pressing your toes and then your heel mindfully into the stone, you inch along. Your arms held in a T-shape waver, but you never fall.

As you near the far side, a thought strikes you…this journey has been like a metaphor for living. When we explore polarity, when we hold opposing and often paradoxical truths, we are able to find balance in the center. If we cling to one side or the other, we tip over. But by remaining in the middle, we can safely and efficaciously move forward in the direction of our goals.

You find yourself on solid footing, the causeway cleared, and you lower your arms. Taking a deep breath, you move away from the ledge, carrying with you what you just learned.

Sometime in my early thirties, I had a realization that would go on to become one of the guiding principles of my life: If something is true, often too is its opposite. You can be weak and also strong. You can be powerful, the helmsman of your destiny and, simultaneously, be powerless, blown haphazardly by the whims of fate. A person could be both good and bad, saintly and sinful, intelligent and naive. Just because two ideas are in opposition, they do not necessarily cancel one another out. Some people might think that only one could exist—that one is the truer view—but it's not so.

Imagine, for example, that a politician could genuinely care about their constituency and want to enact legislation for their betterment, that they have noble aspirations. At the same time, they may be beholden to special interests, realize the complexity of political machinations, and may have to be strategic around what bills they support for consideration. Some people might write this person off as corrupt or double-dealing (and from a certain vantage, they wouldn't be wrong), but others might see their good hearts and view them as virtuous (which, again, from a specific point of view, could also be correct). This is not an either/or situation (though social media would undoubtedly lambast it as such...our contemporary culture is so quick to vilify individuals); it's a both/and. The reality is nuanced and complex. And, in order to see it fairly, we have to see both views as having merit, though they seem contradictory.

This is why I rarely express personal opinions on current world events. Many situations facing foreign affairs, human behavior, and intrapersonal negotiations are so fraught and so layered. Both sides in conflicts have staunch perspectives and opinions with merit. Very often, were we to fully understand each side's point of view, we could agree that there is at least some correctness in their beliefs. And yet, in believing those views, they come into direct contradiction with those of their adversary—whose views we can also agree have justification. It rarely is "either/or"—it is typically more a "both/and" situation. Yes, each side has views that bear weight and deserve consideration.

One of my favorite contradictory truths to consider is that of destiny, free will, and personal agency. It is true that people have agency over their actions; they can set intentions to manifest the lives they desire. They are the helmsmen steering the ship of their fate. Yet, at the same time, it's likewise true that forces much larger than any person—history, nature, cultural currents—shape a person's life in ways that cannot be combatted or sometimes even mitigated. What happens will happen, and all we can do is try to make minor course corrections to steer the boat through the storm.

This idea is beautifully encapsulated in the classic phrase: "Does the man make the times, or the times make the man?" Are we purveyors of fate, or does destiny own us? Perhaps, indeed, both are true. We have control over our lives—simultaneously, we have no control and merely do the best we can.

This is antithetical to how many people navigate the world today. Many of us

XLIV. HOLD PARADOXICAL TRUTHS

are taught to believe that there is a right and a wrong answer. We are asked to boil complex issues down to black versus white, good versus bad, us versus them. We are trained to take sides, believe in absolute truths, and dig into our perspectives like an intransigent mule. We are schooled in defending our viewpoints and rejecting the validity of our opposition's. This rigid dualism inhibits our ability to grow, to see the world with nuance, and to understand complexity.

But what if we learned to hold paradox? What if we could embrace both sides of an argument? What if we could see that opposing arguments are not "wrong" or "bad" but merely an alternative point of view that can coexist? Take, for example, the parable of the five blind men touching an elephant and trying to describe its totality based on what he feels:

One blind man holds its ear and says, "An elephant is like a fan blowing in a breeze."

The second grabs a leg and says, "No, an elephant is like a thick tree."

"No," says the third, holding the tail, "It's like a rope with a tassel on the end."

The fourth says, "No, it's like a snake and coils in all directions." He is grabbing the trunk.

The fifth, at the elephant's side, says, "No, he is like a brick wall. Solid and wide."

All of these perspectives are valid. They seem to contradict one another from each person's limited point of view, yet they are equally true.

Imagine how this could be applied to your own life. You could believe that your body is sacred and perfect just as it is while also believing that you have the freedom to modify and transform it according to your wishes. You could believe that honoring tradition is essential, that it connects with our ancestors and provides meaning. At the same time, you can agree that innovation is necessary and that change is a prerequisite for growth. You can believe that sex is a sacred, intimate act, while simultaneously embracing its joy and freedom when it's shared openly and without reservation.

This exploration invites you to explore in your own life where you feel rigid or dogmatic. Where have you found yourself insisting that there is only one right way? When have you held staunchly to your beliefs, confidently rooted in your own confirmation bias, despite seeing ample evidence to the contrary? When have you willingly stepped beyond your own encampment and genuinely considered how an opposing view can also be ultimately true? By exploring these questions, we begin to approach life with curiosity as opposed to judgment.

One of the great gifts I give myself is to genuinely ponder if what I think could be completely wrong. What if I am entirely mistaken? What if that antagonistic other person may be correct? By stepping into an opposing perspective, it allows me to grow my understanding of the nuance of a situation. It doesn't mean that I abandon my beliefs; I just consider the possibility that I might need to shift them, even if just slightly. The practice of holding paradox helps us grow more humble, wise, and compassionate in our interactions with others.

When we find comfort in the murk, when we find our ease within the paradoxes of life, we free ourselves from the crushing need for certainty. Often, in life, we long for the feeling of righteousness—that our beliefs are undeniably correct. There is tremendous comfort in certainty; it can feel intoxicating, almost impossible to give up. But it's better to be understanding than it is to be right. It's better to hold a broad and complex perspective than to maintain righteous indignation against the possibility of someone's opposing views being accurate. It is better to step into a place of openness where we allow things to be multifaceted and full of contradictions. In this space, we stop trying to simplify the beautiful pallet of life down to a few manageable shades—and, instead, embrace its gorgeous, clashing messiness.

This ability to hold simultaneous paradoxical truths is a sign of spiritual maturity. It means that we approach the world with more compassion, understanding that each person is doing their best with their limited information. Further, we can recognize that each person holds a piece of truth—their mistake is believing they hold the entirety. This practice allows us to engage with those who think differently from us—approaching them with curiosity rather than judgment, empathy rather than malice.

A practice I like to utilize is—when receiving information I disagree with—to assume I am wrong and the other person is correct. Whether in a critical feedback setting, an argument, or a debate...I just say, "Yes, okay, you're right." And then, I strive to follow their logic and see it entirely from their vantage. Sometimes that new information ends up being tremendously valuable. Being a married man who has to daily interact with my spouse, who occasionally has opposing views, this ability allows me to enter uncomfortable conversations with a goal of achieving an understanding that is mutually beneficial.

This universe exists because of opposing forces. Whether it be positive and negative poles on a magnet that allow an energized field to develop or high and low points on a mountain that enable gravity to let water flow downhill, it is the contrast between two things that spawns potential. Gravity is the polarity between mass and emptiness; electricity is the polarity of the buildup between positive and negative charges. We see this polarity expressed on a daily basis between light and dark, day and night, masculine and feminine, strength and vulnerability, stillness and movement. These opposites are not enemies but essential parts of life's intricate design. They create the dynamic tension that is

XLIV. HOLD PARADOXICAL TRUTHS

energetic potential. No rivers would flow if all land was at sea level—we need high and low points to create that kinetic potential. Life unfolds through the dance of opposites, through contrast and tension.

This concept of polarity is present in many spiritual traditions. Whether it's in the creation of a universe via the operation of energy into masculine and feminine, the two churning the oceans of existence with their lovemaking—or matter vs antimatter spawning the galaxy in which we reside—polar opposites sparked life. This is why the mythos around good and evil are so prevalent within religious texts; it demonstrates this natural dichotomy between the forces that pulled the universe into being.

But we, dear traveler, are on the path of reunification. We are moving beyond right and wrong, good and bad, and instead strive to see everything as whole. All things are cosmic energy made manifest in physical form; everything in existence is an aspect of the divine Oversoul made material. There is no positive or negative, there is no light or dark. There simply is. In this non-dualist point of view, everything is God. And, from this vantage, we can embrace all sides and any perspective, for that, too, is divine. That, too, is holy.

As you reflect on this, imagine yourself again on the narrow bridge, holding in one hand an orb of light and in the other an orb of darkness. Neither is good—neither is bad. They are simply counterbalances for one another. By holding and extending both to your sides, you remain centered and steady as you traverse the narrow path. You find your center not by reacting to any perspective but by embracing all. In this delicate tightrope walk, you find your strength.

So, embrace paradox. See all sides as having merit. Enjoy the messiness in contradictory opposites. And, most importantly, develop a sense of humor around all of it. There is no need to become overly serious in maintaining any one vantage; if something is true, so, then, is its foil. This means we can all be a little freer with ourselves, knowing that this is just a great game. Relax. Have fun. Discover your own path toward peace and wisdom by simply saying "yes" and enjoying the view from all sides.

RITUAL:

Invite a friend or family member over for a friendly debate and choose a topic that matters deeply to you. The catch is, you must take the side opposite of what you truly believe. Strive to fully embody the opposing viewpoint. Afterward, reflect on what you learned from seeing the issue from another perspective. How did it feel to challenge your own beliefs? How did it feel to let go of certainty and welcome a more expansive understanding?

JOURNAL PROMPTS:

- When have I encountered two opposing truths that both felt valid? How did I navigate the tension between them, and what did I learn about holding space for contradictions in my life?
- Reflect on a time when embracing paradox helped me grow. How can I become more comfortable with uncertainty and the coexistence of multiple truths?

GUIDED MEDITATION:

Take a deep breath and feel yourself sink inward. Remind yourself that there is nowhere to go and nothing to be. Accept yourself fully as you are here. As you breathe deeper and relax, remind yourself that there is seldom anything in life that is inherently right or wrong. Something that feels good at the moment can end up being a source of regret in the future. Conversely, something that feels challenging right now can end up being a source of pride or joy in retrospect. We can hold multiple emotions and multiple perspectives at the same time.

Think of something that you've encountered recently that you felt either extremely positive or negative about—but someone else felt the total opposite. Can you think of an example? Maybe it made you happy, but another person was miserable—or vice versa? Two things can be true at once. Can you think of a time, perhaps, when you were simultaneously brave and also cowardly, wise but also foolish?

What if you started giving yourself leniency to be multiple things at once? What if we see overlapping truths not as contradictory but as layered? What if we, our loved ones, or the situations in which we find ourselves could be multidimensional and hold conflicting vantages as sacred? What if many things could be true at once? Begin to see things less in opposing shades and instead as a kaleidoscope of colors. See the nuance. See the beautiful contradictions. Dwell on these ideas for as long as it feels comfortable.

MANTRA:

"I peacefully hold conflicting truths."

XLV. BE GRATEFUL...FOR EVERYTHING

The rainstorm came in from nowhere. The sky was blue and sunny, and then, with no notice, it turned to clouds of roiling silver and pelted you with rain from all directions. Sheets of rain, buckets of it. You laugh because you couldn't be more wet than had you jumped into the nearby ravine. Every inch of you, every cranny, is soaked. But, to your surprise, you don't mind. In fact, you feel delighted. The air is warm, and there is something enchanting about an unexpected downpour.

With a whimsical lightness in your step, you begin to dance. "*Let the storms come!*" you shout to the heavens. This is no inconvenience; getting caught in a deluge might make another person miserable, but not you. For you have uncovered a secret to a joy-filled life: no matter what comes, you remain thankful. No matter how intense the storms, you say, "I am grateful for the rain!" You splash through the puddles like a child newly discovering precipitation. This, too, is a gift. As you laugh and spin, the raindrops glow with an inner light. The world around you brightens—not because the storm passes, but because you've embraced it.

When you choose to be grateful for everything that comes into your life, your whole existence becomes a magical experience laden with blessings. Enacting gratitude is one of the most powerful spiritual tools at your disposal—and it begins with simply expressing thanks for whatever comes. Whether pleasurable or painful, sought after or long avoided—can you reframe it in your mind as being a gift? Even if you don't know why you're expressing gratitude, can you just do so and examine what comes of it?

Start in the morning, when you wake up. Getting out of bed is a gift; many on this planet won't be so lucky. Appreciate that you have clean air to breathe, a warm bed in which to sleep, and shelter that keeps you safe while you slumber. As you go into the bathroom, marvel at the wonders of turning on artificial illumination with the flip of a switch. Be thankful that you get to use the toilet in the comfort of an indoor, climate-controlled setting. Stop and appreciate the marvel of indoor plumbing—you can access hot and cold running water on demand! That is something even many of the wealthiest people in history could not lay claim to possessing.

You likely have food to eat, clean water to drink, probably even coffee or tea flown in from some exotic destination across the globe. Even something so easily taken for granted as your physical body—you can move, stretch, reach, and walk around. How amazing is that! Consider how few humans in the course of human history have been as blessed as you are today. No matter your income level, you are one of the most well-fed, technologically sophisticated, educated, and wealthy people when taken in perspective of the last few thousand years.

The very fact that you were born at all is a miracle. In many places and times, childbirth was perilous and surviving into adolescence was hardly preordained. Just two hundred years ago, in the United States, nearly half of all children would perish before their fifth birthday. Think how unheard of that is now; how blessed we are to live at such healthy times. You were likely given vaccines and medical care to protect you from diseases that once claimed millions of lives. You were likely fed food designed specifically for your developing body. You likely received an education and were free to play and explore rather than spend your early years working in fields or factories like many children.

Think of the fact that you have likely traveled or lived beyond the boundaries of the town into which you were born—something rare in human history. You might even have access to a car or public transit; you could hop on a jet and visit nearly any place on the globe. Even a hundred years ago, that would have been unfathomable. You have been given so much that your ancestors would only have been able to envision in their most farfetched dreams. So, how often are you expressing gratitude for these things? Or, do you find that you fall into the trap that many of us do and take them for granted?

It's become too familiar of behavior in our society to bemoan and complain about things. No matter how blessed and abundant their life may objectively be, people have the remarkable ability to find fault and nitpick at what they wish were better. The train is too slow, the government is inefficient, the weather is too hot or cold. The complaints are endless, and people focus on what they lack rather than what they have. They count their inconveniences rather than their blessings. We all have a daily choice: to see life as a blessing or a burden. We get

XLV. BE GRATEFUL...FOR EVERYTHING

to decide if what happens to us is a gift or an ordeal. Our vantage is often the only difference between seeing our lives as harrowing journeys or bold adventures. And, notice, it truly is a choice. I can choose to enact gratitude, I can choose to offer thanks, or I can default to just complaining.

Our minds have been engineered over millions of years of breeding to look for faults. When we were hunters and gatherers, paying attention to potentially life-threatening dangers was critical. We needed to keep vigilant and focus on what could possibly go wrong. But, in today's world of pre-ground coffee, smartphones, and instant downloads, we seldom have to prepare for the worst. Instead, we must strive to reprogram our minds to focus on what is good and beautiful, choosing to see the gifts that have befallen us. Every moment and each experience can either be cherished or endured—the difference is your mindset.

Please, don't mistake this outlook as ignoring the very real injustices and hardships that exist in the world. For many people, oppression, inequality, and suffering are daily occurrences. We should lovingly strive to address these issues with compassion and action. There are real wounds that need healing, real systems that need reforming. The important thing, however, is to keep at the forefront of our minds that, while we work toward change, we must also cultivate gratitude for the good things that do exist. For if we succumb to the heaviness of the suffering and view that as our totality, then that heaviness will become our truth.

All we have control over is our perspective—the same instance can be viewed positively or negatively depending on who is looking. By adopting a mindset of gratitude, positivity radiates from our hearts and ripples of kindness spread into the world around us. Gratitude is a choice; no one's life is so humble that they cannot find something to be grateful for. Just as, unfortunately, no one's life is so lush that they cannot find something to complain about. The choice is ours.

Gratitude, when practiced deeply and in this way, becomes more than just a thankfulness for life's good things—it becomes an appreciation of everything. Yes, even the difficult and painful experiences. Being able to say "thank you" for life's uncomfortable offerings is a gateway toward true growth.

When you are able to thank life for everything it brings—both the pleasurable and painful—you begin to see every experience as a lesson. Every hardship becomes an opportunity for growth rather than a travail to endure. Every setback becomes a blessing in disguise. Spiritual writer Elizabeth Lesser wrote, "When you feel yourself breaking down, may you break open instead. May every experience in life be a door that opens your heart, expands your understanding, and leads you to freedom."

Practice, in your heart, saying "thank you" to the person who insults you—

they are teaching you about resilience and grace. Express gratitude for that injury that forces you to slow down, rest, and reset. Give thanks for that technology issue that is disrupting your workflow, reminding you that even important things aren't as crucial as you might think. This type of radical gratitude is a pathway to true spiritual liberation.

The author Haruki Murakami said, "Pain is inevitable, but suffering is optional." Pain is an unavoidable part of living on this planet; no matter how diligently you strive, you will never avoid it. The suffering, however, is a choice. You can choose to be bogged down by it, allow it to consume your reality, or you can work with it. Move through it. Shift it in some way. How we respond to the pain is what makes the difference. By seeing everything as a blessing, especially the difficult moments, we can often transcend the suffering that frequently accompanies hardships.

Gratitude also pulls you into the present moment. When you're grateful, you are no longer trapped in anxieties about the future or regrets over the past. Gratitude anchors you in the now, permitting you to appreciate the small, sacred moments of everyday life. The way the sunlight falls through your window, the feel of warmth emanating from your teacup into your hands, the laughter of a friend—these are moments worthy of reverence.

To watch a forest is to experience gratitude in action. When you see green leaves reaching for the sun, you feel the gratitude shining off them as they thank the solar light for its gift of sustenance. When those same leaves turn brown and fall to the earth, the woodland critters give thanks for new spaces in which to build their homes. When the leaves decay and return to the soil, the roots give thanks for the nutrients and insulation the former leaves provided.

The cycles of life also remind us that everything is temporary—and part of what makes something worth appreciating is knowing that it, too, is fleeting. The fact that we only have a set number of minutes, days, or years with an object, person, or experience allows us to appreciate it more via the temporality of its presence in our lives. No matter how wonderful or terrible, it will vanish at some point—leaving us only with the memories of how it made us feel. If our memories are ones of gratefulness, how much richer does our life become? Let us always hold front and center in our hearts gratitude for the people who walked the path with us, the experiences that made us laugh or wail, and the lessons that taught us how to become the person we are growing into.

Let us also remember that what brings us pleasure may later bring us pain—and vice versa. There's an old story about a man and his farm. One day, his fence breaks, and his horses escape.

The neighbor next door says, "Oh, what a shame!"

XLV. BE GRATEFUL...FOR EVERYTHING

The farmer says, "We'll see."

The next day, his son finds the horses grazing with a group of wild stallions. They lasso the creatures and bring them home to add to their herd. The neighbor rejoices, "Oh, what a blessing!"

The farmer says, "We'll see."

The following day, his son breaks his leg, trying to tame one of the new stallions. The neighbor again cries, "Oh, what a shame!"

The farmer says, "We'll see."

That week, the nation's army marches through and conscripts all the young men. The farmer's son is left behind because of his broken bones. The neighbor again says, "Oh, what a blessing!"

Again, the farmer says, "We'll see."

And so the story continues...

What truly is "bad" or "good" once enough time has passed? That which initially caused great distress might have been a tremendous blessing disguised. If we simply remain grateful, it allows us to let the experiences evolve and change in the way they ought to, teaching us what we need to learn and providing the lessons we need to grow.

Gratitude reshapes your heart. It makes you more expansive, filling the space around you with loving compassion. It isn't just a feeling or state of being—it's a practice. It is something you can choose to enact each and every day. When you live in a state of appreciation, others are drawn to your light. So, be grateful for...everything. For the sun and the rain. For the light and the dark. For the blessings and the challenges.

Appreciate both the moments of bliss and heartache that stumble into your life. For life, in all her complexity, is a gift. When you embrace it all with gratitude, the world becomes more magical than you could have imagined. You'll notice moments of serendipity and synchronicities blossoming around you. Impossible feats will become everyday occurrences because you are now realigning life; you are inviting more and more things to come into it that reinforce those feelings of gratitude. You step into the great flow, and spirit responds by flooding your existence with more things that will make you feel grateful.

So, go run barefoot in the storm. Splash in the puddles and give thanks. When you can find gratitude for everything, you have uncovered the secret: to live is to be blessed. And for that, we give thanks.

RITUAL:

For one month, each night before bed, take a few moments to write down three things that brought you joy, pleasure, or a sense of ease—things you are deeply grateful for. Then, name three challenges or difficulties that you faced and express gratitude for the wisdom, lessons, or growth they are teaching you. Reflect weekly on how this practice affects your attitude toward daily life.

JOURNAL PROMPTS:

- What challenges in my life have ultimately turned out to be blessings in disguise? How can I express gratitude for both the joys and the difficulties I've faced?
- Reflect on a time when practicing gratitude shifted my mindset or transformed a situation. How can I bring more gratitude into my daily life, even when things are hard?

GUIDED MEDITATION:

Close your eyes and breathe deeply. When you are ready, bring to mind something wonderful that elicits joy from you. It could be a recent work opportunity, a moment with a loved one, or perhaps kindness from a stranger. Feel the emotions here and allow the sensation of gratitude to well up in your heart. Feel gratitude pulsing through you and shining out of your sternum. Take a few breaths to really hold this sensation.

Then, let this memory go and invite a new recollection. This time, imagine something that was a bit challenging for you. Perhaps it was a disagreement at work, a rude moment with a stranger in a parking lot, or a disappointment relating to a goal you were working toward. Allow yourself to feel the discomfort, but then realize how something is possible to be observed even in the discomfort. Perhaps there was a valuable lesson you began to learn, or maybe it redirected you away from what you thought you wanted and toward something more true. Perhaps it is even simply gratitude that you survived the moment.

Can you start to feel a sense of thankfulness for all things? Not just the good—but life in its entirety? Can you shift your vantage to be able to really think, "This too is a gift," even if it doesn't immediately feel that way? Each thing we encounter can be a blessing or a burden, a delight or a source of dismay, and truly, the main difference between the two is often our perspective.

How can we choose gratitude, even when it's not easy? Then, notice what

XLV. BE GRATEFUL...FOR EVERYTHING

happens in your body when you do this. Notice how you feel lighter and freer. Gratitude can transmute our heavy emotions into something lighter and freer. Dwell with this practice for as long as it is comfortable.

MANTRA:

"I am grateful for all things."

XLVI. LIVE WITH INTEGRITY

The forest was burned, scorched by the carelessness of others. Those who did not bother to care if their actions caused harm burnt this once-vibrant forest to the ground. You stand in the still-hazy landscape, planting a new sapling here. The ground is wet and fragrant from the storms that came to dampen the flames; it feels rich and ready to spawn new life. A faithful, devoted dog sits and watches you—he, too, understands the importance of offering a small action that may feel insignificant in the grand scheme but is meaningful to the sentient being experiencing it. Every word of kindness, each scratch behind the ears, and all the scraps of food given to him has mattered a great deal. For those actions of kindness, he has remained devoted to you. He cheers you on as you do this next small thing, planting a small tree amongst the decay. It may not be much, but you are doing your part to make the world the kind of place you know it has the potential to be.

Integrity itself is not some grand gesture but a quiet, steady commitment to live in alignment with your deepest values. It is, simply, to say what you mean and mean what you say. To make sure that your thoughts, words, and actions are congruent. It is akin to honesty and not speaking words that are untrue—but it's more than that. It's about living in alignment with your soul, bringing your values, actions, and words into congruency.

Integrity isn't an external code of conduct; it's an internal compass. It's living in such a way that what matters most to us is expressed in how we interact with the world. Yet, plenty of people do not live in such a way. Far too many are adept at lying—both to others and themselves. They make promises they never intend to keep. They erect facades incongruent with who they believe themselves to be; their exteriors do not reflect who they are within. "Fake it 'til you make it" is an axiom we've all heard, but what happens when we lose all sense of who we really are?

Integrity is about stripping away those layers of pretense and living in alignment with our vulnerable and raw truth. By saying things you don't mean or making promises with no intention of keeping them, you undermine trust in yourself. Your body becomes a place of distrust rather than a home—your physical form betrays you because it knows you will not follow through on what you tell it. "Oh, I will go to the gym tomorrow," but you never do. "I am going to start treating myself better," but you don't. Then, without that internal safety, you begin to project that doubt onto others. You become incredulous if anyone is worthy of trust. Your view of the world gets tinted with hostility and doubt.

To build integrity, start within. Regularly engage in an inner dialogue, a "self-audit" of sorts. Ask yourself: Are my thoughts, words, and actions aligned? Do my external behaviors match my internal beliefs? If I say that I will do something, do I almost always follow through? This regular checking in with yourself can help you pinpoint when you are acting with integrity versus not. Remember that this has nothing to do with societal standards or expectations—this is about you with yourself.

Various cultures have expressed this idea in different ways. In Japanese culture, the concept of *meiyo* (honor) is deeply tied to integrity, representing a person's unwavering commitment to their word and responsibility. First Nations teachings often emphasize living in harmony with the earth, where every action must be taken with the collective in mind. *Ubuntu* is an ancient African word meaning "I am because we are" or "humanity to others"—we are all connected. Though the expressions of integrity may differ, the essence remains the same: honoring one's truth and aligning words with actions is a value that transcends borders.

While making choices that disconnect you from your truth may feel easier at the moment, their weight accumulates over time. Just as one pebble added at a time to a backpack doesn't initially feel significant, their collective accumulated weight will eventually become unbearable. Living without integrity is akin to carrying around this heavy burden. This weight pulls you down and drains you of your energy. Living truthfully, however, lightens the load. Though it may feel terrifying to say that uncomfortable thing or offer honest feedback, the long-term result is much more favorable than the easier route of betraying your feelings and saying that "everything is fine." You become lighter, freer, able to move around the world with increased joy and vitality by living this way.

This journey with integrity also leads us to accept our imperfections. There

XLVI. LIVE WITH INTEGRITY

will be times when we fall short, when our actions do not align with the values we espouse. Integrity doesn't demand we never make mistakes; it just asks that we own them. Speak up and say, "I was wrong...how can I make this right?" It means putting in the effort to make amends. It demands that we do what we must to slowly restore the trust that has been broken. It's an act of acknowledgment and accountability. In doing so, we unveil our capacity for growth through the humility it takes to admit we've gone astray.

What is one action that you can do today to align you better with your deeper values? Could you fulfill a promise that you've been putting off? Perhaps you could let someone know how you were wrong? Maybe you just take time to journal and reflect on where you could be in better alignment with what really matters. Integrity is built one small choice at a time. As researcher and author Brené Brown says, trust is like a marble jar; you fill it one marble at a time. Shoving one giant marble into it won't work. You must be patient and fill the jar through small and deliberate actions.

So, too, must we reestablish trust in ourselves with one tiny gesture after another. Making a tremendous sweeping change today won't likely bring you back into integrity with yourself or others. This practice will take time, patience, and months (if not years) of diligent work. It took many poor decisions to break trust with yourself—it will take a commensurate amount more to come back into alignment with your values.

Like planting a sapling in a deforested area, each act of truthfulness brings you closer to a life lived in harmony with your cosmic self. Pause and notice how you speak to others and speak to yourself. Notice when you can go out of your way to put another person's (or your higher self's) well-being ahead of your transient desires. Observe the promises you make and keep. For it's in the quiet moments when no one is watching that integrity is grown. Choose to act with honesty and kindness, not because it's easy, but because it's simply the right thing to do.

"When is the best time to plant a tree?" a Chinese proverb asks. "Thirty years ago. When is the second-best time to plant a tree? Today." Regardless of how many decades have passed where your integrity could have been stronger, you can still start today to make the meaningful changes you seek. Nurture that sapling of truth, water it, and trust that it will turn into a beautiful, strong tree that gives you shade in time.

RITUAL:

For one week, take time each evening to reflect on moments when your actions did not align with your stated values. For example, if you value family but spend hours on your phone instead of being present, or if you claim to prioritize health but repeatedly choose to purchase junk food. Make note of these moments of incongruence and ask yourself why they happened. At the end of the week, reflect on how you can make changes to better align your time and actions with what you truly value, and observe the impact on your sense of integrity and fulfillment.

JOURNAL PROMPTS:

- In what areas of my life do I feel misaligned between my values and my actions? What small steps can I take to bring more integrity into those areas?
- Reflect on a time when I acted in alignment with my deepest values. How did it feel, and what impact did it have on my sense of self-respect and authenticity?

GUIDED MEDITATION:

Close your eyes and imagine yourself walking through a dense forest. Feel the moss under your bare feet; smell the fecund scent of decaying leaves birthing new soil. Hear the sound of the birds. Now, envision the path before you. You walk it steadily and easily. Feel how effortlessly you are in alignment with your goal: reaching your destination. Sense how you and your path are in alignment.

Now, a short distance ahead, the path splits. One path is the one that will lead you toward where you wish to go, the other will not. Go ahead and take the wrong path. How does it feel walking in this direction? Does the space between your shoulder blades itch? Does your stomach tie itself into knots? Recall times in your life when you knowingly moved out of integrity and chose the wrong path. Feel yourself exhaling out those memories and dropping them like pebbles on the roadside.

Reflect and take a few more steps in this direction; then, when you are sure you have deeply felt the wrongness of this choice, turn around and retrace your steps. Return to that fork in the road and, this time, walk the other route. Notice how everything feels clearer, brighter, and easier. Feel how your breaths come and go more effortlessly.

Reflect on times in your life when you chose the right thing, even if it was

XLVI. LIVE WITH INTEGRITY

difficult, even if you were the only one and everyone else chose the other way. Remind yourself how your integrity is everything—you need to be a person of your word so others will trust you, but more importantly, you will trust yourself.

Keep walking the right path for as long as you need. And if you need another reminder, go ahead down another wrong turn and see where it leads.

MANTRA:

"I honor my truth in all that I do."

XLVII. RECLAIM YOUR POWER

The lightning flashes in blinding bolts, pummeling the ground in the distance. The storm has risen into a tempest, but despite the ground-rattling thunder, you are unafraid. You stand here, bare-chested, in the dim evening light—spine proudly erect, head held high. You will be beaten back no longer. No more will you cower and sulk in the periphery; tonight, you are reclaiming your space. You are demanding the respect you deserve as a living, breathing being, and no storm will drive you into hiding.

In the flashes of light, you spot a mighty creature in the distance. A large, lumbering, hulking shape padding through the dense forest, cracking branches under their paws as if they were twigs. Some type of bear? In the next lightning strike, the light illuminates its colors: black and white. A giant panda. He makes you smile. This panda reminds you that, as powerful as he may be, he doesn't lord it over others. He can be playful. Power doesn't need to be domineering or forceful; in fact, it can be quiet, reserved, even silly. "Speak softly and carry a big stick," the saying by Theodore Roosevelt pops into your mind.

How often have we struggled to find this balance in our own lives? How frequently have we erred in one direction and forsook the other? Sometimes, I will see people trying to reclaim their power—and in so doing, end up hardening and losing their tenderness. Conversely, I have witnessed those who utilize humor and kindness as a defense mechanism—they wield it as a shield to deflect or mitigate injury when they really should be fighting back. It is entirely possible to be soft *and* strong—powerful *and* also flexible. One does not negate the other.

Many of us grew up in a world where we were taught to give away our power.

We were told that we shouldn't shine so bright, that we should settle for less because it was all we deserved. We were told we weren't all that intelligent, insightful, talented, or capable. And so, believing these falsehoods, we allowed ourselves to become diminished. We accepted those poorly-paying jobs because we thought it was all we were entitled to receive. We treated ourselves unkindly because we didn't think we deserved better. We settled for toxic friendships because we supposed no one else would love us.

If you grew up being bullied, you may have learned to make yourself smaller. You may have found that it was easier to disappear or to hide. You may have come to believe that being seen was dangerous, and you'd best lurk along the periphery or hide in the shadows. If this describes you, I see you. That was my journey too, which I wrote about extensively in my book, *I Dreamt of Flight*.

On the other hand, maybe you went the other way and became a bully yourself. Perhaps you decided you must crush and dominate others before they have the opportunity to do so to you. But even this is a negation of your true power—you are enacting the role of a tormentor because you don't fully believe that you can keep yourself safe without malice and causing pain first. True power is quiet, respectful, and has nothing to prove.

Or, perhaps you became an over-achiever. You proved your worth to society through your output, accolades, and productivity. Maybe you graduated valedictorian, got into an Ivy League school, won a position at a top law firm. Maybe you have a shelf full of awards and diplomas. This can be a negation of your inherent value because you are constantly striving to assert your worth. You are trading in your time, focus, and life-force for signposts of validation because you don't necessarily believe you are valuable in and of yourself. If you stopped producing at a high level, would anyone respect and love you, you wonder?

Another route you might have taken is making yourself the perpetual victim. No matter what happens in life, other people are at fault. You are always the one being oppressed, maligned, and marginalized. While identifying with being the victim can temporarily feel good because, in so doing, you get to enact righteousness (it can be a rush to feel entirely innocent and right while others are the villains), it ultimately does you a tremendous disservice. If you are only ever the victim, then other people have all the power—they can do whatever they want to you, and you are powerless to stop them. That means they also have all the power to block your healing—you are perpetually subservient to their whims. Until they tell you you can recover from your traumas, you never will.

Instead, if you own your part in all situations—if you learn to see that you were never a victim but a co-contributor in creating your suffering—then you were the one who got yourself in that position, so you can also get yourself out. You begin to call your power back to you and say: *I am the creator of this reality. I get*

XLVII. RECLAIM YOUR POWER

to choose how I respond, and I teach other people how to treat me. I don't need your permission to heal; I don't need anything from you to be able to move on. Going forward, I am creating environments where people treat me well. I will not settle for less.

This is recalling your power back to you. It is realizing that you are the divine co-creator of this universe, and you can manifest whatever life you wish. It is recognizing the truth that you are worthy of respect, being treated well, and being loved. Because, deep down, you know that all sentient creatures are worthy of this. Everything that lives deserves to be treated with dignity. All beings are worthy of compassion and kindness. In a more harmonious world, we would treat each human, animal, plant, and spirit with patience, kindness, and understanding. We aren't asking for anything extraordinary when we demand it for ourselves—we are just believing that we are equally as deserving as everyone else.

Reclaiming our power is learning to see our inherent worth. We are alive—therefore, we are worthy. There's nothing we need to prove, achieve, or do to earn worth—being born was enough. The sheer fact that you exist means that you should be treated with respect. Reclaiming your power isn't showboating and lording it over others; instead, it is a quiet sort of resilience. It's a soft affirmation that "I deserve to thrive, and I will be treated accordingly." It's to say, "I do not need to deflect by using humor or hide in the shadows—I can stand proudly and share all of myself because I am the divine embodied in the physical, and this is my birthright."

Numerous spiritual traditions from Tibet to the western hemisphere have created practices called "soul retrieval," where a shaman or a healer calls back to you all the pieces of your energy body that you have lost at various points in your life. With each trauma, each moment of indignity, a part of your energy body was surrendered—given away to the situation or the person who you allowed to hurt you. After years of losing ourselves to others, we find ourselves depleted—chronically sick, overtired, lacking luster and vibrancy. The healer brings that energy back and reintegrates it into our aura/energy field.

How often have you given away your power without meaning to? How frequently have you let difficult situations or other people's poor actions result in the diminishing of your life-force? It's time to call these parts back. While there are aspects of soul retrieval that we can do on our own, reaching out to a practitioner who is trained in this topic may be beneficial in providing you with the complete experience. In the meantime, it can be helpful to imagine golden strands of energy rushing back toward you like threads pulled from a tapestry reintegrating themselves back into the weave.

Some people purposely avoid power because they think it's dangerous. Many of us grew up hearing the phrase, "Power corrupts; absolute power corrupts absolutely," but this is tremendously misleading. To be powerful doesn't mean we will become some totalitarian dictator. Power itself is neutral—it is neither good nor bad. Power is simply energy; what matters is how you choose to use it. Will you use it to create, uplift, or offer healing? Some of the mightiest souls I've met are also incredibly kind, quiet, and demure. Power doesn't need to brag, boast, or domineer. Those who feel compelled to behave thus are actually often disconnected from their power and compensating. They are often akin to scared children roleplaying as competent adults; their accrued power is just revealing the immaturity and tumult within. In the words of author Robert Caro, "Power doesn't corrupt, it reveals"—it strips away the façade to show who we are underneath.

At our deepest core, we are the divine creators of this universe. Our thoughts, words, and actions are incredibly powerful—they spawned this whole galaxy in which we reside. If you want to manifest a beautiful life for yourself, that is entirely possible. When you stand in your true power, a magical connection with this reality unfurls. Granted, it may take years of mental training—learning to quiet your mind and reconnect with source—before you see monumental change in your life. But, speaking from personal experience, it is entirely possible to shift your reality in profound ways.

It is possible to draw into existence energy so potent that who you are changes in unimaginable aspects. You can manifest a life that rewrites your entire history—that you become someone almost entirely new. Not because you're trying to outrun or bury your past, but because you've grown so bright and expanded so vastly that the old vessel can no longer contain your revealed truth. A new physical form has to take its place to contain your rediscovered radiance.

I know this, too, from personal experience. People who meet me nowadays cannot envision my younger self; they find it inconceivable that such a person even existed. This soul journey has opened me so vastly that innumerable blocks and tensions have fallen away. How I look, how people respond when I enter a space, the vibe people feel in my presence…all of it is vastly different than it used to be. When I was twenty years old, I would have given almost anything to become someone other than myself. Years later, I learned that being me was the best person I could be—and in that acceptance of myself and finding home within, I began to change. By accepting where I was, I went somewhere new. By rooting down, I lifted up. By stopping my search to become someone different, I evolved into a truer version of me.

Life requires us learning a deftness and finesse when dealing with force. The more effort you apply to move in one direction, the greater a resisting force will push back at you. It is Newton's third law of motion: "Every action has an equal and opposite reaction." By striving to wield great power, you will fail to attain it—too much reciprocal force striving to shove you back. By giving up and accepting where you are, great power will naturally arise within you. By moving forward gently and unhurriedly—by *inviting* things to manifest rather than *forcing* them—the universe's potential opens before you. You can become anyone, experience anything. But to do so, you must find contentment with your present circumstances. By wanting nothing, you gain everything. By being at peace with being where you are, you can instantly travel anywhere.

You have the power to manifest any life you choose—you can find full liberation and enlightenment right here and now. But to do so, you must reclaim your power by realizing that you've always already had it. It never left you. It was always inside of you because you are God incarnate—you've never been anything other. Yes, you thought yourself to be small, weak, and incapable—but those were stories spun of shadows. They were ephemeral cobwebs, not your truth. Now, you are reclaiming who and what you truly are—the divine Oversoul in physical form. You are the master of the universe, the creator itself.

In that knowledge, you've learned the secret: everyone and everything on this planet is God. We are all the divine in fleshy bodies. We are all deserving of respect, dignity, power, and living a wonderful life...because we are the dreamers experiencing this dream. We are the makers of this world. And ultimately, we are all one—we are all the same being experiencing different dreams. And as you are, so am I.

If I can do it, so can you. If I can reclaim my power and open into a more confident and radiant person, then it is within your purview, too. You have infinite power to have an amazing life. So, are you going to claim it? Are you going to reawaken to the wisdom that all that exists also dwells within you? Are you going to realize that power isn't something hard, domineering, or dangerous? It is the soft, sweet, playful flow of creation. For, after all, another term for this reality is "The Great Game." We came here to create, explore, play, and not take things so seriously. So, as you reclaim your power, find your softness, sweetness, and silliness. Realize that you can be strong and pliable at the same time.

Be like the panda—mighty yet gentle, powerful yet playful. Let your power flow through you, not as something that dominates others, but as a light that shines from within. Your power does not need to be loud or aggressive; it can be quiet, steady, and unwavering. You are reclaiming your truth. You are reclaiming your strength. You are not just a human being; you are God. The same energy that created the stars flows through your veins. You have never been separate from this infinite power—you are it.

As the storm settles, you feel a deep peace well up within you. The crackles of lightning fade, but the energy remains. You have called back every part of yourself that has scattered; you have reawakened to your divine self-knowledge. You stand whole, complete, and ready to shine.

You are powerful. You are enough. Reclaim your power and unveil your light.

RITUAL:

Envision yourself encircled by an orb of light. Write down a list of people, events, or situations where you feel you've given away your power—moments where others' opinions or actions defined your sense of worth, or where you felt small or diminished. Once you've written them out, draw a large circle around each one and, next to it, write: "I call my power back." Cross through the names or events, symbolizing the release of their hold on you as you envision bursts of light returning to you, making your orb shine brighter. Keep this paper somewhere visible as a reminder that you are reclaiming your agency in life.

JOURNAL PROMPTS:

- Reflect on a time when you felt disempowered or when someone else made decisions for you. How did it feel to give up your power, and what thoughts or beliefs led to that experience?
- What would it feel like to cultivate the life I desire, to step in my power unabashedly? What holds me back from reclaiming my full radiance?

GUIDED MEDITATION:

Breathe deep and let go of your sight; turn your mind's gaze inward. Breathe and feel the erectness of your spine, the strength in your shoulders. Bring your hands together and hold them in front of your chest. Imagine that in the space between your hands is a vessel of some kind: a small urn, a jar, a chalice. Allow it to be something that can hold liquid. Allow the vessel to be translucent and yellow in color.

Now, from the middle of your chest, envision a small, floating version of your highest self. The version of you that is fully united with cosmic consciousness. Allow this mini you to float up and out of you—notice how it, too, is a yellowish gold that matches the vessel. As it hovers before you, ask it to please travel off

XLVII. RECLAIM YOUR POWER

and recover parts of your energy body, your soul, that you have left with others due to traumatic events. Perhaps there even was a painful romantic break-up, a malicious attack, or a time of great fear. See the mini you zoom off into the distance.

When they come back, they are glowing more brightly, carrying that fragmented energy in their hands. They rush over to the vessel you hold and toss that energy within. Notice how the vessel grows brighter. Then, they zoom off again in a new direction to reclaim another part of you.

Again, they return, add the contents of their search to your vessel, and it glows yet brighter. Send them off a third time. If memories arise, that's fine. If no memories float to the surface, that's great, too.

Allow this mini you to zoom off as many times as needed until your soul's vessel grows so luminous that it is almost blinding. When you feel you've reached a conclusion point and are ready to close the meditation, draw the vessel into you, allow it to return into your heart, and feel the contents mingle with and reattach themselves to your energy field.

You have called your full self home.

MANTRA:

"I am opening up to my vast power."

XLVIII. JUST BE

You've come so far—you've journeyed so hard. Think of all the mountains you've climbed, the rivers you've waded through, the caves you've explored. But now, after all this adventure, it is simply time for rest. You settle yourself on this lily pad floating atop a tranquil pond and close your eyes. Breaths come and go in steady succession. A light of peace wells up from the center of your chest and shines brightly out of you. A little nudging at your knee causes you to look down; a small tamarin monkey has settled itself beside you, looking contentedly at you. You smile remembering how many spiritual traditions have described the "monkey mind"—the state of being chronically mentally unsettled, the mind jumping from branch to branch. But not now, not here. At this moment, your mind is quiet and peaceful, like this small creature. There is nothing to do, nowhere to go, and nothing to achieve. You have completed your tasks, and now you simply exist. Here and now. Present.

Welcome, my dear traveler, to the long-awaited principle of simply being. It is said that the most advanced spiritual technique is that of simply existing. No mantras, no affirmation, no visualization or things to write about. There are no exercises or new perspectives to attain. All you have to do is simply let go and experience.

Everything has led to this moment. All the searching, learning, growing, healing—it has brought to the stillness of now. The water flows, as water always does, but you are not trying to direct its course. You are a part of it. The movement of the current is within you, as is the pulsing of the earth. You are no longer striving for change, for enlightenment, or for some greater achievement.

You are no longer striving to become anything. Now is the time where you remember that you are already whole.

This is the paradox of spiritual growth. We spend so much time believing that we need to do more—meditate more, learn more, heal more, expand more—yet, in the end, the great lesson is that there is nothing to be done. The essence of great wisdom is the recognition that you are already complete. The divine has been within you all along, and you access it not through effort but through surrender.

A phrase I often use is: *we grow by subtraction*. We become more not by layering new things on, but by letting go of that which limits us. But even in this letting go, it is not an effort. It is an action-less action, an effort-less effort. Letting go is the antithesis for striving. Surrendering to what you are requires no work at all.

In this moment, as you sit precisely where are, feel the vastness of the sky overhead and the ancientness of the planet beneath you. Realize that everything you need is right here, already with you. There is nothing to achieve and nowhere to be because you already have it all. Release any feelings of need; allow the weight of striving to fall away like autumn leaves drifting on the wind. There's no longer any pushing forward or pulling from behind. You aren't trying to shape yourself into something. You are simply sitting, breathing, and being. That is enough.

There is peace that comes from knowing there is nothing else to do. The jaguar, sated from its hunt, does not seek out more prey—she lounges on a branch in the shade of a canopy. Her body is full and happy. The flower doesn't exert strain in forcing its petals to open; it effortlessly blooms when the time is right. The river doesn't flow because it wills itself to do so; it just follows gravity and sinks to where it is low and tranquil. The same can be true for you. The magic of life exists in this very breath, in the simple act of being.

This journey of becoming is actually a journey of unbecoming. We peel away the layers, the false facades, the striving, and the endless desire to be something more than we are. We strip ourselves bare until we are left with only our essence—the pure, simple light that burns brightly within our hearts. In many of the eastern spiritual traditions, there is this notion of paths being either *sutric* or *tantric*. *Sutric* paths ask us to give up everything (meat, alcohol, sex, money, etc.) until all we are left with is God. The *tantric* paths ask us to embrace everything until we realize God is in even the most fearsome, loathed, or taboo places.

Though both paths seem to lead in opposite directions, they ultimately lead to the same place. And, interestingly, both paths ask us to keep letting go (whether it's of external things like money or internal things like prejudices and limiting beliefs) until all that remains is light. That is the reason the *sadhus*, or the wild, sometimes naked, holy men wandering the streets smear themselves in twice-burned ash: it is the physical representation of physical matter transmuting into light. It is representation of clothing one's self in starlight because all that we are is light, once we transcend everything.

In this stillness, in this silence, you rediscover the truth that was always there within you: you are whole. The universe is within you and also around you. It holds you, and you hold it, just as the riverbed holds the river and the sky holds the stars. You have always been and will always be—you are an eternal, inexorable part of this reality.

What if this moment is all there is? What if enlightenment is not a distant peak to be reached but a quiet realization that you are already there? What if the divine and the infinite Oversoul is not hidden in some distant, far-off place but is right here and now in the soft flutter of your breath. What if God is here between the beats of your gently pulsing heart?

This is the final lesson we all must face: to stop searching, striving, or trying to control the flow of life. There is nothing that needs fixing. There's no attainment to be had. Watch the trees grow and see how they are a representation of you, ever growing down into the soil and up into the heavens—always effortlessly expanding. They just exist and allow life-force to flow through them. Watch the ocean churn and allow that massive power that undulates the waves to roll through your body. You are the conduit, the vessel—you don't need to do anything to make it move. Let the currents of life carry you onward. Your soul knows the way. Your guides will protect you and keep you safe. All you need to do is trust and let go.

More effort doesn't necessarily mean faster progress; often, it means more challenges. When we approach spiritual work with force, will, or effort, we meet with equal resistance. But when we enter a state of flow and release the need to control, we are effortlessly carried. Imagine a high-diver poised at the edge of a pool, ready for a twenty-foot leap into the waters below. If they enter the water with a tremendous amount of force—say, in an unskilled belly-flop—a tremendous amount of force will rise up to greet them. Not only will they generate a giant splash, but it will also feel as if they catapulted into concrete. However, if they dive elegantly through the surface, generating as little resistance as possible, there will be hardly any waves created, as well as no pain. The difference between the two is not in the effort but in the grace with which they move.

As the aphorism goes, "we are human beings, not human doings." Can you release the need to be perpetually in motion, ever-improving, always chasing after the next thing...even when used in a spiritual context? I think we've all seen those people who drift from ceremony to ceremony, from retreat to retreat, accumulating empowerments, teachings, and initiations...but never really attaining anything of value. They continue seeking out that higher enlightenment, that greater awakening, without ever realizing that their most profound realizations were already housed within. Can you give over your aspirations and simply realize that you are already perfect, healed, enlightened, and whole? Can you let the water carry you and stop trying to direct the flows?

You are a part of this. All of this. Everything that exists…that is you. As you sit and watch the ripples on the water, breathe in the firefly-laden air, realize that you have already reached your goal. You have won. You attained it all already. Now, it's time to simply *be*. You are not separate from your enlightenment; it was already you. You are the pond, the moon, the stars, the peaceful monkey beside you. You are life itself, in all its beauty and mystery.

There is no goal beyond this moment, no higher achievement than the pleasure of being alive. You realize that was why you chose to incarnate here: for the love to be shared, the lessons to be learned, and the joy to be felt. And now that you've come to know this, you can simply be. You have done the work. You have walked the path. Now, just let go of the need to strive. Trust that you are being held by the divine, that the universe will carry you where you need to go. You are already there.

Shine bright, dear star. In the words of the ecstatic Sufi poet, Rumi, "Do not feel lonely, the entire universe is inside you. Stop acting so small. You are the universe in ecstatic motion. Set your life on fire. Seek those who fan your flames."

Let yourself be.

RITUAL:

Set aside time to sit or lie down outside in nature, whether on the grass, under a tree, or by a body of water. Let the earth cradle you. Resist the urge to "do" anything—no phone, no music, no distractions. Simply exist in the moment, breathing in sync with nature around you. Let the natural world hold you as you release all striving. Feel the connection to the earth beneath you, the sky above, and allow yourself to just be. Reflect on how it feels to let go of constant doing and simply rest in being.

XLVIII. JUST BE

JOURNAL PROMPTS:

- What drives my constant need for doing and achieving? How can I begin to practice the art of simply being, without feeling guilty or unproductive?
- Reflect on a time when I allowed myself to rest in the present moment without striving or pushing. How did that experience change my understanding of peace and contentment?

GUIDED MEDITATION:

Close your eyes and breathe. For this meditation, all that is required is to savor. Whatever you imagine, whatever you feel, whatever you hear, drink it in. Let it linger within you. You are simply being present to the experience of life, of your mind, of your body, of your surroundings. There's nothing else to do, nowhere else to be. All that is being asked of you is to give into this moment, relax, and be.

You've done so much; now is your time to just be. That is enough. You are enough. No more striving; now you just exist. Be here. Be now. Savor this moment. All is well. All has been well. All will be well.

MANTRA:

"I am."

THE BRIGHTENING SKY

We linger at the edge of the woods. Behind us, the glowing portals dim as daylight brightens. Traveling through the forest together, we have uncovered parts of our truth buried by the passage of time. We have rediscovered our existence as cosmic beings, incarnated into the dance of life—eternal souls journeying in the flesh to learn, to grow, and to shine.

We have come closer to reuniting with our joy-filled selves. We have danced, we have mourned, we have raged, we have sung. We have examined the beliefs that held us prisoner for too long and have found greater freedom through this exploration.

And now, it is time to retake the paths that lead us home.

The sky brightens to majestic fuchsias and tangerines as the lights from the forty-eight portals wink out entirely. The gateways merge once more into this woodland of the soul, which in turn begins to fade back into mist. Another twilight will soon come when some intrepid traveler will summon these mossy, vine-strewn ways with their need, searching for their Ecstatic Self. That traveler may be you—these pathways are ours to return to at any point we choose. We can come back whenever we need new guidance, require grateful remembering, long for a new understanding of where we are, or must uncover a compass to show us the way.

These gateways, these pathways, these portals are yours now. You have done the soulful work; you have courageously ventured through them, shedding your old beliefs. You have reconnected with your inner gatekeeper and now know how to find your way back through the winding paths toward your luminescent self. Be confident in your ability to return whenever your heart calls to find your ways again through the woodlands of spirit.

But that is for later. At this moment, you are being drawn to return to your daily life, to the world from whence you came before you met me at the crossroads at twilight—which was both a breath and an eternity ago. It's time to take this newfound wisdom and integrate it into your circles, your home, your places of work. It's time to find peace, joy, ecstasy, and belonging in the world that feels familiar yet also newly strange to you. You have grown and no longer fit within the chrysalis of your former life—your wings have unfurled and dried.

Peace is a blessing when you can find it in the quiet of the forest, away from the hum of human habitat—but it becomes even more remarkable when you can carry it back to civilization and maintain that hard-won tranquility. Return to your family, your friends, and your colleagues, holding fast to this peace, this openness, this kindness within you. Go be a flame that sparks many other candles alight; remind others of their own divine light, their worth, their eternal beauty. Be the ember that glows and sets the world alight with the brilliance of remembering our inherent worth.

Thank you for your patience, your trust, and, most of all, your time. Time is the only resource you cannot cultivate more of, so I hope our journey together was worth the investment. Remember that you can always find me lingering here, on the edge of the wild, where the less-traveled roads converge. Here, in the deepening dark, we will rediscover our primal, untamed souls—and through that rediscovery, our connection with the cosmos and each other. After all, the highest purposes of this life are to experience joy, to share love, and to create meaningful connections with one another. It has been an honor to share that with you.

Thank you for traveling these winding, wyrd ways with me this past night. It has been a sincere privilege to walk beside you and to open the paths to these portals. I am forever your humble servant. And I hope to meet you again on another eve, under a deepening sky that calls us toward adventure. There, our radiant hearts will reveal themeless, nestled deep within a forest of soul. Until then, my dear traveler, be well and shine bright. "We are starlight wrapped in skin," says the ecstatic poet Rumi. "The light you have been seeking has always been within."

You have always been that light.

With all my love,

Kaelan

ALSO BY KAELAN STROUSE

If you enjoyed walking the 48 Gateways, there's more to explore. Kaelan's other writings deepen the path of embodied joy, sacred aliveness, and divine remembering:

JOURNEY TO THE ECSTATIC SELF

Part workbook, part memoir, this is Kaelan's foundational offering—sharing the tools and insights he uncovered on his journey toward healing shame, reclaiming his sensuality, and remembering the divine within.

I DREAMT OF FLIGHT

A fantasy allegory of growing up different in a world that didn't understand. This poetic tale transforms trauma into self-discovery—a journey home for anyone who was born an outsider.

ACKNOWLEDGMENTS

There is no way I could ever thank the innumerable guides and teachers who have illuminated the paths we now tread. There have been countless chance encounters, bits of wisdom dropped at the right time by unseen sources. These magical happenings boggle my mind to fathom how they happened so serendipitously.

I should begin with my parents. My mother and father were my first guides, setting the course for me to walk in my early development. Both magical beings in their own right, I am awed and inspired by the wisdom they imparted to me.

My husband would be next. I often call him the greatest gift that I have ever received. His soulful musings as we amble down the sidewalks with our dogs fill my heart, enliven my spirit, and structure my thoughts and plans. He has imparted so many deep, meaningful insights—I am inspired by and in awe of his genius daily. I have learned so much from him over the course of our ten trips around the sun together. I am so thankful for another beautiful adventure together.

There have been many teachers who have come and gone from my life—some of the greatest, unfortunately, left without any sort of kind regard in their departure. I still appreciate and am grateful for what they taught me. And to all the many soul guides who have not incarnated on this planet but still lead me through their presence and wisdom, I am profoundly and humbly thankful. I look forward to rejoining you in our combined work when this trip aboard this crazy blue dot is over.

To my Patrons, readers, followers, subscribers, clients, and retreat attendees—you all teach me on a daily basis through your stories, messages, comments, and kind words. We are all wandering the path together and en route on the journey home.

To my talented graphic designer/illustrator, Alfred Obare, and editor, Kayli Baker—thank you for the magic you bring. The project would never have made it to the finish line without your fantastic support and contributions.

And most of all, you. You who hold this project in your hands. Thank YOU for taking this walk with me and doing your part to grow and evolve. We are all striving toward that divine remembrance that we are one—and it's a privilege to share heart-space and to be with you on this exploratory journey.

May you be blessed; may you be well. May you know your strength. May we cultivate a place of peace and harmony where everyone knows their worth and all beings are treated with respect.

All the best to you!

PATRON SAINTS OF THE ORACLE

Thank you to these Kickstarter Backers who went above and beyond to help bring this project to life!

Adam Medlin
AJ Phillips
Andy Mommabear
Melichar
Bryan
Budi Gunawan
Christopher
Dharma
Felix Borges
Gregory Chapman
Henrik Sturesson
Jim Grimnes
John Kannisto
Joshua Heard
Matthew
Matthew Henriksen
Neal Frick
Nick Kasovac
O-Ren Williams
Oliver Willcox
Patrick Hewitt
Ploynapat
Rich Walton
Richard Lawyer
Ryan Christensen
Stuart McGeoch
Tim Veihl

THANK YOU: KICKSTARTER BACKERS

Alanna
Alejandro Ignacio
Alejandro Sordo
Alex Kirschenbaum
Alex Rountree
Alexander DuBois
alexandra
Ally Smith
Amanda McCullough
Amanda Salas
Amy Speck
Andrew Barker
Andy Yang
Arg'ach
Asian Tarzan
Auser Jann Fernandez Pagunsan
Ave Joe
Ayren Mann-Martin
Barry Sabo
Ben Conrad
Benj Wise
Benjamin SMITH
Biany Isabel
Bill Sive

Brandon Brown
Brian Blevins
Brian Jones
Brian Michaelsen
Brian Snell
Carlos Montague
Carmen
Chad Hendry
Charles Aguilar
christan Fleres
Christian
Christina Riggio
Christopher Benitez
Christopher H. Merrell
Christopher John Sullivan
Christopher Williams
Christy Bertuglia
CJ Pankey
CJ Van Der Klontz
Colin Israel
Connor McNamara
Cordell Jenkins
Corin Wyatt Seah
Corry Parker

Courtney Clark
Cyd Foley
Dalton Privitt
Darin Thomas
David Iorio Izzo
David Stepney
David Zeager
Desi Valentine
Dirk Burns
Dominador Arquelada
Edgar Ponce
Eileen Halecki Corwin
Elizabeth
ElkWhistle
Emerald Orchid
Emilio
Emily Fernandez
Emmanuel
Enrico Gomez
Eric Chiu
Eric Daniel Saulters-Wood
Eric Shupert
francisco romans gomez
Frank Serio

Franklin Henry
Garrett McClure
Geert-Jan Borgstein
Gerard Frost
Greg McDougall
Guillermo Murillo
Hans Abplanalp
Heather Erickson
Jack Aubert
Jake Johnson
James
James Welch
Jancarlos Del Valle
Jannah Salter
Jasper
Jeff Embree
Jeff Marshall
Jeremiah McCurry
Jerome Farley
Jessica Buckles
Jim
Jim Nash
Jim Roberts
Jim Steuterman
Joe
John Brock
John Smith
John Stevens
John Wingweaver
Jon Carl Lewis
Jon Vigne
Jorge
Jorge

Joseph Etheredge
Josh Hufford
Joshua
Joshua Allton
Joshua Buckman
Jostin Schimmoeller
JT
Juan Miranda
Jurgen Schoevaerts
Karla Quezada-Torres
Kathy Higgins
Kaz
KB77
Keith J. Farmer
Ken
Kerynn
Kristi
Kyle
Kyle Wagg
Leroy Flint
Lorraine Mathews
Lynda Lampert
Vanderhoff
Mal
Marcel P.
Marinus Ouwerkerk
Mark Stephens
Matt Bach
Matt C
Matt Jeske
Matt Scott
Matthew Gerlach
Michael

Michael Grogan
Michael L Lester
michael stern
Michael Strauss
Nic Altavilla
Nicole
Nicole Mires
Noah Harris
Omar Padilla
Paul Dehlin
Paul Lindsey
Peter
Peter Mansfield
Peter Swann
Pierre
Pippo
Procedural_Nomad
RA Atthewsmay
Randy Johnson
Riccardo Muzzioli
Rick Silverman
Rita A Kalmar
Rocky Matthews
RoJo
Ron Kirby
Russell Green
Sandra April
Sean Levahn
Shawn
Shawn Hollenbach
Sherwin Sng
Steph Waters
Steven L. Sanders

Steven Nordberg
Stuart
Susie
Sytse Monsma
Terry Knowles
thomas roberts
Tim
Timothy Alberts

Tj
Tommy To
Tony Ortega
Topher
Tot
Van Morse
Vanessa Vasquez-Witcher

W
Walter
William Stookey
Zachary "Pup GIR" Ledbetter
Žarko Ristić
求宏 谢

ABOUT THE AUTHOR

Kaelan Strouse is a spiritual guide, author, and teacher dedicated to helping others rediscover their Ecstatic Self—a life brimming with joy, authenticity, and connection to the divine. Since 2008, Kaelan has guided individuals through meditations, coaching, and transformative practices, blending ancient wisdom with modern insights to inspire deep, soulful growth.

A seven-year residency in a meditative ashram shaped Kaelan's approach to spiritual exploration, alongside his study of diverse traditions such as Tantra, animism, and mystical Christianity. His books—*Journey to the Ecstatic Self, I Dreamt of Flight,* and *48 Gateways to the Ecstatic Self*—offer practical tools and profound reflections for personal transformation. Through his teachings and nearly a million followers online, Kaelan encourages seekers to embrace their light, dance with their shadows, and embody the vastness of their being.

Kaelan lives in Washington, DC, with his husband, Anthony, their two dogs, one cat, and more plants than he dares count. When not creating heartfelt content or leading transformative retreats, you'll find him wandering through nature, curled up with mystical books, or practicing rituals that connect the cosmos to the everyday. *For more info visit: EcstaticSelf.com*

www.ingramcontent.com/pod-product-compliance
Lightning Source LLC
Chambersburg PA
CBHW070750230426
43665CB00017B/2315